Blues on Stage

SUNY Press Jazz Styles

Blues on Stage

The Blues Entertainment Industry in the 1920s

JOHN L. CLARK JR.

EXCELSIOR
EDITIONS

Cover credit: BenCar Archives. Public Domain.

Published by State University of New York Press, Albany

Printed in the United States of America

Excelsior Editions is an imprint of State University of New York Press

For information, contact State University of New York Press, Albany, NY
www.sunypress.edu

Library of Congress Cataloging-in-Publication Data

Name: Clark, John L. Jr., author.
Title: Blues on stage : the blues entertainment industry in the 1920s / John L. Clark Jr.
Description: Albany : State University of New York Press, 2023. | Series: SUNY Press Jazz Styles | Series: Excelsior Editions. | Includes bibliographical references and index.
Identifiers: LCCN 2022021049 | ISBN 9781438491554 (hardcover : alk. paper) | ISBN 9781438491561 (ebook) | ISBN 9781438491547 (pbk. : alk. paper)
Subjects: LCSH: Blues (Music)—To 1931—History and criticism. | African Americans—Music—History and criticism. | African American women singers. | African American singers. | Sound recording industry—United States—History. | Music and race—United States—History.
Classification: LCC ML3521 .C54 2023 | DDC 781.64309/042—dc23/eng/20220503
LC record available at https://lccn.loc.gov/2022021049

10 9 8 7 6 5 4 3 2 1

Contents

Introduction

In the introduction to their book, *Embodied Voices: Representing Female Vocality in Western Culture*, Leslie Dunn and Nancy Jones stated that the meanings of songs and the voices that sing them "cannot be recovered without reconstructing the contexts of their hearing" (Dunn & Jones, 1994, 2). While their focus was specifically on women singers, the same principal holds for men as well. In the study of blues in the 1920s, women artists are generally more visible and thus seen as more important than their contemporary male counterparts; while this point is true on many levels, male performers of blues and African American popular music of the 1900–1935 era were great influences as well.

The definition of the blues of this period is somewhat flexible. While sometimes called "Classic Female Blues" to limit the style to the careers (and recordings) of the great blues women of the 1920s, the era can in fact be seen to begin with the development of the Black entertainment industry in the late nineteenth century and continuing through the jazz-influenced swing and jump blues of the 1930s (the so-called Bluebird Sound in honor of the company that issued recordings of many classic performers of the genre). From the late 1910s until the end of the period, blues and jazz were closely associated and mutually influential in terms of style, sound, and even instrumentation. The common strain with most of the blues repertoire and performance styles discussed here is that they were developed on the stages of the Black entertainment circuits of the first twenty years of the twentieth century.

In its earliest days, the music that has come to be known as blues was an amalgam of folk songs, ragtime, and popular Tin Pan Alley fare, including the subgenre of "coon songs," which became popular in the 1890s and early 1900s, but can be seen to have originated in the White minstrel tradition predating the Civil War. A complicated admixture of racial and gender stereotypes was interpreted through the musical prism of the popular syncopations of ragtime and a highly developed professional apparatus that was almost unbelievably accelerated by the travels of Black entertainment troupes, which lead to the adoption of the folk form that coalesced into the blues. The appearance of the rural Black folk music tradition that gave its feeling and musical expression to the blues structure, codified by sheet music publications and recordings beginning in the mid-1910s, was a happenstance that, in turn, influenced virtually all American popular music for the next hundred years.

When interviewed by folklorist John Wesley Work III in 1929, Ma Rainey ("The Mother of the Blues") claimed to have been the first professional entertainer to sing blues on stage after hearing the style for the first time in 1902 (Abbott & Seroff, 2017, 162). This early date does not seem likely, because press notices of Rainey's performances do not mention her singing anything other than standard popular fare before 1913, and the first publications of blues songs dated from slightly later (Abbott & Seroff, 2017, 170). Prior to that, Rainey occasionally had been advertised as a "coon shouter," singing that repertoire of songs, which as Abbot and Seroff have pointed out, share many characteristics with popular blues of the 1920s: humor, perspective, language, feeling, and occasionally even structure.

The popular concept of the blues as a pure folk form is a simplification of little importance to what became known as "Classic Blues." Sometimes also called "Vaudeville Blues," the style codified during the 1910s when Tin Pan Alley published numerous songs with the word *blues* in the title and the use of what came to be known as traditional blues lyrics, occasionally utilizing Black dialect. These songs were performed both by Black and White performers in highly professional settings: vaudeville theaters, cabarets, tent shows, and even circuses as part of larger entertainment companies presenting comedians, dancers, dramatic sketches, animal acts, and much more. Peter Muir calls this style "popular blues" and separates it from folk blues, largely due to transmission: written music for popular blues and oral music for folk blues. While this is a neat distinction, many Black singers of the 1920s clearly had feet in both camps (Muir, 2010, 3).

My own connection to the blues comes as a performer, historian, and academic who values the power of the music not only for what it represents but as a personal mode of expression. While as a White middle-class person raised in New England I cannot claim the direct experience of blues culture, I can value it for its endless capacity for reinvention and appreciate it for its central location in American culture, both looking back and forward. The recent focus on critical race theory (CRT) across many disciplines makes application to Classic Blues and the Black entertainment world before 1935 at once both illuminating and essential. Two particular elements of the CRT construct are of particular relevance to the study of African American vernacular music of this period.

First is the idea of "intersectional theory," which was developed by Kimberle Crenshaw in 1989 as a way of identifying and exploring the complex overlapping of gender, race, class, sexuality, and many other identifiers. Through this theoretical lens, a performer like Ma Rainey must be simultaneously heard/seen as a woman, an African American, an entertainer, a southerner, and possibly an individual who was sexually fluid, combination of which both greatly enhanced and complicated the narrative.

The second is the concept of "storytelling" as a means to unlock the lived experiences of musicians and entertainers. Very few contemporary interviews were done with participants in the Black music tradition prior to the Swing Era (1935–1945), and only a handful of film appearances (mostly silent) exist before this as well. The two sources of consistent documentation of these performers are commercial recordings that allow us to hear some of the most significant voices of the period (sometimes performing their own original material) and contemporary press reports and reviews. While the vast majority of these records were produced by White-owned companies primarily concerned with sales figures, enough echoes (however dim) of the on-stage and touring experiences of Bert Williams, George Walker, Ma Rainey, Bessie Smith, and W. C. Handy emerge to allow for interpretation and conclusions to be drawn. According to Bryan McKinley Jones Brayboy (2005), "Tribal Critical Race Theory . . . honors stories and oral knowledge as real and legitimate forms of data and ways of being. Stories are not separate from theory; they make up theory." He further points out that these stories (which are, in essence, what many of the blues songs and show tunes of the period consist of) "are not separate from theory; they make up theory and are, real and legitimate sources of data and ways of being" (15).

Any historian embarking on an overview project is necessarily standing on the shoulders of giants. My research would have been much more difficult and in many ways utterly impossible had it not been for the work of many researchers and enthusiasts who came before me, beginning with the interviews conducted in the 1940s and 1950s by William Russell, Len Kunstadt, and Derrick Stewart Baxter. These interviews have proved invaluable for preserving the stories and voices of participants in the 1910s and 1920s Black entertainment scene. This research and investigation took on professional proportions by the 1960s, at which point periodicals such as *Storyville* and *Living Blues* aimed at jazz and blues audiences began publication with intrepid volunteer staffs fanning out over the entire United States and Europe to find more interview subjects. Book-length studies like Walter C. Allen's *Hendersonia* and Chris Albertson's *Bessie* sought to contextualize this plethora of information, while discographies by Brian Rust and, later, Dixon, Goodrich, and Rye identified thousands of recordings done during the period.

By the 1990s, even more in-depth work was being done. The extraordinary documentary work by Lynn Abbott and Doug Seroff began with a series of articles and extended to three books (so far) that developed from a close reading of contemporary Black newspapers, creating layers of detail previously unknown. This was combined with a truly monumental CD reissue project by the Austrian Johnny Parth, who started Document Records in 1985, which by 2000 had released over a thousand CDs of blues, gospel, and African American entertainment and roots music recorded before 1950. These resources, plus the many jazz reissue projects, have made available virtually all recordings made during the 1910s and 1920s easily available and accessible on YouTube as well as streaming platforms.

I have chosen to divide the singers of this period into three categories. First is the "Cabaret Blues" style, which was the first to be recorded, beginning with Mamie Smith in 1920. The singers I include in this category were active primarily in cabarets, nightclubs, and smaller entertainment venues in the North during the late 1910s. Many (Mamie Smith, Ethel Waters, Mary Stafford) were born in the North or Midwest, as well, and did not bring a traditional southern sensibility to their performances. Others (Alberta Hunter and Lucille Hegamin) were born in the South but largely raised in Chicago.

The second category is "Vaudeville Blues." These singers began to appear on record by 1923, and were led by the twin epigones of the era: Bessie Smith and Ma Rainey. For the most part, these singers had been raised in the South and had a great deal of exposure to southern folk music, including early blues. They were active performers on the Black vaudeville, tent show, and even minstrel circuits, and were often (unlike the Cabaret Blues singers) considered to be stars of the industry before they began recording, although some (Ida Cox and Rosa Henderson) became famous because of their recordings. The distinguishing factor uniting these performers is their professionalism and long-term stage experience, which allowed them to work well in the high-pressure atmosphere of the recording industry, which often required them to learn songs on the spot and create spontaneous performances.

The third category ("Down-home Blues") begins to emerge around 1925 and gradually takes over the industry, launching the various blues styles of the 1930s and beyond. This category was driven in large part by economics and the need to present new material to the record-buying public. Almost exclusively southern, these singers typically brought their own original material (a cost-saving method, meaning record companies did not need to pay copyright fees) and worked either alone or in smaller combinations. Female singers (Victoria Spivey, Sippie Wallace, and Luella Miller) and males (Blind Lemon Jefferson, Papa Charlie Jackson, and Blind Blake) usually did not have as much professional stage experience as their vaudeville counterparts and were accustomed to making music in "temporary" entertainment venues such as at house parties and on street corners. Nevertheless, performers such as Jefferson and Blake became some of the most popular and widely recorded stars of the period.

Some performers do not fit neatly into any single category. Trixie Smith recorded extensively during the first period (where I have discussed her, largely on the basis of her influence being felt more strongly there), but is much more in line with the vaudeville singers. Eva Taylor made many records during the first period, but her partnership with Clarence Williams (her husband) made her far more influential during the second. Papa Charlie Jackson is the first successful recording artist of the Down-home period, but he (virtually alone among those performers) had extensive stage experience in tent and medicine shows.

I have decided to deal with the singers in the individual sections in the order of their first recording session, except for a general listing of "other singers" whose influence was limited due to their limited recordings, who I address at the end of the chapters.

Chapter 1

Beginnings

The Rise of the Black Entertainment Industry

Black Minstrelsy

Authentic African American entertainment did not make a significant impact on American culture until the last decades of the nineteenth century. Entertainers such as pianist Blind Tom Wiggins Bethune and dramatic actors such as Ira Aldridge and James Hewlett had toured White theaters and played other venues prior to the Civil War. Others earned renown in southern slave communities for their abilities, but broad opportunities for a professional career did not exist until the period following Reconstruction. In the wake of the Civil War and the comparative ease of travel, Black troupes began to tour the country performing a version of blackface minstrelsy. Robinson uses the terms *blackface minstrelsy* to refer to White performers and *Black minstrelsy* to refer to African American entertainers (Robinson, 2007), both of which I will utilize here.

The origins of blackface minstrelsy has been traced and analyzed in detail, with the uneasy agreement that the beginning came in the early 1830s with the performance of Thomas Dartmouth "Daddy" Rice.[1] Rice

1. Many books and articles have been written about the development of blackface minstrelsy, but good overviews are Robert C. Toll, *Blacking Up: The Minstrel Show in Nineteenth-Century America* (London: Oxford University Press, 1974) and William J. Mahar, *Behind the Burnt Cork Mask: Early Blackface Minstrelsy and Antebellum American Culture* (Urbana: University of Illinois Press, 1999). The University of South Florida also maintains an informative website on "The History of Minstrelsy," http://exhibits.lib.usf.edu/exhibits/show/minstrelsy/jimcrow-to-jolson/jump-jim-crow/.

evolved a character he called "Jim Crow," supposedly modeled after a Black stable hand, and his comic representation of the man's dress, gait, and speech patterns largely directed the next thirty years of his career. Part of his imitation involved donning blackface, which had in fact been an established stage convention for centuries. Rice's combination of black makeup, ragged dress, and exaggerated movements suggesting slow motion were as important as his use of Black dialect, speech patterns, and music to create the image of an uneducated but canny Black character who could then comment on social and political issues from behind the characterization.

Rice found almost immediate popularity with his Jim Crow character in variety shows and plays, inspiring other performers to develop similar characters based on Black and slave stereotypes such as Zip Coon and various mammy figures. By the early 1840s, entire programs were being developed around the theme of these representations, with the Virginia Minstrels being perhaps the first to develop a unified stage persona using blackface, costume, and particularly music (the members were all musicians and singers), with the banjo figuring prominently. They were followed later in the decade by Christy's Minstrels, who popularized the original music of Stephen Foster (composed specifically for minstrel shows) and also solidified the structure of the minstrel show into a three-act form, both elements continuing in blackface and Black minstrelsy for the rest of the century and occasionally beyond as well.

The general order of the program began with the cast seated in a semicircle on stage, with the interlocutor (essentially the straight man or master of ceremonies) in the middle. On either end were the comics (the "endmen" known as "Tambo" and "Bones") who provided the jokes based largely on misunderstanding and spoonerisms generated by their apparent lack of education. Often most of the actors would also be singers or instrumentalists and musical selections would be interspersed with jokes. The second part of the show focused on the individual talents of the cast, with singers, dancers, comics, and jugglers all doing short turns. This became the "olio," which was an important precursor to vaudeville and variety programs in the first half of the twentieth century. The final act would be a short play, often in a plantation setting to further utilize the costumes, makeup, and music, with a grand finale involving everyone in the cast.

Echoes of part or all the minstrel shows of the mid-nineteenth century can readily be seen in the various Black entertainment units that will be discussed leading up to the Stage Blues era. For example, accounts of the shows led by Ma Rainey in the 1920s describe a sequence of solo acts (comics, dancers, and instrumentalists) leading to Rainey's performance, after which the entire cast would come on stage to dance the Charleston. From the prior decade, the Original Creole Band brought early jazz to the White Orpheum vaudeville circuit, with its members dressed in rags and playing in a plantation setting (Gushee, 2010).

Blackface has been seen as a mask for White performers in the obvious sense that it would give them license to mimic Black society, or at least their idea of Black society. By emphasizing the negative and unseemly elements of that group they could assert their own superiority. (Later developments in minstrelsy and vaudeville mirrored this, with the social groups being stereotyped moving from racial to ethnic focus.) William J. Mahar has made the important observation that blackface in its earliest inceptions was "a vehicle to express the disappointment and doubts of those 'others' (including Whites themselves) who dwelt on the margins of political power, economic comfort, and relative security in jobs, homes, and private life," although his earlier point that it "did *not* reflect white perceptions of black culture" is more problematic (Mahar, 1999, 41).

African Americans initially began using blackface to mask their own Black skin, thereby appearing less threatening or exotic to White audiences. The first account of an African American performer using blackface was from 1841, when William Henry Lane (aka Master Juba) was hired by the showman P. T. Barnum to replace a White dancer who had left his show. It was thought necessary for Juba to use the burnt cork that had been an identifying factor of White minstrelsy for a decade in order not to offend White audience sensibilities and to allow him to travel with an otherwise White minstrel troupe.

When Black minstrel companies began to attract attention on national tours, their White owners often insisted on blackface for reasons of racism and segregation, particularly when performances occurred in the South (Barlow, 1989, 1191–20). Barlow places much blame on the White owners and financial backers of the Black troupes for perpetuating blackface and minstrel stereotypes into the early 1900s. The continuation of the tradition through Black minstrelsy is more difficult to explain. When the next generation of entertainers transitioned from minstrelsy to tent shows and circuses, many still "blacked up" for their performances, even when the primary audience was rural African Americans. Mel Watkins suggests that the lower-economic and -social strata of Black society (the primary audience for these traveling shows) could laugh at themselves through the representations of minstrel humor while knowing that there was more to their existence than the stereotype (1994).

The trope of "Signifyin(g)," as described by Henry Louis Gates Jr., is helpful in understanding the reception of blackface by Black audiences at this point (1989). Gates's description of signifyin(g) is summed up in a general way as "repetition with a signal difference," although the full weight of its use in African American humor, literature, and ordinary discourse carries simultaneous elements of misdirection, exaggeration, insult, and irony—all of which are illustrative of Black minstrelsy and how it both expressed Black culture and commented on White imitations of it. Samuel Floyd in *The Power of Black Music* likewise uses signifyin(g) in a refinement of Houston Baker's idea that the mask not only protected Black performers but also afforded them an entry into White society, as well as a way to reject modernism, which was seen as a move to make younger (and more financially successful Blacks) reject their folk and cultural roots (Floyd, 98).

While the obvious use of blackface makeup is the focus of modern scorn regarding racist stereotyping, the use of sonic cues was no less important to the style and evolution of both and blackface minstrelsy. The development of "Black dialect" used in Tin Pan Alley songs from the time of Stephen Foster through the blues era and even beyond was enhanced by the popularity of blackface minstrelsy in the north and perhaps even Black minstrel shows in the South later on. Jennifer Lynn Stoever has pointed out that minstrelsy was "an array of sonic stereotypes," even considered apart from blackface, and that ideas of race (both positive and negative) could be summoned by sounds as effectively as visual representation (Stoever, 2016, 84). She notes that the introduction of recordings by Black performers made the idea of a "black sound" possible and ultimately even more evocative than blackface itself (11). The unprecedented success and subsequent universality of Stephen Foster's minstrel songs such as "Old Folks at Home" and "Oh! Susanna" is a testament to the effectiveness of such sonic representation.

By the mid-1870s, White minstrel companies were beginning to change their entertainment focus. Still using blackface in order to maintain the consistency of the tradition, these groups gradually began deemphasizing the depictions and characterizations of African American life that had been an integral part of the style before the Civil War. Instead, they began to explore representations of other ethnicities and racial groups; skits and shows presenting Italians, Irish, German, Jewish, Chinese, and Native Americans became stock resources, eventually leading to vaudeville conventions.

At the same time there were also numerous Black Minstrel groups performing around the country. These groups continued using blackface and, contrary to the direction taken by their White counterparts, began featuring more African American themes and entertainment styles in their shows. Plantation settings, Jubilee singers, and broad folk humor became identifiable characteristics in these shows, exemplified by the new-style companies led by William Foote and Sam T. Jack (Toll, 1974, 160–61, 226–27; Abbott & Seroff, 2002, 145). This emphasis was not necessarily designed to retain the White audience, because the largest constituency following these groups was apparently lower- and lower-middle-class Blacks. According to Robert Toll, "New minstrelsy, in the hands of Black performers, acquired the capacity and occasion to transport its audiences towards a more profound comprehension of slavery and racism," although the question remains as to whether such a transport was entirely intentional (Robinson, 2007, 147).

Likewise, the musical component of these new style Black Minstrel shows advanced in terms of technique and presentation. From the late 1870s vocal groups, beginning with the original Fisk Jubilee Singers, began presenting concert arrangements of Black folk music and traditional spirituals along with classical selections, influencing similar groups who were touring in minstrel shows. One of the most consistently successful of the "high-class" minstrel troupes was led by Matilda Sissieretta Jones (1868–1933). Known as "Black Patti" in tribute to Italian singer Adelina Patti, Jones was trained as a concert singer and attracted the attention of composer/conductor Antonin Dvořák when he was in New York in the early 1890s. Finding most concert venues closed to African American artists, Jones founded the Black Patti Troubadours, which toured from 1896 to 1915. This group represents a transitional period between blackface minstrelsy, and later vaudeville/variety shows, and it toured all over the United States and Canada, performing for both Black and White audiences (Abbott & Seroff, 2007, 38). As the female lead of a large company, Jones was the direct predecessor to the "Blues Queens" of the 1920s, demonstrating vocal power, a galvanizing stage presence and a sartorial panache (Abbott & Seroff, 2002, 214, 438). In the same way, the popularity of the bands that toured with these minstrel companies led to a measure of celebrity for their leaders (P. G. Lowery, Fred

Figure 1.1. Black Patti, ca. 1899. Metropolitan Printing Co. Library of Congress, Prints and Photographs Division. Public domain.

Simpson, and Henderson Smith were popular bandmasters, as reflected in contemporary advertisements) and brought regional and folk styles of African American music, as well as classics to Black and White audiences around the country.

These Black Minstrel groups toured internationally as well as the entirety of the United States (not just the South) and the response by both transplanted African American populations as well as White audiences produced the first generation of recognized Black entertainment stars (Abbott & Seroff, 2002, 62, 65, 106). Companies such as the Georgia Minstrels toured Europe and the Far East from 1865 to 1902, while Mahara's Colored Minstrels (1892–1909, for a while featuring bandleader W. C. Handy) and Pringle's Georgia Minstrels (1887–1903, with Billy Kersands) toured primarily in North America. Sam Lucas (ca.1840–1915), Billy Kersands (1842–1915), and Ernest Hogan (1865–1909) were all key performers, and in Kersands's case, producers of traveling shows. Hogan was also a successful songwriter, composing the enormous hit "All Coons Look Alike to Me" in 1895, although later in life he admitted regret over his role in cementing the word *coon* in the culture. Unfortunately, none of these three lived long enough to make recordings, and only Lucas (who was also known as a fine dramatic actor) appeared in a film. (Lucas starred in the 1914 Vitagraph film *Uncle Tom's Cabin*, making him among the first African Americans to star in an otherwise White film. He also may be seen in existing film footage from the unreleased 1913 Biograph film *Lime Kiln Field Day* that starred Bert Williams and had an all-Black cast.)

The popularity of these traveling companies served to alert African American audiences to the possibility that their own experience could be presented on stage in a recognizable way. Smaller touring troupes tended to stay primarily in the South and play to exclusively rural and poor Black crowds, while the larger ones starring the entertainers mentioned above would move throughout the country, playing for both Black and White audiences. While African Americans took pride in seeing the success of these groups and could laugh at their jokes by seeing their own experience and life reflected from the stage, knowing that there was more to their existence than the stereotype (Watkins, 1994, 128). The 1893 Columbian Exposition in Chicago brought the idea of African culture (albeit in a highly stylized and often racist way) to mainstream public attention (Abbott & Seroff, 2002, 296). In addition, it fostered a burgeoning level of racial pride and interest in African American folk and traditional culture, which acted in tandem with the developments in the Black Minstrel shows. When these Black shows played for White audiences, they were seen as, in Mel Watkins's words, a kind of "peep show" drawing back the curtain on the existence of a foreign culture (Watkins, 1994, 121).

Canvas Shows: Tent Shows and Circuses

For the most part, minstrel shows during the 1880s and 1890s were indoor affairs, being performed in permanent theaters for a time before moving on to the next town. By 1900, theaters (particularly in midsized and large cities) were closing their doors to African American acts. This retraction caused smaller and newer companies to begin carrying their own theaters—large tents that could be set up and taken down quickly—allowing for single performances and limited runs in rural areas. Allen's New Orleans Minstrels (1899–early 1920s), the Rabbit's Foot Minstrels (1900–late 1950s), the Florida Blossom Minstrels (1906–1920s), and especially the long-lived Silas Green from New Orleans (1904–1957) show became touring staples throughout the South, combining minstrel structure, popular music, parades, public concerts, and even exhibition baseball games (Abbott & Seroff, 2007, 209–210).

Tent shows were a familiar presence in American entertainment from the second decade of the nineteenth century. Beginning with traveling circuses that had become too large and unwieldy to present indoors, various performing groups found that traveling with their own venue was economically feasible as well as allowing them to take their tours further afield than had previously been the case. By 1856, variety shows had begun to explore the possibilities of touring with their own tents and the development of commercial rail travel during and immediately after the Civil War further expanded possibilities. By the end of the century, audiences ranging from urban people to those living in the most rural sections of the country could avail themselves of a range of entertainment possibilities, including minstrel shows, opera, vaudeville, Chautauqua performances, and repertory theater, in addition to circuses and variety programs "under canvas." These shows developed rapidly due to the seasonal aspects of traditional indoor theatrical performances; the lack of air conditioning forced most permanent theaters to close during the summer and early autumn, and the facilities themselves were often inadequate in terms of size and amenities to allow for large-scale or ambitious performances.

After a temporary lull caused by the Panic of 1893, which greatly impacted tours to rural areas (both agriculture and the railroad industry were severely hurt), tent shows staged a comeback during the first two decades of the twentieth century. Coinciding with the Golden Age of the Circus (lasting until the early 1920s), variety and minstrel tent shows featuring popular music of the day began to make regular tours through the South and Midwest, focusing primarily on rural audiences, which did not have easy access to permanent theaters. As radio and sound film were not to become available until the mid- to late 1920s, people outside of urban areas were limited in terms of entertainment choice, and the traveling tent shows provided a needed outlet. For three or four years following the end of World War I, traveling tent shows achieved their greatest commercial success; more disposable income in rural areas, lack of other entertainment opportunities, and the popularity of the automobile allowed for greater range of movement for both performer and audience. Until the development of extensive national and regional radio programming and the explosion of the popular record industry, combined with the availability of affordable radios and record players in the mid-1920s, tent shows were the only venue for much of the country to experience African American popular music.

Indeed, music had been a key element of tent shows from the beginning. Circuses almost always traveled with bands that played incidental music during performances, but more visibly the bands played for parades, which were staged as the troupe arrived in a new town. Important Black bandleaders in the circus tradition include James Wolfscale (1868–1921), who led the sideshow band for Barnum and Bailey from 1912 to 1918, and P. G. Lowery (1869–1942), who took over from Wolfscale when that circus combined with Ringling Brothers from 1919–1941. Both leaders employed many Black musicians who were to become better known as jazz players in the next two decades, including Zue Robertson, William Thornton Blue, and Charles Creath.

Variety and minstrel tent shows often pressed their musicians into service for parades as well, and inevitably the popular music of the day would be featured. The repertoire of the various acts would reflect the trends in pop music of the day, at least as far as their immediate audience might be willing to go. By the early 1900s, these groups were featuring instrumental versions of popular ragtime and cakewalk performances, and by the 1910s blues and other African American folk styles were also being introduced in both Black and White shows. In an interview with John Wesley Work in 1932, the singer Ma Rainey (who had been touring in tent shows since 1900) claimed to have first been aware of the blues as a particular style by 1902, and featuring music that she recognized as blues shortly thereafter.

While most of the literature on tent shows and circuses has focused on White shows, there was an active tradition of Black troupes traveling the country under canvas as well. From the late 1800s to the first decade or so of the twentieth century, there was also a tradition of White circuses presenting African American musicians in their sideshows, performed outside the main tent. There was a fluid movement of these musicians and their performance style between circuses (both Black and White) and minstrel shows, and this intersection provided one of the first socially accepted opportunities for the White public to hear African American popular music (Abbott & Seroff, 2007, 373–75). Perhaps more important, African American audiences were now able to hear music created and performed by other Blacks. This was a vital and unique form of cultural dispersion until 1920, when African Americans were finally given the opportunity to make recordings on a large scale.

By 1900, tent shows directed and sometimes produced and funded by African Americans began to tour throughout the South. These shows initially combined aspects of traditional minstrel organization—the tripartite structure beginning with the introduction (which might still include the interlocutor and endmen); the olio (which eventually became the most important component, featuring as it did the individual talents of the performers); and the skit portion (which often provided the continuity of the show). Such shows as the Rabbit's Foot Minstrels and Silas Green from New Orleans were perennial favorites in rural southern areas until as late as the 1950s. These shows were noted for their music: the bands and singers were frequently mentioned in reviews as well as publicity materials in Black newspapers. Shorter-lived shows such as the various Smart Set Companies were also important in bringing contemporary trends in popular music to areas in the South largely ignored by theater-based vaudeville and musical comedy troupes (Abbott & Seroff, 2007, 4–6).

Perhaps the first "modern" tent show to tour was Alexander Tolliver's *Big Show* in 1914. Initially called *Tolliver's Smart Set*, this show was developed on the heels of the well-known and more formal *Smart Set* founded by legendary Black entertainers Billy McClain and Ernest

Hogan in 1902. This show consciously sought to deemphasize the traditional minstrel elements considered indispensable to a Black show and to freshen up the presentation of the acts with more contemporary music (initially, ragtime). The success of this approach can be seen in a backhand way by *Smart Set*'s unofficial ban from New Orleans after its 1903 appearance, probably due to local officials' discomfort with the new and more respectful presentation of African American entertainment. This show continued to tour successfully throughout the 1910s, led first by Sherman Dudley and, from 1913, by Salem Tutt Whitney (1875–1934).

Whitney, a popular comic and singer in various shows (including with the *Smart Set* since 1910) was a particular force in African American entertainment during the 1910s, by virtue of his regular column "Seen and Heard While Passing," which ran in the African American newspaper *The Freeman* from 1911 and continued in the *Chicago Defender* until Whitney's death in 1934. His shows were seen as the apex of Black entertainment during this period, and he took pains to present a quality, "high-class" show using Black popular music such as ragtime, spirituals, and quartet singing, and even occasional forays into vernacular music. Whitney was furious when Tolliver began presenting his show as *The Smart Set*, and a lively argument was waged between the two in the pages of *The Freeman* beginning late in 1914, when reports of Tolliver's success in the South began to reach Whitney.

Tolliver's show shared little in common with Whitney's beyond the name. While the Whitney *Smart Set* was an elaborate show performed in theaters and featuring formal presentations of dramatic recitations and classical and concert music along with comedy and ragtime, Tolliver's show was aimed at a much less sophisticated southern audience, both Black and White. Partnering with the White show business financier C. W. Park in 1914, Tolliver developed a broad-based variety show with a definite southern slant in terms of both music and humor. Traveling with a tent that could seat up to 1,200 people, the Tolliver/Park show ranged from Virginia through the Carolinas and Georgia during its initial, abbreviated fall season before wintering in Atlanta.

Typically, a tent show would find winter quarters in some warm location from December through February or March, during which time it would organize the entertainment and line up acts for the following season (capable performers would occasionally do short tours in vaudeville to fill up the empty calendar space). The touring season would begin in the early spring and usually extend through the fall, with the company moving through the South to maximize both the good weather and the planting and harvesting seasons. This would allow the traveling companies to take advantage of the disposable income of the newly paid agricultural workers following a planting or harvest. During the winter of 1914–1915, Tolliver began pulling together a show that was far more ambitious in terms of size and scope than any tent show that had come before it. For the 1915 season, the Tolliver *Big Show* (which was occasionally still booked as the *Smart Set*) featured future blues stars Clara Smith, Jodie Edwards, and Susie Hawthorne (who later married, billing themselves as "Butterbeans and Susie"); Leola "Coot" Grant; Wayne "Buzzin'" Burton (who had toured vaudeville teamed with Bessie Smith for a few seasons previously); Alec Lovejoy (who had a busy career in films following the introduction of sound); Frankie "Half Pint" Jaxon and Trixie Smith. But their principal attraction was the team of Rainey and Rainey.

Gertrude and Will Rainey had been touring the tent show and vaudeville circuit since their marriage in 1904, and had amassed a degree of celebrity, particularly in Virginia, the Carolinas, and Georgia. Not known as "Ma and Pa" until 1913, the Raineys had led their own companies (such as the Alabama Fun Makers and the Georgia Sunbeams), as well as performed in shows such as the *Rabbit Foot Minstrels* and *Benbow's Chocolate Drops* before being hired by Tolliver. The larger show and the increase in the audience encouraged Tolliver to get a larger tent capable of holding 3,000 patrons and locating the main stage in the center. Following a resoundingly successful season, the show wintered in New Orleans, making the acquaintance of numerous musicians and entertainers while performing at local theaters and cabarets. Several native New Orleans players were engaged to go on tour with the revamped Tolliver *Big Show/Smart Set*, which was being billed as a "Circus and Musical Extravaganza." Willie Hightower (trumpet), Alvin "Zoo" (also known as "Zue") Robertson (trombone), David Jones (saxophone), Eddie "Rabbit" Robinson (drums), and John Porter (bass) were signed to play with the band led by the well-traveled clarinetist Fred Kewley, suggesting that this band might have been capable of playing some early forms of jazz, although it is unlikely that at this date they would have had the opportunity. In addition to the Raineys, Jodie Edwards, Daisy Martin, Susie Edwards, and Clara Smith, there was a collection of singers, dancers, and more circus-oriented acts such as jugglers, clowns, and high-wire performers. Ma Rainey was frequently mentioned in reviews as a "blues singer" with great popular appeal (Abbott & Seroff, 2007, 127–31).

The popular Tolliver shows of 1915 and 1916 were afforded the luxury of remaining in locations for a week or more, as well as by traveling in relatively comfortable Pullman cars. Following the close of the 1916 season, the show went into winter quarters in Birmingham, Alabama, where Tolliver and Park had a falling out that resulted in the show losing its financing. This immediately reduced the *Big Show* significantly, with many of its acts leaving or being let go. The 1917 season was a much less comfortable affair, with the tours being more representative of the usual tent show experience: frequent successions of one-night performances, and crowded sleeping and traveling conditions with occasional layoffs. Any possibility of recovering in 1918 was defeated by both the entry of the United States into World War I, resulting in travel restrictions, new taxes, and the draft (Tolliver himself was drafted in 1918) and the Spanish influenza pandemic, which caused quarantines and further travel restrictions.

Nevertheless, for the 1914–1917 period and immediately thereafter, tent shows touring the South became prime deliverers of Black popular culture—music, dance, and humor—throughout the southern portion of the country, and that influence was reflected in the development of Black vaudeville and stage shows for the next decade, culminating in the blues and jazz of the 1920s.

Black Broadway

By the early 1890s, the next generation of Black entertainers was beginning to come to prominence. Generally more urban than their predecessors, these performers benefited from more education and professional training in music as well as theater, and saw themselves in a different light than did the first generation of Black minstrels who were often self-taught and raised in much more restrictive circumstances. This generation of stage actors was led by Bob Cole (1868–1911), George Walker (1872–1911), J. Rosamund Johnson (1873–1954), Bert Williams (1875–1922), and Aida Overton Walker (1880–1914), among others.

Sam Lucas figured prominently in the success of *That Creole Show*—a minstrel show produced by the White entrepreneur Sam T. Jack in 1890—that began to reject the standard format of the classic minstrel show (particularly its reliance on plantation themes and settings) and move toward both vaudeville and burlesque by incorporating women in prominent roles. Despite this move, the show still had its cast wear blackface and preserved the role of the interlocutor (Woll, 1989, 4–13). *The Octoroons* (1895), presented by the White producer John W. Isham, likewise furthered this transition, using the older minstrel Tom McIntosh (who had also toured with Sissieretta Jones) in the lead role.

One of the first successful attempts to update the traditional minstrel entertainment and to bring to it a level of formality and respectability was *A Trip to Coontown* (1898) by Bob Cole and Billy Johnson. This show was the first musical show created and presented by African American composers and entertainers and was closely followed by *Clorindy: The Origin of the Cakewalk* by Will Marion Cook and Paul Lawrence Dunbar, a single-act musical that was the first all-Black production to run on Broadway. The participation of Cook is significant, as he figured prominently as a composition student of the Czech composer Antonin Dvořák during his 1892–1895 residence as director of the National Conservatory of Music. In a famous and influential interview published in the *New York Herald* in May, 1893, Dvořák cited in particular "the Negro melodies of America" as the source of an indigenous American school of musical composition (Tick & Beaudoin, 2008, 308–15).

Perhaps in part due to the awareness and grudging recognition of traditional African American musical forms initiated by Dvořák, the 1890s saw a move to include more facets of African American entertainment within the confines of the minstrel show structure. Sissieretta Jones ("Black Patti") was widely respected for introducing European concert pieces (including operatic arias) into the olio of a minstrel performance. Jones moved easily between stage shows and concert performances during her career and found immense (if temporary) success leading her "Black Patti Troubadours." This move toward "higher class" or cultural entertainment was fed by the increasing self-awareness of the performers mentioned above and their racial as well as professional pride.

Following this trajectory were the shows produced by the fruitful partnership of Bob Cole and J. Rosamund Johnson (and to a lesser extent his brother, James Weldon Johnson). Cole and Johnson were highly successful Tin Pan Alley songwriters from the beginning of the 1900s, with hits in numerous White and Black shows. They also toured as a singing and comic duo in some of the more lucrative vaudeville venues, eschewing any minstrel trappings. They performed their own songs while dressed in tuxedos and maintaining a level of sophistication taken on twenty years later by Noble Sissle and Eubie Blake. In 1907, the team produced *Shoo Fly Regiment*, followed by *Red Moon* in 1909, each of which was a plot-driven Broadway show presenting African American characters who were far less beholden to minstrel stereotypes and even engaged in romantic plot elements. Cole unfortunately committed suicide by drowning in 1911, following a long battle with the effects of syphilis and depression, ending one of the most successful partnerships in Black entertainment of the period.

The performer who was most vocal about attempts to advance Black stage productions was George Walker. After several unremarkable years of touring in minstrel shows in the Midwest, Walker found himself in California in 1895, at which point he met Egbert "Bert" Williams, a native of the Bahamas who had likewise been touring in various minstrel companies. Walker was known primarily as a dancer and Williams a comedian, although both sang and could act as foils for each other. As "Two Real Coons" they toured vaudeville, making their way to New York, where they began to attract attention by 1896. After being featured in several White productions, they launched a series of musical comedies featuring all-Black casts, beginning with *Sons of Ham* in 1900. In addition to the formal aspects of the show, the individual characterizations were more sympathetic and human than had been the case in the minstrel shows of the previous decades. *In Dahomey* (1902) was the first all-Black show to be launched on Broadway, and was a remarkable success, even touring England and performing for Edward VII in 1903.

Walker was quite outspoken in press interviews about his vision for future shows. He felt that he, his wife Aida Overton Walker, and Williams were responsible for elevating the idea of the African American entertainer and set *In Dahomey* and its successor *Abyssinia* (1906) in Africa, in an attempt to celebrate the history of Blacks in America (Woll, 1989, 38–42). Walker said: "The one hope for the colored performer must be in making a radical departure from the old 'darky' style of singing and dancing. . . . There is an artistic side to the black race, and if it could be properly developed on the stage, I believe the theatergoing public would profit much by it" (quoted in Gilbert, 1963, 284). Unfortunately, Walker was forced into retirement during the run of *Bandanna Days* in 1908, suffering from the effects of advanced syphilis. Williams made an attempt to continue in *Mr. Lode of Koal* in 1909, but his extraordinary popularity with both White and Black audiences (helped in no small way by numerous recordings he made of his signature stage numbers) secured him a job with the otherwise all-White Broadway show *Ziegfeld Follies* of 1910, with which he remained until 1919.

The deaths of Cole, Walker, Kersands, Lucas, and Hogan, as well as Williams's move into White Broadway shows severely hampered further development of Black Broadway productions, although the constantly evolving and changing tastes of the public would probably have had the same effect. All-Black shows returned to Broadway ten years later with *Shuffle Along* (1921), but in the interim other entertainment possibilities assumed prominence.

The 1910s: Recordings and Syncopated Dance Music

The sudden collapse of the African American musical theater scene after 1910 coincided with the equally sudden rise of the commercial recording industry. While White performers such as John Philip Sousa, Arthur Pryor, Al Jolson, John McCormack, and Enrico Caruso dominated the sales charts, a surprising number of Black entertainers were also given the opportunity to record. Brooks estimates that there were at least 800 commercial records made and released by African American performers prior to 1920 (Brooks, 2004, 10).

The first successful foray into recording came with Thomas Edison's 1877 experiments with a foil-wrapped cylinder. Edison did not see his invention as having any practical application to the entertainment industry, instead imagining its future as a tool for business, education, and historical archiving. By 1886, Chester Bell and Charles Sumner Tainter improved on the model by inventing a wax cylinder recorder they called the Graphophone, spurring the competitive Edison into answering with his vertical-cut cylinder phonograph two years later (Roland Gelatt, 1977, 21–38; see also, Millard & Brooks).

Perhaps the most significant technological development (although one that did not become evident for twenty years) was Emile Berliner's development and patent of a lateral cut disc that could be played on his "gramophone." These discs were far more portable and easier to store, as well as being generally more durable. By 1896, the first budget-line phonographs were marketed and made available to the public, which further encouraged recording and consumption as well as the development of the "Big Three" companies: the Columbia Phonograph Company (1889), the National American Phonograph Company (incorporated by Thomas Edison in 1896), and Victor (1901). These three were the beneficiaries of the patents taken out by Edison and Berliner, in particular, which effectively allowed them to monopolize the industry until the expiration of those patents in 1917 (Gelatt, 1977, 49–50).

The primitivism of recording and reproduction technology is something difficult to comprehend today. At first, cylinders could not be mechanically duplicated, necessitating multiple performances into numerous horns to produce a stock of any recording. It was this situation that existed at the dawn of the commercial recording industry, which effectively began in the early 1890s. Very few cylinders from this first period still exist, but a study of contemporary advertisements and catalogs show a panoply of whistlers, piano players, monologists, and wind bands, with small detachments of John Philip Sousa's band being early popular favorites. The perception of what sounds recorded well was an important factor in who would be brought before the horn in a studio.

Remarkably, African American performers were present virtually from the beginning of the commercial recording era. The Unique Quartet recorded a long series of minstrel and folk tunes from 1890 to 1893 (followed by the Standard Quartette in 1894), while George Johnson began his long and odd career making whistling and laughing records in 1890 (Brooks, 2004, 5–8). Johnson was a former slave who had gained some notice in New York by the 1880s as a performer. He continued recording until about 1910, although the new processes of mechanical duplication severely curtailed his recording activity (he was only required to record a selection once, rather than multiple times), and he died in poverty in 1914. The New Orleans banjo player and minstrel Louis "Bebe" Vasnier was making cylinders of monologues and comic numbers by the mid-1890s, and mention is often made of a cylinder supposedly recorded by the legendary New Orleans cornet player Buddy Bolden, presumably in the 1890s as well.

In the years following the turn of the century, more of the professional class of Black entertainers began making recordings that were distributed around the country. First and foremost in terms of influence and popularity were the Victor and Columbia recordings of Williams and Walker, and after George Walker's death, by Bert Williams alone. Williams was the most frequently recorded African American performer prior to the 1920s, although his discography was complimented by Carroll Clark (who recorded spirituals and southern songs for Columbia beginning in 1908 and extending to art songs in the 1920s), the Fisk University Jubilee Singers (beginning in 1909), and Daisey Tapley (the first African American woman on record, singing mainly classical selections in 1911;

Brooks, 2007, 7–9). Recordings at the end of the decade by concert singers Roland Hayes and Florence Cole-Talbert continued the tradition.

Recording Black vernacular music was a slower proposition, although ultimately a far more important one. Although Black musicians and bands had been key in performing ragtime and syncopated dance music since the 1890s, the first authentic recordings by African American performers of popular music were not made until 1913 and 1914, when both James Reese Europe and Dan Kildare were brought into the studios of Victor and Columbia, respectively. The Jamaican Kildare directed the band for White dancer Joan Sawyer, under whose name his first recordings were made in New York in 1914 (a further handful was done by his Ciro's Club Coon Orchestra in London two years later). Performers who might previously have had to wear blackface were not required to do so in the recording studio. Lisa Gitelman has commented that records allowed for "blackness" to survive "without the sight of minstrel blackness," leading to the development of new signifiers of Blackness through sound (Gitelman, 1999, 134–35).

Europe, on the other hand, was the driving force among Black musicians in New York in the 1910s. After a stint as a conductor for both Ernest Hogan and Cole and Johnson's shows, Europe became the music director for the sensationally popular White dance team Vernon and Irene Castle in 1913. At the same time he was an organizing member of the all-Black Clef Club (a loose guild of African American dance band and society musicians), which elected him as its first president in 1910 (he was replaced by Kildare in 1913). In addition to booking musical groups all over the city and promoting concerts devoted to the works of African American composers, Europe was active in introducing syncopated dance music to the White New York public, at first through his work with the Castles. In 1913 and 1914, a reduced version of Europe's Clef Club Orchestra made several recordings for Victor under the name of "Europe's Society Orchestra," including ragtime songs "Too Much Mustard" and "Down Home Rag" (Victor 35359, December 29, 1913). These sides were relatively successful and might have led to a longer discography had World War I not intervened, taking Vernon Castle, Europe, and many of his musicians into the service. Europe became one of the most visible and successful Black musicians of his time through these recordings and engagements, and his career as a band leader during the war (and subsequent series of recordings for Pathe in 1919) cemented his position in the industry. It is one of the numerous tales of unfulfilled promise that his early death (at the hands of one of his musicians in 1919) robbed the African American musical community of one of its most accomplished leaders.

Following the successful example of Europe's Society Orchestra, dance bands led by Ford Dabney (beginning in 1917 for Aeolian) and Wilbur Sweatman (1916 for Emerson and 1917 for Pathe) recorded an intriguing mix of ragtime and what came to be known as "jazz," following the Victor recordings of the Original Dixieland Jazz Band in 1917. (Dabney had played piano on Europe's 1913 and 1914 records, and Sweatman had recorded clarinet solos as early as 1901; Brooks, 2004, 7.) The "Father of the Blues," W. C. Handy recorded ten sides as "Handy's Orchestra of Memphis" in 1917, with what was largely a pickup band playing his arrangements of material (including one of his own tunes) either similar or identical to what he had been playing on the minstrel circuit for at least a decade.

Black Vaudeville

The period following the retirements or death of so many of the brightest lights of the Black musical theater coincided with an economic downturn in the industry. Referred to as a "lull" by Thomas Riis, the second decade of the twentieth century saw traveling Black shows relegated to theaters far inferior in terms of prestige and structure than the ones occupied by both the Williams and Walker, and Cole and Johnson shows of the first years of the century (Riis, 1989, 159–60). This made touring (especially in the South) far more difficult, with rising costs, racism, fewer available venues, and the loss of financing combining to put an end to the big touring shows for the next few years.

Several entertainment outlets rose to fill the gap. "Legitimate" theatrical productions of classical works as well as plays by African American authors began to appear during this period. The Lafayette Players (initially known as the Bush Company) presented works from 1915 to 1932, primarily in New York. Various Black acts toured the so-called Big Time (meaning, "White") vaudeville circuits. Charlie Case (1858–1916) was an anomaly: a Black performer (although perhaps attempting to pass for White, while donning blackface) touring White vaudeville as a single as early as the 1880s (Gilbert, 1963, 176). Bill Johnson's Original Creole Orchestra from New Orleans was touring the usually all-White

Orpheum circuit by 1912, bringing both early jazz and African American performance styles to White theaters throughout the Midwest and West Coast (Gushee, 2010).

The success of Black entertainers on the White circuits, coupled with the virulent racism they encountered, encouraged the organization of several Black theater guilds and employment agencies. The roots of Black vaudeville can be seen as early as the 1890s in saloons and outdoor venues known as park pavilions, presenting a combination of minstrel acts, ragtime, and vocal quartets. By 1910, there were more than 100 theaters presenting Black vaudeville in the southeast and Gulf Coast states and the need for more central coordination became apparent (Abbott & Seroff, 2017, 7, 55). In 1907, the White theater manager Fred Barrasso established the Tri-State Circuit—a small network of all-Black theaters in Arkansas, Mississippi, and Tennessee, which in 1909 became the Theater Owners Booking Agency and seemed poised to expand before Barrasso's death in 1911. Other organizations followed, including the Afro-American Vaudeville Booking Association (1910), William Foster's agency (also 1910), and the Colored Vaudeville Exchange, founded in 1912 by songwriter and producer J. Leubrie Hill, although it is unclear if these groups were attempting to create circuits of Black vaudeville theaters or simply to place Black acts in White vaudeville (Breaux, 2019, 43–48).

Perhaps the most successful (and groundbreaking) of these groups was the Southern Consolidated Vaudeville Circuit, founded by comedian and producer Sherman Dudley (1872–1940) in 1909. The first Black-owned and -run theater chain, Dudley's creation expanded throughout the 1910s and was virtually the only such outlet until it was challenged by the 1921 establishment of the Theater Owner's Booking Association, run by the White theater owner Milton Starr. Dudley soon bowed to the greater resources of Starr's conglomerate and joined forces with it, creating a Black vaudeville monopoly that continued until 1929, when vaudeville in general was essentially finished by a combination of the Depression, sound film, and radio.

According to Eileen Southern (1971, 369), Black vaudeville began to replace the touring Black minstrel companies from the first years of the twentieth century until around 1920. This is slightly misleading; the line between minstrel companies (and their successors) touring in circuses and tent shows in the South during the summer and fall was a fluid one, and often included the same performers and acts that would tour the Black vaudeville theaters in the winter and spring. As will be seen, blues singers and personalities such as Ma Rainey, Bessie Smith, Ida Cox, and Clara Smith all went back and forth between vaudeville and canvas shows well into the 1930s, depending on the season and economic need.

Chapter 2

"Yonder Come the Blues"

The invention and development of the blues has been discussed by virtually every author of a text on American popular music. These discussions are invariably underpinned with the politics of race and economics, emphasizing certain points while dismissing others along the way to develop a theory of creation.

"Blues," in fact, represents a variety of cultural expressions. Similar in a way to the porous delineation of "rap" and "hip-hop" in more modern popular sensibility, blues can refer to a style of music, a specific form, or even an entire cultural spectrum. When a musician refers to playing the blues, he or she is generally referring to one of the myriad variations of the twelve-bar musical structure understood as blues since the 1910s. In the blues style, musicians use the structure extensively but not exclusively; in that case, blues is an approach to playing any song by emphasizing certain "blue notes," emotions, and familiar instruments (electric or acoustic guitar and bass, harmonica, drums, voice). On a sociological level, blues can refer to a mode of living, interacting with others, dancing, and, of course, emotion.

Even isolating the first instance of the word *blues* in a musical context is difficult. The term itself existed in England in the 1600s as a contraction of "blue devils," usually referring to the effects of alcohol abuse. By the 1800s, it was also used to describe a state of sadness or depression over the course of time. In African American culture the term was used as a description of sadness or desperation as early as 1893 (Abbott & Seroff, 2002, 302–3). The first published musical composition with "blues" in the title that used the twelve-bar progression was "I Got the Blues" by the

Italian American composer Anthony Maggio in 1908, which became a regional hit in his hometown of New Orleans (Lief, accessed 2021). In New Orleans, Maggio had heard an African American playing guitar and singing a lament described by the performer as blues, which inspired Maggio to compose a tune in the same style and using the same three-note motif. The 1911, Tin Pan Alley standard "Oh, You Beautiful Doll" by A. Seymour Brown and Nat Ayer based its verse on a standard blues progression, indicating the reach of the style beyond its African American folk roots even by that point. By 1912, numerous compositions had been published, cementing both the musical form and the style of blues in the popular consciousness (Abbott & Seroff, 2002, 302–3).

What led to the development of the blues as a musical form? Michael Coolen suggests the distant reaches could be in the Senegambian *fodet*: "A *fodet* is a recurring musical structure (in some ways a musical template) of a fixed number of beats (from six to twenty-four), with specific melodic, rhythmic, and even harmonic characteristics. While some *fodets* are composed of only one phrase, it is more common to encounter *fodets* composed of two to four phrases. Like the blues, *fodets* are cyclic, repeated as many times as the performer chooses to play them." Coolen goes on to comment on the similarity of the AAB phrase structure and multiple tonal centers of the *fodet* to the standard blues structure (Floyd, 1995, 85).

Somewhat at odds with this line of thought, Samuel Floyd has suggested that both jazz and blues were beholden to European musical forms superimposed on African elements, although he supports Coolen's claims in general. Floyd gives ragtime, spirituals/jubilee hymns, work songs, and vernacular dances (such as the cakewalk) as Black folk elements leading to the blues style. The work song in particular he sees as a key ancestor, bringing traditional African elements of call and response, regular meter, and extra-musical sounds (such as grunts, whistles, and groans; Floyd, 1995, 50). Along with this line of reasoning is the argument Peter Muir makes for the "Blues Ballad" form, represented by the traditional song "Frankie and Johnny" (Muir, 2010, 190–99). The first song of this type to be published was "You Needn't Come Home," by blackface minstrel Hughie Cannon in 1901. The numerous songs in this category feature at least one twelve-bar section, which is different from a traditional blues by the inclusion of an IV chord instead of a tonic on the seventh measure. This harmonic difference was likely generated by a more active melody line emphasizing a narrative tale, possibly derived from the ballad tradition of Scots-Irish White settlers (Muir, 2010, 200).

Perhaps of more immediate importance to the nascent blues in the early 1900s was the nexus with religious music. Spirituals had been important elements of religious expression among African Americans since the beginning of their conversion to Christianity. Initially, these songs were developed from standard White Protestant hymns that were then interpreted stylistically, using performance practices that would be carried into the twentieth century with blues and gospel music: "blue" notes, rhythmic accompaniment (clapping, foot stomping), repetition, call and response, performer interaction with the audience (or congregation), improvisation, and so on. "Sorrow Songs" were religious laments that often combined a longing for earthly freedom and justice as well as eternal peace, clearly leading to the more secular lyrical focus of the blues. "Jubilees," on the other hand, were more up-tempo and focused on triumph rather than tragedy. Robin Sylvan points out this combination and how the components of celebration and observance are common to both gospel and blues, demonstrating how blues singers were "more priestly than artistic" in their role as conduits of the music on stage—a point made by people describing both Bessie Smith and Ma Rainey in their stage appearances (Sylvan, 2002, 62–63). Angela Davis makes a similar point that blues singers such as Rainey and Smith functioned like preachers as well as mothers in their performances (Davis, 1998, 127–28). James Cone calls them "new priests" of African culture, allowing for gathering places outside of church (Cone, 1991, 102).

Improvisation was also an important connection. James Cone relates that slaves made up words to preexisting hymns, reflecting their day-to-day experience of suffering rather than deliverance, even creating a genre of "seculars," which protested against God and mankind, leading quite obviously to blues (Cone, 1991, 102). This sense of adapting both structure and melodic content became one of the most important (and influential) elements of the early blues period.

The First Blues Performers

Reports from the Black press during the first two decades of the twentieth century are a gold mine of information about the individuals engaged in touring at the most grassroots level in African American entertainment during that period. By tracing expressions such as "coon shouter" and mention of specific songs, we can see the gradual evolution to "blues singer" and the universal acceptance of the term as both a style and a specific form.

While it is virtually impossible to isolate the first blues song prototype, determining the first performers who might have developed the repertoire is somewhat easier. The word *blues* appears in song titles as early as 1897, even though no specific blues were published for another fifteen years, demonstrating at least a cultural consciousness of the term. As will be seen in the discussion on Ma Rainey, she claimed to have become aware of blues as a specific style as early as 1902, although this seems very early during her professional career indeed. Folklorist John Jacob Niles cited Ophelia Simpson as a Black medicine show performer he heard singing something resembling blues in 1898, although his account and transcription (done in 1930) might have been informed by subsequent developments (Niles, 1930, 519). He also claims to have heard a White mountain singer performing blues in 1908, and points to 1910 as the beginning the public consciousness of the blues form (523). W. C. Handy recalled that in 1903 he heard "a lean, loose-jointed Negro" who was "plunking a guitar" using a steel bar as he sang a repeated refrain about where "the Southern cross' the Dog" (a train crossing in Morehead, Mississippi; Handy, 1941, 74). A slightly later experience in Cleveland, Mississippi, demonstrated to Handy that Black audiences in the South responded to folk music he described as "haunting," which developed into the blues that influenced his compositions and arrangements during the 1910s.

Prior to singers being singled out as "blues singers," the expression "coon shouter" was used to describe performers specializing in songs supposedly evoking African American themes and performance practice, although a certain amount of this description obviously comes from minstrelsy and the "coon songs" in vogue during the 1890s. White singers like Clarice Vance, Mae Irwin, and Artie Hall were marketed as coon shouters in the late 1890s, although by that time "Ragtime Coon Songs" were beginning to present more of the African American perspective, as opposed to a strictly comic stereotype, opening up the gates for Black performers as well. So-called Up-to-Date Coon Shouters including Ma Rainey, Bessie Smith, and Clara Smith replaced earlier Black women singers like Rosa Scott, Bessie Gilliam, and Carrie Hall (who were not accorded the "up-to-date" title, whether by reason of style or age; Abbott & Seroff, 2007, 12–23).

Sherman Dudley's *Smart Set* show of 1906 featured a song titled "All In, Down, and Out," which Abbott and Seroff have proposed as a precursor to stage blues, having much in common with the later blues-era song "Nobody Knows You When You're Down and Out" (Abbott & Seroff, 2007, 98). By 1910, Butler "String Beans" May was singing blues songs in Black vaudeville productions and would likely have become a force in the next era had he not died in 1917. Vaudeville in general was hospitable to male blues singers and instrumentalists (such as pianist Baby Seals) at this time, although there was always a tincture of "smut" about the music, which might have helped its popularity.

By 1915, the transition had been made from "coon shouter" to "blues singer" in the Black press, with such forgotten names as Rhea Wilson, Lizzie Crosby, and Mrs. T. H. Dumas being complimented on their performance of blues or blues-influenced songs (Abbott & Seroff, 2007, 241–44). The unrecorded Katie Price was a significant success in the *Florida Blossoms* show of 1914, singing "I Wonder Where My Easy Rider's Gone," which may have been similar to "See Rider" (discussed below). By 1916, her place had been usurped by Bessie Smith. Likewise, the "female baritone" Ada Lockhart was feted for her version of "St. Louis Blues" with the *Silas Green from New Orleans* show in 1915 (Abbott & Seroff, 2007, 322), while the soon to be better known Clara Smith was advertised as the "Queen of the Blues" when traveling with a Tolliver company the year before. As well-reviewed and successful as some of these singers were, it was Ma Rainey who reigned supreme, first as a coon shouter and then as a blues singer under canvas.

Ma Rainey

Of the singers of the Classic Blues Era, it was Ma Rainey who had the longest career prior to her first recording. Dubbed "Mother of the Blues" during the 1910s, she had been touring since the first years of the twentieth century, referred to as a "coon shouter" as early as 1909, was reported to be singing blues by 1912, and called a "Blues Singer" by 1915. The point is that of all the blues singers recorded during the 1920s, it was Rainey who had the most varied career, as well as one that extended almost back to the nineteenth century, so it can be concluded that she had perhaps the widest repertoire of blues and preblues of any other such performers.

Recording for the relatively small, race label Paramount, Rainey was allowed to record many of her own compositions (as well as those

Figure 2.1. Ma Rainey, ca. 1917. Ben Car Collection. Public domain.

credited to her, which were probably more in the line of traditional material) and a relatively high proportion of theatrical blues and even ragtime tunes that singers such as Bessie Smith (recording for the large, nationally distributed Columbia label) could not. As such, Rainey's discography includes a variety of material that possibly reflects songs and song forms she had been performing in tent shows and circuses for two decades, giving us a unique glimpse of an earlier era, as well as some candidates for early blues prototypes.

"Shave 'em Dry" (Ma Rainey and H. Jackson; recorded August 1924, in Chicago for Paramount)

Rudi Blesh, mentioned "Shave 'em Dry" as an early (he referred to it as an "archaic") form of blues (Blesh, 1946, 19). Consisting of only an eight-bar structure (the second half of which was a refrain), "Shave 'em Dry" is one of two short-form blues recorded by Ma Rainey, along with "Yonder Comes the Blues" (Paramount 12357, December, 1925), which had a one-bar refrain but also included a four-bar instrumental tag after each chorus. Credited to Rainey and "H. Jackson," this tune is likely a much older song assembled from various common stock lyrics, many of which found their way into later blues compositions. "H. Jackson" was probably Papa Charlie Jackson (1898–1938), a remarkable blues and ragtime banjo player and singer who had a successful series of recordings during the 1920s (he will be discussed in chapter 5). He also recorded "Shave 'em Dry" several months after Rainey did and was quite possibly one of her unnamed accompanists. The harmonic structure of the song is essentially a compressed version of the twelve-bar blues, with the usual first eight measures telescoped into four.

Shave 'Em Dry Blues

Ma Rainey/H. Jackson

1. Have one thing I don't understand / why a good looking woman likes a working man (*Refrain*: Hey Hey, Daddy let me shave 'em dry)
2. Goin' away to wear you off my mind / you keep me hungry and broke baby all the time (*Refrain*: Hey Hey, Daddy let me shave 'em dry)
3. Don't see how the hungry women can sleep / they shimmy all day but not a bite to eat (R)
4. Goin' downtown to spread the news / State Street women wearing Brogan shoes (R)
5. It wasn't for the powder and store-bought hair / State Street gals couldn't get nowhere (R)
6. There's one thing I can't understand / some women drivin' State Street like a man (R)
7. Went to the show the other night / everybody on State Street was tryin' to fight (R)
8. I'm crazy 'bout my yellow, ain't wild about my brown / but you can't tell the difference when the sun goes down (R)
9. When you see the women running hand in hand / bet your life one's got the other's man (R)
10. Come here daddy, lay in my arms / when your wife comes tell her I don't mean no harm (R)

"Titanic Man Blues" (Ma Rainey; recorded December 1925, in New York for Paramount)

The sinking of the Titanic on the morning of April 15, 1912, and the resulting loss of 1,500 lives was one of the first great tragedies of the new century and found widespread fame by the new developments of wireless telegraph, film, newspaper reporting, and song. The sheet music and recording industries also preserved numerous ballads based on either historical or fanciful representations of the sinking. As early as March 1913, the Black singer Moses Graham was reported as singing a "Titanic" song in North Carolina, closely followed by Virginia Liston (identified as a blues singer) in Indianapolis the following May (Abbott & Seroff,

2017, 181–82). Numerous other singers were also reported singing songs about the disaster, including Ma Rainey, Ida Cox, and String Beans May, although the reports are generally unclear as to whether these songs were similar, different, or identical.

Both Liston and Rainey recorded versions of "Titanic Man Blues" (Rainey in 1925) and "Titanic Blues" (Liston in 1926), which share melody, structure, and refrain, although the interior lyrics differ significantly. Each version uses a sixteen-bar form, which is sometimes called a folk blues and may have derived from the nineteenth-century ballad tradition that was still popular in African American vernacular music until almost completely replaced by the twelve-bar blues by the 1920s. Rainey, and to a lesser extent Liston, had been headliners in Black tent shows and vaudeville from the early 1910s, and were each identified in press reports as "coon shouters" before that expression was superseded by "blues singer" around 1913, making them direct links to the earlier era. Presumably, "Titanic (Man) Blues" was representative of a popular type of song form that predated the standard blues. For example, Rainey recorded several tunes made up entirely of similar or identical sixteen-bar structures, including "Jealousy Blues" (Paramount 12364, February 1925), "Blues Oh Blues" (Paramount 12566, August 1927), and "Oh My Babe Blues" (Paramount 12332, December 1925).

Titanic Man Blues

1. Rig you up like a ship at sea, / but you certainly made a fool of me
   It's the last time Titanic, fare thee well
   It's a hard and a bitter pill, / but I've got somebody else that will
   It's the last time Titanic, fare the well

2. Now I won't worry when you're gone, / another brown's got your water on
   It's the last time Titanic, fare the well
   Now I'm leaving you there's no doubt, / mama's gonna cut you out
   It's the last time Titanic, fare thee well

"See See Rider" (Ma Rainey and Lena Arant; recorded October 16, 1924, in Chicago for Paramount)

While I have already discussed the publishing history of blues, it is clear that twelve-bar structures existed at least by the turn of the century. The song recorded in 1924 by Ma Rainey as "See See Rider" has also been called "C. C. Rider," and "Easy Rider" and contains many common stock lyrics as well, as having been cited by earlier sources. For example, Big Bill Broonzy recalled a blues singer from his youth (about 1908) called See See Rider who was the first person he heard perform blues, including "See See Rider," before the term was in vogue (House, 2010,19). Jelly Roll Morton claimed to have heard the song as early as 1901, performed by a saloon pianist named Josky Adams in New Orleans (Lomax, 1970, 20). Rainey is credited with the composition, although Lena Arant apparently composed the first verse, which is essentially an introduction. The lyrical structure of the tune varies from chorus to chorus—after the verse by Arant (a twelve-bar, nonblues form in the key of F, before modulating to Bb for the main section)—the three choruses are, respectively, ABB, AAB, and ABC, which is an unusual departure from our common assumptions about published blues maintaining one structure for each successive chorus.

[verse] I'm so unhappy, / I feel so blue— / I just feel so bad
I made a mistake / right from the start, / oh it seems so hard to part
All but this letter / that I will write, / I hope he will remember / when he receives it

See See Rider

Ma Rainey/Lena Arant

1. I'm goin' away baby, / won't be back till fall (Lawd, Lawd, Lawd) [2x]
   If I find me a good man / I won't be back at all
2. I'm gonna buy me a pistol / just as long as I am tall (Lawd, Lawd, Lawd)
   Kill my man and catch the Cannonball
   If he don't have me he won't have no gal at all

The Business of the Blues

Recording the Blues

Much of what has come down to us about the "Classic Blues" period has been because of recordings made by entertainers active on the various Black entertainment circuits in the 1910s and 1920s. Since the 1990s, scholarship has been attempting to reclaim the lost history of the pre-1920s blues culture. Lynn Abbott and Doug Seroff have been vital to this scholarship, with their three books (as well as numerous articles) uncovering reams of articles and advertisements in the Black press, presenting a nuanced picture of the traveling companies and shows that nurtured the talent of the famous blues singers of the 1920s.

As has been mentioned, there had been virtually no market for African American singers of popular songs prior to 1920; the perception that female voices would not record well had long since been replaced by the assumption that, while Black consumers would buy records by African American male entertainers, they would not accept those by females. Perry Bradford was a force in Black entertainment in New York during this period as a songwriter and entrepreneur and was nothing if not determined (his nickname was "Mule"). He badgered numerous recording companies in New York to give his songs and singer Mamie Smith (who was singing in one of Bradford's shows at the time) a try. With at least one (Victor), he progressed as far as making a demo record of "That Thing Called Love," which was turned down by the company executives who may have feared backlash from southern distributors.

As we have also seen, the expiration of the general patents involved with lateral cut recording technology in 1919 opened the doors for smaller companies to challenge the commercial stranglehold that had been held by Victor, Columbia, and Edison during the previous twenty years. One of the first companies to jump into the fray was OKeh, founded by Otto Heinemann as a producer and distributor of record players in 1916. The small size and limited budget of a company such as OKeh precluded hiring top-flight entertainers or large orchestras, so when they began recording and issuing their own records in 1918 (initially vertical cut, they switched to the more easily produced lateral cut recordings after the expiration of the patents), the directors tried to focus on smaller musical forces. Because of this, the most OKeh records from 1918 to 1919 were by small chamber music groups, vocal soloists, jazz or dance bands (attempting to capitalize on the runaway success of the 1917–1918 Victor records by the Original Dixieland Jazz Band), and occasional novelties, such as saxophone ensembles or xylophone solos (Laird & Rust, 2004). The first months of 1920 were in fact ripe for some new commercial opportunities.

Enter Bradford. Following his round of failures convincing the major record companies to take a chance on his songs and Mamie Smith, Bradford was given an introduction to Fred Hagar, who was the recording manager (probably equivalent to an "A&R" man in more recent times), and went to plead his case at the beginning of February 1920. Hagar listened to Bradford's pitch about the marketability of African American music, particularly in the South among a White southern audience and was intrigued enough to listen to several of Bradford's songs (Miller, 2010, 78–81). Hagar's assistant from 1919 to 1925 was Ralph Peer, who went on to develop the concept of "road trips" to remote southern locations to record local talent and was largely responsible for the development of what was then called "Hillbilly Music," but gradually developed into the modern idea of "Country Music." According to Peer, the music being recorded by OKeh by 1920 was a stale collection of Americana and nineteenth-century parlor songs (Mazor, 2015, 35).

While Hagar was impressed with the songs, enough to commit to recording two of them, he stipulated that the White performer Sophie Tucker be engaged as the singer. Tucker was a major star at the time, and it is doubtful that OKeh would have been able to afford her fee even if she had not been already under contract with Aeolian-Vocalion, but Bradford duly inquired. When he returned to deliver the bad news to Hagar, he renewed his pitch to use Mamie Smith in her stead. Having no other reasonable option, the recording director agreed to take a chance and booked Smith and Bradford to record two tunes ("That Thing Called Love" and "You Can't Keep a Good Man Down," OKeh 4113, February 14, 1920).

The success of this record (it was reputed to have sold 100,000 copies) encouraged OKeh to bring Smith back to the studio in September to record two more tunes, including "Crazy Blues," which was the first official blues recording by an African American singer. This recording sent shockwaves through Black communities who bought copies like hotcakes, encouraging OKeh and the other recording companies to begin what came to be known as "Race Records," with larger companies such as Victor and Columbia eventually issuing both ethnic and Black music with their own dedicated catalog numbers. These series were aggressively marketed to Black and other ethnic communities.

For the first two years or so of this recording boom, female African American singers were contracted by individual companies on the basis of their vocal qualities (clarity of diction seemed to be a prime concern) and ability to adapt to sometimes complicated musical settings. In several instances (even as late as Bessie Smith's first recordings in 1923), singers were occasionally credited as "comedienne" on the record labels in nonrace record lists, presumably to make the music more accessible to non-Black, nonsouthern audiences. For the most part, these singers (who were often stars of Black stage shows in New York, or performers in more upscale nightclubs and cabarets) were presented on records backed by arrangements done by in-house arrangers. Lizzie Miles recalled the Black pianist and arranger Bob Ricketts doing orchestrations for the White reading bands that accompanied her on her early records (Miles interview, 1951). The arrangements done by musicians like Ricketts for OKeh (and possibly Fletcher Henderson and William Grant Still for Black Swan and others) were apparently created specifically for the recording dates and seem not to have been used for other singers or published as stock arrangements. In general, they were very straight orchestrations of the sort large theater bands would use, which required little or no improvisation and could be rendered by Black or White studio musicians who were not necessarily regarded as jazz players.

By the beginning of 1923 the market had apparently changed, and many of the singers who had been frequent visitors to the recording studio were either being phased out or eliminated entirely. Mary Stafford, Lucille Hegamin, and even Mamie Smith all saw their contracts ended by the early months of 1923, with only occasional recording sessions occurring for the balance of the decade. Even singers who continued apace saw their accompaniments change significantly. Alberta Hunter and Ethel Waters both continued busy careers in the recording studio, but only rarely with larger groups and even more rarely with fully realized arrangements. Instead, singers were far more likely to be supported by only a pianist with possibly one or two horns. These groups were often playing only from published lead sheets (in the case of Tin Pan Alley songs or commercial blues) or nothing at all (as with original blues). Both clarinetist Buster Bailey and trumpeter Demas Dean remembered sessions with Bessie Smith being casual affairs from an organizational standpoint.

This development probably stemmed from the realization that having specific orchestrations done for single use was not an economically sustainable model and that singers who were comfortable in such settings were not numerous. Likewise, the flexibility of a single pianist and a horn or two conversant in the jazz style and comfortable with improvising backgrounds allowed for more productive recording sessions, as well as a wider variety of material.

1923 also saw a change in the singers brought into the studio. While Cabaret Singers were still in evidence (Hunter and Waters in particular), southern singers who were more used to being featured in tent shows and on vaudeville stages were favored, and their more narrative approach to material became standard. Ida Cox, Clara Smith, and Rosa Henderson became stars in large part due to their recordings, while Butterbeans and Susie, as well as Trixie Smith renewed their careers and found a much larger audience by means of their records. Bessie Smith

Figure 2.2. Bessie Smith, ca. 1928. New York Public Library, Digital Collections. Public domain.

and Ma Rainey (and, to a lesser extent, Trixie Smith) represented an earlier, earthier style of entertainment that was originally thought to be popular only with rural Black audiences, but by 1923 was found to have much broader appeal. Bessie Smith, for example, had been turned down several times by recording companies due to her coarse manner and, one suspects, her deep-South accent and occasionally muffled diction. The commercial success of recordings by the Smiths, Rainey, Cox, as well as earlier efforts by Hunter and Mamie Smith inspired smaller companies to engage singers to cover the most popular songs, with singers like Lillian Harris (Banner) and Sister Harris (Pathe) essentially having their entire recording careers devoted to songs done by others.

The success of the first series of Bessie Smith Columbia recordings probably led to Rainey's employment by Paramount in December 1923. In October of that year, veteran singer Sarah Martin recorded two songs with only guitar accompaniment, creating what was in effect the first country blues recording. Her accompanist, Sylvester Weaver, went on to record some of the first solo blues guitar works several weeks later. This began the parallel recording history of country, "Downhome" Blues singers and players such as Blind Lemon Jefferson, Papa Charlie Jackson, Blind Blake, and others, as well as initiating the series of rural recordings known in some catalogs as "Hillbilly" or "Old Time Tunes" featuring White musicians. The popularity of those records inspired other companies to imitate that setting and Bessie Smith, Clara Smith, and Ma Rainey (among others) issued recordings accompanied by a range of fiddles, guitars, jugs, saws, and kazoos during the early months of 1924.

In the spring of 1925, the larger companies began tentatively to explore electric recording, as opposed to the prevalent acoustic process. Now, rather than grouping around a horn and having to balance the sounds by proximity, singers or soloists could step closer to a microphone, guaranteeing higher fidelity and much more accurate sound separation. This allowed for larger bands to be used behind singers in a more efficient fashion. There were already examples of contingents of larger bands (for example, Fletcher Henderson using five or six pieces from his large group behind Bessie Smith, Clara Smith, and Ma Rainey), but these were relatively rare and often created a muddled soundscape. A bandleader like Chicago's Lovie Austin would generally use a small combination (piano, trumpet, and clarinet) in support of a singer and then add pieces (trombone, percussion, banjo) for instrumental records.

Columbia began its electric experiments in a surprisingly methodical fashion, recording Bessie Smith and Maggie Jones in May 1925. Smith's session did not go especially well, with the band, singer, and engineers crammed into a tent inside the studio. When the tent collapsed after one number, so did the session (along with Smith's patience and her never abundant good nature). Jones's session went better and demonstrated how a singer with a smaller voice could now be heard over a larger group of improvising musicians. Successes like this one encouraged companies to begin marrying the older blues-vaudeville style of singing with the more current jazz style of playing, an innovation that also encouraged some of the more popular (and financially secure) singers to take larger bands (quintets, sextets, etc.) on tour with them.

By 1928 or so, the vogue for blues and even the Vaudeville Blues popular early in the decade had fallen off dramatically, with recording opportunities for many singers becoming fewer and fewer. Rural, or "country" blues singers such as Blind Lemon Jefferson, Papa Charlie Jackson, and Blind Blake were selling more records and at far less cost to the companies; they generally performed on their own, without backing musicians and were valued by recording directors for the fact that they produced their own songs, making copyright payments unnecessary. The fact that most of them were essentially uneducated and sometimes completely illiterate put them at the mercy of the producers, some of whom became wealthy at their expense.

The female blues singers found it necessary to change their material to the "salacious" blues songs ripe in double entendre and metaphor. Bessie Smith had recording successes with the two-sided "Empty Bed Blues," as well as songs such as Andy Razaf's "Kitchen Man" and "Need a Little Sugar in My Bowl," which included imaginative lines such as

When I eat his doughnuts
All I leave is the hole
Any time he wants to
Why, he can use my sugar bowl
Oh, his baloney's really worth a try
Never fails to satisfy
I can't do without my kitchen man

("Kitchen Man" by Edna Alexander
and Andy Razaf, 1929)

Other even more clever songs in this genre were "Loud Speakin' Papa" (Yellen and Pollack) sung by Ethel Waters and Razaf's "My Man O'War" sung by Lizzie Miles. The first explores images of the newly popular radio technology, and the latter uses various military and bellicose metaphors to extol the prowess of the singer's mate. Victoria Spivey's version of Oscar Jefferson's "Toothache Blues" and Laura Bryant's recording of her own "Dentist Chair Blues" also contain clever (if a bit overwrought) wordplay.

It was a stroke of good fortune that the blues recording boom came at a time when many of the stars of the Black theater and tent show circuit were not only still active but at a peak of their abilities. The fact that so many female singers were recorded at something close to their peaks also tends to obscure the fact that very few males had that opportunity. Stars such as Butler "String Beans" May (1894–1917) and H. Franklin "Baby" Seals (1880–1915) were among the biggest draws in Black vaudeville but died before they might have had the chance to record. May was a first-rank performer who was acknowledged to be an influence through his comedy, singing, and piano playing. He was vital in introducing Black entertainment styles into northern theaters, clearing the way for other Black singers to tour the north and spread his influence by the secondhand performances of associates like Butterbeans and Susie (Abbott & Seroff, 2017, 170).

Female singers like Evelyn White (Abbott & Seroff, 2007, 346), Estelle Harris (Abbott & Seroff, 2007, 216–29), and Princess White (Bernhardt, 208–12) were overlooked by the recording industry, but had significant impact through their live performances. Evelyn White is a mysterious figure (her birth and death dates are unknown) who appears in numerous press releases between 1909 and 1930. A featured performer with various Tolliver shows—where she was mentioned along with Bessie Smith, Clara Smith, Ma and Pa Rainey—and Susie Edwards, she performed with *Silas Green from New Orleans* through most of the 1920s, retiring in 1930 due to ill health. Harris (1885–1934), not to be confused with the blues singer Estella "Mama Yancey Harris," was credited with being among the first to sing songs designated as "blues" on stage. From the beginning of the century she was active in a succession of the most successful Black shows and troupes, including Mahara's Minstrels, Black Patti, and the *Smart Set*. She may have recorded under the name "Sister Harris" for Pathe, accompanied by White groups and covering a variety of popular blues numbers by better-known singers. New Orleans pianist Jelly Roll Morton recalled that Harris and Laura Smith were the two best blues singers in vaudeville during the 1920s. Princess White (1881–1976) was a busy performer on the Theater Owners Booking Association (TOBA) circuit through the 1930s (after tours to Europe and Australia), leaving the business in the late 1940s to pursue church activities. She was "rediscovered" in the 1970s by trombonist Clyde Bernhardt, who recalled being impressed with her performances as a boy, rating her as an equal to Bessie Smith, Clara Smith, and Sara Martin. She spent the last four or five years of her long life performing with the Harlem Blues and Jazz Band before collapsing backstage during a concert and passing away at the age of ninety-five.

The Depression and the inevitable change in popular taste greatly changed the fortune of the popular blues recording stars of the 1920s. Those with wider repertoires and more "sophisticated" outlooks were able to reinvent themselves, sometimes multiple times. By the late 1920s, Ethel Waters and Alberta Hunter were exploring Broadway roles, with Waters advancing beyond that to successful ventures in radio, film, and later television, while Hunter returned to her roots as a supper club and cabaret entertainer. Bessie Smith's single foray on Broadway (*Pansy* in 1929) was not a success, but occurred at the same time she made her first (and only) film, *St. Louis Blues*, which suffered from poor distribution and a gritty setting some found offensive. She remained a fixture on the tent show circuit as well as in theaters until her death in 1937. Trixie Smith, Victoria Spivey, and Mamie Smith all made films in the 1930s, with Mamie Smith developing a fairly significant career. Some of the later entries into the blues recording scene of the 1920s such as Hattie McDaniel and Edith Wilson became far better known for their screen and radio roles in the next two decades.

Sadly, the touring life of entertainers was not conducive to a long life. By the end of the 1930s several prominent singers (such as Ma Rainey, Rosa Henderson, and Lizzie Miles) had retired to home or church work and several (Clara Smith, Virginia Liston, and Evelyn White) had either died or been incapacitated by illness. Numerous others (Princess White, Ida Cox, and Alberta Hunter) retired from the entertainment industry by 1950, although many were brought out of retirement later on for a final curtain. A very few (Ethel Waters and Butterbeans and Susie) maintained consistent professional careers until the ends of their lives.

A short flurry of retrospective activity in the late 1930s brought several 1920s stars back into the recording studios and temporary prominence. Mary Mack recorded for Bluebird in 1937, and John Hammond introduced Ida Cox to audiences for his *Spirituals to Swing* concert in 1939, following up with several recording sessions on Vocalion, which also had Lizzie Miles the same year. Grant and Wilson, as well as Trixie Smith recorded for Decca in 1938, and Alberta Hunter for the same company the following year, while Victoria Spivey recorded for both Decca and Vocalion in the mid-1930s. The 1940s saw a further nod to nostalgia with Bertha "Chippie" Hill, as well as Grant and Wilson being again recorded, but singers of the tent show generation were largely forgotten until Chris Albertson and other producers began to seek them out in the early 1960s with albums devoted to re-creations of the era by Ida Cox, Victoria Spivey, Alberta Hunter, and others. Only Hunter was, by good health and superior business sense, able to fashion an entirely new career in her old age, becoming a popular singer again in her eighties.

In one way our perception of blues recordings of the 1920s is inverted. In most historical accounts, the accompanists have been viewed at least as equals to the singers, when for the first half of the decade at least the singers were the stars. With the "second wave" of singers engaged early in 1923, established stars of both the TOBA and the tent show circuit such as Ma Rainey, Bessie Smith, Sara Martin, Virginia Liston, and Butterbeans and Susie were brought into the studio, in many cases to record their regular repertoire. These performers were the focus—the accompanists were often in awe of the singers they were backing, as memories by Louis Armstrong, Garvin Bushell, Buster Bailey, Demas Dean, and others demonstrate. Clyde Bernhardt recorded a particularly interesting perspective in his autobiography about his interactions with blues singers and comedians in Black shows when he was doing errands and delivering telegrams in Badin, North Carolina, at the age of fourteen (Bernhardt, 33). Bernhardt, like many other classic jazz players who accompanied these singers in the mid-1920s, was barely out of short pants at the time and these entertainers were the superstars of the day.

Ma Rainey

While chronologically a part of the "Vaudeville Blues" chapter, Rainey's career transcends category. As one of the oldest performers to record in the 1920s (Laura Smith, Essie Whitman, and Billy McBride were of the same vintage), Ma Rainey brought to the table twenty-five years of professional touring experience and a range of material that was second to none. She was able to record a variety of blues and blues-related songs from her entire career and stands as living monument to the development of the music, more than justifying her honorific "The Mother of the Blues."

The woman who came to be known as "Mother of the Blues" was born Gertrude Pridgett in Columbus, Georgia, at the end of the nineteenth century. Her death certificate gave her birth date as November 20, 1892, although the 1900 census suggested April 26, 1882. Her brother Thomas gave what might have been the most authoritative date in an interview after her death as April 26, 1886 (which more or less agrees with her given age of "25" in the 1910 census as well). Several accounts cite one of Gertrude's grandmothers as being a stage performer, but no documentary evidence has been found to date to support this claim.

The eldest child born to Thomas Pridgett and Ella Allen (who were both Alabama natives), Gertrude was joined by Malissa (known as Lizzie, who with her husband Frank Nix remained close to her sister and even allowed her and her husband to board with them when not on the road), Essie (a son whose adventures on the far side of the law led to a violent death in Detroit in 1924), and Thomas Jr. Thomas Sr. died in 1896 and it was left to Ella to support the family as a laundress, although Gertrude began her career as an entertainer by 1900, performing with the *Bunch of Blackberries* show at a local theater (Reeves, 1927). By February 1904 she was touring and married fellow entertainer Will Rainey, with whom she performed in vaudeville and tent shows for the next dozen years.

From 1905 to 1906, the Raineys traveled with their own *Alabama Fun Makers* company, putting on shows in the South before they were engaged by producer Pat Chapelle, who put them in his *Rabbit Foot Minstrels* show until 1908. It was during this time that press first recognized Gertrude as a "coon shouter" and commented on "Billy Rainey and Gertrude Rainey—Sketch Artists" and their prowess at the cakewalk and a blackface act (Abbott & Seroff, 2007, 262–63). Early 1909 found the duo with *Benbow's Chocolate Drops*, but by the fall they had their own show (managed by Will), sometimes called *The Georgia Sunbeams* and toured the South (Florida, Georgia, and Alabama) with as many as eighteen performers on stage and a nine-piece band until 1915. It was during this period that Gertrude became identified even more closely as a "coon shouter" and was occasionally teamed with other singers, including Bessie Smith for a brief period in Atlanta in the fall of 1910. (This was perhaps the short engagement that led to the myth that Smith was somehow "kidnapped" by the Raineys to be in their act.)

By 1913 the act was known as "Ma and Pa Rainey," although Will was beginning to be affected by ill health, largely retiring by 1916 and dying in June 1919. In the spring and summer these companies would travel throughout the rural South, playing in tents, while the late fall and winter (and also occasional fallow periods) would see the principal performers go into vaudeville, playing the southern theater circuit and occasionally venturing to New York or Chicago. It was at the Monogram Theater in Chicago that the duo (sometimes known as "The Rainey and Rainey Big Musical Comedy Four") was reviewed in the early summer of 1913, with Ma Rainey being credited for the first time with singing blues on stage (Abbott & Seroff, 2017, 170). By the following year, the Raineys were billed as "The Assassinators of the Blues," although several other duos were also described that way.

The Raineys had achieved significant success and recognition on both the tent show and Black vaudeville circuits in the South, and in 1915 they were engaged to appear in Alexander Tolliver's *Smart Set*, by far the most prestigious show the Raineys (now billed as "Ma and Pa Rainey") had been a part of. Ma was billed as "The Great Blues Singer" and toured the southern states in a company that at various times included future blues performers Trixie Smith, Leola Grant, Clara Smith, and Jodie Edwards, as well as comic Alec Lovejoy who had apparently taken Will Rainey's place on stage during one of his illnesses.

As with many touring tent shows, *The Smart Set* wintered in a warm climate while preparing for the next season. Tolliver housed his company in New Orleans during the winter of 1915–1916, and the occasional performances by Rainey and others were remembered by jazz musicians Zutty Singleton and Willie Humphrey in later years. During this time Tolliver developed a show that was significantly more ambitious than the usual tent show. Called *Tolliver's Circus and Musical Extravaganza*, the show left New Orleans in the spring of 1916, with a huge cast and one of the largest tents ever seen on the circuit. In addition, he engaged a band largely staffed by New Orleans musicians, including Zue Robertson, David Jones, and Willie Hightower, suggesting a connection to early jazz (Wells, 1916). The show opened in New Orleans on February 26, 1916, in its full form under canvas after a month or so of tryouts at the Temple Theater. Following that they toured through Georgia, the Carolinas, and Virginia. This show toured with great success through the summer and into the fall when a fight between Tolliver and his financial backer caused it to lose its funding and break up.

From early 1917 until the beginning of her recording career in December 1923, Ma Rainey toured both vaudeville and the tent show circuit at the head of her own shows, often called *The Georgia Smart Set*, to capitalize on the name recognition of the several *Smart Set* shows that had gone before. In general, these were large shows featuring a band, chorus line, comics, and a soubrette (a young girl singer) in addition to Rainey, who would have a featured spot singing a set of currently popular songs as well as contributing to the finale, which often involved the entire cast in a fast dance number (Abbott & Seroff, 2017, 174).

When Ma Rainey made her first recordings for the Paramount label in December 1923, she had arguably been the most popular and influential Black singer in the United States for most of the previous ten years. The fact that "blues" singers had been making recordings for over three years at that point demonstrates the reluctance of record companies to bring southern, country-based singers into the studio, assuming that their music would be too "rough" for the public. Bessie Smith's success proved that theory wrong, and there was a rush to find other singers with similar backgrounds. Rainey's recordings ran the gamut of popular music styles of the first three decades of the twentieth century. In December 1927, toward the end of her recording career, she also recorded several sides that are remarkable in that they were apparently done by her touring band and featured a coupling of a ragtime tune, "At a Georgia Camp Meeting" (here titled "Georgia Cake Walk") and "Ma Rainey's Black Bottom" (Paramount 12590), done instrumentally with vocal asides that might have been part of the finale of her stage show. Also, "Ice Bag Papa" (Paramount 12612) features a male vocalist who may have been her longtime stage partner, Fred Walker. These records are perhaps the only documents of parts of an actual Black stage show from the period not focused on the headliner.

While both Bessie and Clara Smith are usually looked at as fortunate in recording for one of the largest companies—Columbia—and benefiting from superior sound quality, distribution and budget in terms of hiring accompanying musicians, the association may have cost something in restricting their repertoire. Rainey was signed by Paramount, a small label operated as a subsidiary of the Wisconsin Chair Company, making records to be marketed along with their furniture. Just as it was about to sink into bankruptcy, the label changed its talent policy to a primarily African American one, with the product marketed as "race" records by 1922. For most of the 1920s, the primary talent procurer (in modern terms, an "A&R man") was J. Mayo Williams, nicknamed "Ink," who signed Rainey to her recording contract; the agreement included signing all her compositions over to the Chicago Music Publishing Company, which he owned (Barlow, 1989, 131).

Rainey had appeared in Chicago as early as 1913, but her vaudeville tours had taken her to the Monogram Theater throughout the decade, and it was there that Williams probably approached her about recording for Paramount. Of the eighty-five-odd titles released by Paramount under Rainey's name during her recording career, slightly more than half were credited to her, with perhaps half of the remaining number listed as by one of her music directors, Thomas A. Dorsey or Lovie Austin. While some of the songs (such as "See, See, Rider" and "Titanic Man Blues") were probably of indeterminate origin, Rainey clearly brought a great deal of original material to a public awareness far beyond that which she had as a live performer. It is also clear that she, virtually alone among the Black singers of this period, was able to capture on record a significant part of her repertoire stretching back at least a decade. We can gather from these dim and in some places incomprehensible sounds a great deal of what made Ma Rainey the premiere Black performer of the 1910s.

First, her forthright delivery and powerful voice, which was an important part of her live communication in preamplification days, comes across remarkably well on all her recordings, whether her accompaniment is a small jazz band, a piano, a jug band, or some combination of folk instruments. Second, her emotional expression is particularly well represented in songs like "Little Low Mama Blues" (Paramount 12419, December 1926) with her hypnotic humming calling to mind religious ecstasies supported by a country fiddle and guitar or "Blues Oh Blues" (Paramount 12566, August 1927), which consists of a melodic moan, accompanied by what may have been her touring band. Third, and possibly most important (if usually least acknowledged), is her humor, and the connection she had to the ordinary people who made up her fan base and their shared life experiences.

In several recordings, this connection is manifested in what we might today call "product placement." By citing commercial products familiar to poor and rural African American families, Rainey both established and reinforced the connection with her audience. In Rainey's own "Those Dogs of Mine" (Paramount 12215, March 1924) the singer references "Sapolio," an aggressively marketed brand of soap familiar to all households in the first thirty years of the twentieth century,

[verse] Look here people, listen to me / believe me I'm telling the truth
If your corns hurt you just like mine / you'd say these same words too
Out for a walk, I stopped to talk: / oh how my corns did burn
I had to keep on the shady side of the street / to keep out the light of the sun
[chorus] Oh lord, these dogs of mine: / they sure do worry me all the time
The reason why I don't know, / sometimes I soak 'em in Sapolio
Lord I beg to be excused, / I can't wear me no sharp toed shoes
Oh lordy how the sun does shine / on these hounds of mine

The pain of sore feet was a familiar presence in the lives of working-class people. Likewise, her "Soon This Morning" (Paramount 12438, November 1926) references "Poro," an African American hair-care program that included a college of cosmetology founded by Annie Malone, who was celebrated as being one of the first Black female millionaires in the United States.

He ain't good looking, ain't got no Poro hair [2x]
He's got a disposition to take him any old where

Rainey's talent with broad comedy was also demonstrated in a song composed by Paul Carter: "Wringin' and Twistin' Blues" (Paramount 12338, December 1928). Here, after the singer is told that her man is being unfaithful, invites her rival to dinner, intending to poison her with a witches' brew of a menu!

He told me that he loved me, I found it wasn't true,
he has gone and left me; there's nothing else to do
but if I know that woman, that's caused my heart to moan;
I cooked and served her dinner, invite her to my home
I had some green cucumbers, I had some half-done tripe and greens;

Some buttermilk and codfish, some Sauer's kidney beans
When she eats what's on my table, she will be graveyard bound;
I'll be right there to tell her when they shove her in the ground
It's because of me having those wringin' and twistin' blues

Another familiar domestic product (Sauer's beans) is included here as well.

The combination of all these factors is represented in Rainey's "Bo Weevil Blues," recorded on her first session and redone as the "New Bo Weevil Blues" exactly four years later (with only cosmetic differences, demonstrating a consistency of approach to her own songs).

1. Hey . . . Bo Weevil, Don't sing those blues no more [2x]
   Bo Weevil's here, Bo Weevil's everywhere you go
2. I'm alone Bo Weevil been out a great long time [2x]
   I'm gonna sing these blues so even Bo Weevil knows they're mine
3. I don't want not man to put sugar in my tea [2x]
   Some of 'em so evil, I'm afraid he might poison me
4. I went downtown and bought myself a hat, / brought it back home and laid it on the shelf
   Looked at my bed, getting' tired of sleepin' by myself
   (last four measures done as an instrumental coda plus an additional two-bar coda)

Rainey's lament connecting her faithless man with the traditional scourge of the southern cotton crop surely resonated with her rural audience, who would be directly affected by the insect until it was largely eradicated in the 1950s. How long Rainey had been singing this song is open to conjecture, but the unusual structure of the last verse (eight measures answered by an instrumental passage following the standard blues progression) suggests a holdover from an earlier era.

The remainder of the 1920s was probably the most lucrative time in Rainey's professional career. The success of her recordings and the regular publicity of Paramount's advertisements in the Black press allowed her to concentrate on the relatively easier work in vaudeville theaters rather than the grind of the tent show circuit, which she apparently left until the 1930s. Press announcements and reviews from this period are entirely about TOBA theaters with no mention of tent shows or such until 1929.

Al Wynn recalled that all the places he performed with Rainey were theaters (Wynn interview, 1958). He also recalled Rainey as a particularly nice person with an earthy sense of humor, particularly regarding bodily functions. She had to have his mother sign a consent form to allow him to tour with her in 1924, when he was only sixteen.

In April 1924, she premiered a show at Grand Theater in Chicago, which capitalized on her recording fame: "The feature attraction of the program was Madame 'Ma' Rainey, a Paramount Star. This is her first Chicago appearance and she was well received. She clearly proved that she was far superior to any of her predecessors. The curtain goes up and finds her concealed in a Victrola box. While her Jazz Wild Cats played, she sang her first number. Her gowns were most wonderful creations of the dressmaker's art" (Hayes, 1924). The popularity of her recordings (only four months after her first session) encouraged the Grand to book her as an added attraction at the beginning of the month. The Grand was a much more prestigious theater than the Monogram, which attracted a more working-class audience more recently connected to their southern rural roots that Rainey had played for several times during the previous decade. (Several performers, including Ethel Waters, gave damning accounts of the Monogram's facilities [Harris, 1992, 87–89].) The "Wild Cats" had been put together by pianist and blues composer Thomas A. Dorsey, who had been active for several years in Chicago. He left a particularly vivid account of Rainey's show and her instant connection to the audience.

> When she started singing, the gold in her teeth would sparkle. She was in the spotlight. She possessed her listeners; they swayed, they rocked, they moaned and groaned, as they felt the blues with her.
>
> The curtain rose slowly and those soft lights played on the band and picked up the introduction for her first song. I arranged the music for the band. We looked and felt like a million. Ma was hidden in a big box-like affair bult like a Victrola . . . This stood on the other side of the stage. A girl came out and put a big record on it. The band picked up "Moonshine Blues"; Ma sang a few bars inside the big Victrola, then she opened the door and stepped out into the spotlight with her glittering gown that weighed twenty pounds, wearing a necklace of $5, $10, and $20 gold pieces. The house went wild. (Harris, 1992, 93)

Likewise, poet Langston Hughes compared her singing at the Monogram Theatre in Chicago to music in the Holiness Churches in terms of audience response (Levine, 1977, 180).

Dorsey had assembled the five-piece band (trumpet, trombone, clarinet/saxophone, piano, and drums) that, with some personnel changes, toured with Rainey for the next four years, even after he left at the beginning of 1926 due to ill health and the beginnings of a religious conversion. He was also responsible for directing and arranging the music for the stage show that the singer would take out on tour during the summer and fall of 1924, and then again through 1925. In February 1925, her show at the Monogram featured a dance team, several comics, and her band, which may have been similar to her touring show (Hayes, 1925). By the next year, her company included her "son" Danny Rainey (probably informally "adopted" by her) as a dancer, comic Fred Walker as her stage partner, an assortment of comics and dancers, a dramatic sketch, and even a whistler (Hayes, 1926). By the spring of 1927, business was so good that Rainey bought a touring bus (cited in different press accounts as costing either $6,000 or $13,000) that could accommodate her eighteen-person troupe in relative comfort (Jones, 1927).

Changing tastes and market saturation combined to end Ma Rainey's recording career at the very end of 1928, although Paramount continued to run newspaper advertisements for her records for a full year after her final release. She continued to tour with her own shows (often called the *Paramount Flappers*) until the beginning of 1929 and occasionally into 1930, but was more often called on to return to her roots as a featured performer in tent shows and carnivals, occasionally losing even her headline status. In 1935 she retired from touring to return to Columbus, Georgia, to take care of her mother following the death of her sister. After her mother's death she apparently lived a quiet life; although various sources have asserted that she owned several theaters in the area, no documentary evidence supports this, and her 1939 death certificate lists her as a "housekeeper."

Ma Rainey occupies a unique space in the history of the blues specifically, as well as the history of American music in general. As a performer who was active at the very dawn of the twentieth century (and possibly earlier), she represented the first generation of truly professional African American entertainers and as a woman she represented the first generation of female performers who were industry headliners. More than even Bessie Smith, she exemplified the vernacular culture of southern Blacks, and fortunately was able to preserve elements of her musical and stage show repertoire on records, leaving posterity a remarkable document of an earlier generation. As Daphne Duval Harrison points out, "The record industry did not develop Rainey as an artist; she was already an artist when they 'discovered' her" (Harrison, 1988, 39).

Behind the Microphone

The popularity of the blues and African American popular music during the 1920s allowed for a proliferation of Black publishers and songwriters in New York. By 1928, the Gayety Theater building on Broadway was home to the publishing companies of Clarence Williams, Perry Bradford, and W. C. Handy; the songwriting team of Bob Ricketts and Porter Grainger; the arranger Will Vodery; and the booking agency of bandleader Wilbur Sweatman. Williams, Bradford, and Ricketts and Grainger in particular were key players in the development of the blues industry of the early 1920s, and have not been given their due as players in that development. Ricketts (1885–1936) and Grainger (1891–1955) published "How to Sing and Play the Blues—Like the phonograph and stage artists" in 1926, as well as composing scores for several shows and accompanying scores of singers on record during the 1920s, performing their tunes as well as others. Another figure worthy of further study is Texas pianist John Erby (1899–1981), who with Erby's Fidgety Five accompanied Victoria Spivey and other singers. Under the pen name "J. Guy Sudoth," as well as other pseudonyms, he composed many blues numbers recorded by numerous singers, including Ma Rainey ("Those All Night Long Blues"), Ida Cox ("Graveyard Bound Blues"), and Trixie Smith ("Praying Blues"), among others. The early contributions of Black Swan, OKeh (with Ralph Peer), and Ajax (with producer Joe Davis) in New York and the Paramount company (with Richard M. Jones and Lovie Austin) in Chicago also helped popularize the blues.

In a 1923 article discussing the sudden popularity of the blues industry, "Clarence Williams Music Co." and Perry Bradford were cited as leaders in the field who were "cleaning up from mechanical royalties with the sheet music angle almost negligible and practically incidental." The article lists prominent artists for each company (Victor, Columbia, OKeh, Vocalion, and "minor companies"), as well as Sophie Tucker and Elizabeth Patricola as White blues singers ("Fame and Fortune . . ." 1923). Further publications were issued by individual companies as marketing devices. Paramount brought out their "Paramount Book of the Blues" in 1924, with a reprint in 1927 featuring photos and short biographies of their principal artists. The fact that so much of the information is the fanciful work of press agents (to put it mildly) makes much of the rest suspect, but in some cases these blurbs represent virtually the only information or pictures we have of performers like Blind Blake or Blind Lemon Jefferson. Along the same lines (although more directly related to selling records) was OKeh's *Twelve Room House for Blues*, issued in time for Christmas, 1924, and featuring interviews with artists as well as lists of OKeh recordings (selected by Clarence Williams!) to put in the binder.

Clarence Williams

One of the most influential figures in jazz and blues of the 1920s was Clarence Williams. Born in Plaquemine, Louisiana, as early as 1893 (according to draft records in World War I), Williams was raised in a hotel, where he began to sing with visiting bands, including one led by the legendary Buddy Bolden. By his early teens he had hoboed to New Orleans where he began a lifelong tradition of hustling in various businesses, including dry cleaning and shoeshines, until he had learned enough piano to play at local restaurants. A need to improve compelled him to take a handful of lessons at a local music store, in order to advance his technique as well as to learn new songs.

By the mid-1910s, he had studied the playing of local pianists like Jelly Roll Morton and Tony Jackson and was good enough to play in Storyville at various brothels. In 1916 he began an association with bandleader and violinist Armand Piron to publish their own songs, as well as ones appropriated from local sources. Another associate during this period was the Houston pianist George Thomas, who was active in New Orleans in the mid-1910s and whose composition "New Orleans Hop Scop Blues" was an early Williams publication. Williams also began touring and performing in local theaters, such as the Lincoln, with clarinetist Sidney "Basha," actually Sidney Bechet ("Lincoln Theater, New Orleans," *Freeman*, October 7, 1916, 4).

An unexpected royalty check for his first song, "Brownskin, Who Ya For?" encouraged Williams to dissolve his partnership with Piron and move to Chicago, where he resumed his publishing activities until leaving for New York in 1919, in the wake of the Chicago race riots. Shortly after arriving he established his own publishing company, which scored a hit with "Sugar Blues," cocredited to Williams and Lucy Fletcher. In later years, Williams said that "Sugar Blues" was the only tune he ever really composed (Rose, 213); in the 1920s, it was accepted practice for the publisher to list his name on compositions he published, which made Williams one of the most prolific "composers" of the decade.

Williams had begun his recording career singing several of his own tunes with a White band in October 1921, and within a year had started booking recording dates for singers and bands with the primary objective of publicizing songs from his catalog. The first was "Sugar Blues" (OKeh 8041, October 17, 1922) by Sara Martin, recorded for OKeh, the company for which Williams did more work than any other during the decade. The success of this recording (on which he also played piano), encouraged both him and the recording companies in New York to focus on using records as publicity arms, and for the next three or four years he was almost constantly in the studios backing virtually every singer of note in the style. Martin and Williams's wife Eva Taylor were the two most prolific recording artists used to promote these tunes, with other singers (such as Bessie Brown in 1926–1928) making periodic appearances. Taylor continued her recording career into the 1940s, almost never without Williams.

In addition to vocal accompaniments, Williams began assembling bands to play instrumentals, the first of which was his own "Wild Cat Blues" (OKeh 4925, recorded on July 30, 1923), featuring Clarence Williams's Blue Five, including his old New Orleans running mate Sidney Bechet. This led to some of the most influential and interesting instrumental recordings of the 1920s, including Louis Armstrong, King Oliver, Jimmy Harrison, Buster Bailey, Coleman Hawkins, and virtually every Black jazz musician of note in New York City.

Recollections of Williams as an employer were mixed, to say the least. Negative memories by Barney Bigard and Red Allen (Chilton, 1989, 23 and Bigard 1985, 60) are balanced by those of Willie "the Lion" Smith and Alberta Hunter (Cushing 2010, 47–48). The general consensus was that he was not a particularly good musician (his contributions to blues records run from competent to nearly inept) but an exceptional promoter. In the 1940s, he sold his publishing catalog to Decca, retiring on the proceeds and living comfortably until his death in 1965.

Black Swan Records/Harry Pace

One nonmusician who had a significant impact on blues recording in the 1920s was Harry Pace (1884–1943). Beginning life in Georgia, he acquired an excellent education (graduating from Atlanta University) and worked primarily in insurance, moving to Memphis in 1907.

While in Memphis he was exposed to popular blues and made the acquaintance of W. C. Handy, who became a close friend. They started the Pace and Handy Music Company shortly after this and published music and booked bands for several years before Pace moved the sheet music part of the business to New York in 1918. Forming the Pace Phonographic Company in 1921, following the breakthrough success of Mamie Smith, Pace decided to branch out into making recordings of African American artists and named the record division of his company after the noted nineteenth-century Black singer Elizabeth Taylor Greenfield, known as the "Black Swan."

He decided to create a company that appealed to race pride: "Every time you buy a Black Swan record, you buy the only record made by colored people" (Davis & De Loo, 2002), and the following appeared on his newspaper advertisements: "The only genuine colored record—Others are only passing for colored." At first, everyone involved with the label was Black, including the financial backers, and Pace strove to hire musicians such as William Grant Still and Fletcher Henderson, who were known for their breeding and manners in addition to their abilities. The label began issuing records in May 1921, and at first favored "classical" or concert artists such as Revella Hughes and C. Carroll Clark but soon realized that their audience was perhaps not as "high toned" as they had hoped.

Vaudeville Singers Lulu Whidby, Katie Crippen, and comedy duo Creamer and Layton also made records that first month, as did Cabaret and Blues Singer Alberta Hunter. It was not until the relatively unknown New York nightclub singer Ethel Waters recorded "Downhome Blues" and "Oh, Daddy" (Black Swan, 2010, April 1921) that people began to notice the label. Waters's first recordings were so successful that she was brought back in August to record more prior to being sent out on a vaudeville tour called the Black Swan Troubadours and backed by the Black Swan Jazz Masters, led by Fletcher Henderson. Waters combined the enunciation and diction necessary for a singer to be understood on the early records with a blues sensibility and an earthy sense of humor that made her records accessible to a wide range of people.

In some ways, Black Swan and Pace was defeated by its early success. Pace was never completely comfortable with popular music (he famously turned down Bessie Smith after she auditioned for him, probably because she was obviously less refined vocally and personally than he wanted) and the supply chain getting records pressed from the studio masters became hopelessly clogged, meaning orders were left unfilled. In an attempt to deal with that problem, Pace bought a record pressing plant, overextending his finances to a degree.

The market was also changing, with companies like OKeh, Columbia, and Victor introducing "Race Record" series in their release schedule, focusing on Black music. In March, 1923, Pace renamed his entire operation the Black Swan Phonograph Corporation and attempted to regroup, but it was too late. By the summer, recording activity had ceased and the company went into bankruptcy by the end of the year, with Paramount issuing the backlog of titles Black Swan had amassed. A significant part of the problem was the conflict arising between Pace and the older generation of Black businessmen, who were not fans of the newer blues or jazz (seeing it as a development, if not a holdover from earlier times), and the artists themselves, who were far more attuned to the popular tastes of the Black working class (Vincent, 1989).

Black Swan arrived at a crucial time, shortly after the introduction of Black vernacular music on record. For a year it provided a source of popular music that was then being heard in vaudeville and stage shows performed by singers who had a wide perspective of the entertainment world. By the time of its eventual cessation, Black Swan had issued 180 records, about half of which were blues or blues songs by female vocalists (Vincent, 1989, 367–68). It seems certain that the efforts of other companies to create separate catalogs of "Race Records" and discover more and more authentic blues artists were directly inspired by the successes of OKeh and Black Swan. Black Swan was also a pioneer in advertising, taking ads in forty Black newspapers while it was issuing records, causing the larger companies to use those resources as well.

Perry Bradford

The contributions of Perry Bradford in getting Mamie Smith to be the first African American woman singer on record are discussed elsewhere, but he had been an active force in the Black entertainment industry for a decade at that point.

Born in Alabama in 1893, Bradford was raised in Atlanta and began playing piano and entertaining by the time he was in his early teens. After an early start in vaudeville, he was in Chicago by 1909 and New York by 1910. In 1912 he had developed an act with a partner, Jeanette Taylor, billed as "Mule and Jeanette" singing his original songs (Abbott &

Seroff, 2017, 88). Bradford was already demonstrating his talent for self-promotion by writing regular articles about the entertainment industry for *The Freeman*, one of the most popular Black newspapers of the day, and by his dogged determination to get ahead is what won him his nickname.

After Mamie Smith's success (she had been appearing in Bradford's show *Made to Order* when she made her first recording), Bradford toured with her and managed her career for a while until they had a falling out. He maintained an office in New York during most of the 1920s, from which he badgered singers and recording executives to record his songs. By the end of the decade he had led bands on records, backing Alberta Hunter, Sippie Wallace, Laura Smith, Louis Vant, and Mary Jackson, as well as doing a short series of instrumental recordings featuring Louis Armstrong, Johnny Dunn, Charlie Green, Buster Bailey, and James P. Johnson. He also appeared in numerous shows and even Bessie Smith's film *Saint Louis Blues* (1929). That same year he and Johnson collaborated on the show *Messin' Around*, which ran for about two weeks.

Bradford always seemed to exist on the fringes of the law—in 1923 he was sentenced to jail for four months for subornation of perjury in trying to maintain copyright on "He May Be Your Man, but He Comes to See Me Sometimes," which was a hit for Lucille Hegamin ("Perry Bradford Sent to the Penitentiary," 1923). By the late 1920s he was facing financial difficulty and the loss of his home. During the 1930s he ran afoul of the law several times, being accused of running an illegal cabaret and forcing a girl into an "abnormal act" ("Perry Bradford Will Face Jury," 1932).

By the late 1930s, Bradford had largely slipped from view and was making a living with occasional engagements and residuals from his song catalog. His autobiography *Born with the Blues* came out in 1965, five years before he died, and was an effort to redress his grievances about jazz history overlooking his contributions. Many of the claims he made in the book are along the lines of Jelly Roll Morton's pronouncements about his role in jazz history, but Bradford's account is valuable in recounting the role of music publishers and songwriters in the tapestry of the 1920s music industry.

OKeh/Ralph Peer and Richard M. Jones

The OKeh record company was a division of the General Phonograph Company and began operations in 1918, focusing primarily on popular singers and Tin Pan Alley fare. Having very little market success in competition with Victor, Columbia, and Edison, chairman Otto Heinemann began issuing foreign-language records targeted at ethnic communities around the country. The moderate success OKeh found with this strategy encouraged the company to begin considering other possibilities.

After Perry Bradford introduced Mamie Smith to the recording studio in 1920, and the response from African American people proved overwhelming, OKeh began a methodical program of recording Black singers on their 8000, "race" series. The recording director Ralph Peer was savvy enough to realize that an enormous market had opened. Realizing that he did not have the expertise to produce sessions and find talent, he hired Clarence Williams to find new singers and produce sessions, which he did for the rest of the decade. With singers like Sara Martin, Eva Taylor, and Virginia Liston, Williams recorded hundreds of sides for OKeh that became classics of the genre.

By 1923, Peer and OKeh were interesting in branching out and so began the habit of taking field-recording units to southern cities to seek out local talent. The first was Atlanta in June of 1924, and followed by St. Louis, New Orleans, and Dallas, recording many local blues and jazz artists as well as folk musicians who became the first country performers to record. This model was copied by other companies, including Victor and Columbia, which made regular pilgrimages to the South to find new entertainers.

Peer continued being the recording director for the company but remained in New York. The realization that Chicago was also a center for African American talent (both in residence and passing through the theaters there) encouraged OKeh to open a branch office there, run by the Black New Orleans pianist Richard M. Jones. Jones began recording touring stars like Butterbeans and Susie by the fall of 1924, and then local singers Hociel Thomas and Sippie Wallace in February 1925. Jones began to hit his stride in November of 1925, recording his own group as well as taking advantage of the return of Louis Armstrong after a year with Fletcher Henderson's band in New York to record him with Thomas, Bertha "Chippie" Hill, Blanche Calloway, and with his own Hot Five in the space of four days.

In 1926, OKeh was bought by Columbia, but continued issuing race sessions from New York, Chicago, and its field unit into the 1930s, with a few resurgences into the 1940s with early Rhythm and Blues.

Ajax Records/Joe Davis

The Ajax record company was owned by Compo, a Canadian firm that did some recording in Quebec. Founded to be primarily a "race" label, Ajax began issuing records at the end of 1923, although some may have been from leased masters recorded earlier for other companies. The label's short life (it finished its run in August 1925) produced about 150 released sides, almost entirely recorded in New York, and focused on Vaudeville Blues singers of the second rank. Notable exceptions were Mamie Smith, who moved to Ajax when her OKeh contract expired, and Billy Higgins, one of the most popular Black comics of the decade.

The prime mover regarding Ajax's artist signing seems to have been the White promoter, producer, and songwriter, Joe Davis. Davis was an early entry into the field of publishing African American music. Seeing the potential success for blues and vaudeville music coming out of the fertile atmosphere of Black vaudeville and stage shows, he established Triangle Music Publishing Company in 1919, as a direct competitor to Black-run companies like Handy and Clarence Williams. He was apparently respected by the talent he contracted and had long relationships (both professional and personal) with Fats Waller, Spencer Williams, Fletcher Henderson, and other well-known songwriters and bandleaders. By the early 1920s he was also finding success having songs he published recorded by a variety of companies, but he seems to have forged a primary partnership with Ajax.

Most recording companies during this period employed one or two musicians to direct recording sessions and they usually kept a stable of musicians they trusted to be on call to back singers. At OKeh, Clarence Williams used a floating cast during the 1920s that included Louis Armstrong, Sidney Bechet, and Buddy Christian in the early years and Ed Allen, Cyrus St. Clair, and Arville Harris later on; while Lovie Austin had Tommy Ladnier, Bob Shoffner, Jimmy O'Bryant, and Johnny Dodds at Paramount in Chicago. Fletcher Henderson directed groups for Black Swan, Paramount, and others that were made up of musicians such as Elmer Chambers, Joe Smith, Charlie Green, Don Redman, and Coleman Hawkins, who became the core of his influential orchestra beginning in 1924. The prime music director at Ajax was Canadian pianist Louis Hooper, who had been raised in Michigan and classically trained before becoming a dance band pianist in New York in the late 1910s. He played piano on many of the Ajax releases of the time (occasionally spelled by

Arthur Ray), directing bands (called, at various times, the Choo Choo Jazzers, Kansas City Four or Five, or the Sawin' Three) that usually included either Bubber Miley or Louis Metcalf, Elmer Snowden, Jake Frazier, and Bob Fuller, many of whom also played in dance halls in bands often led by Snowden.

Record sales had replaced sheet music as the chief yardstick of a song's popularity in the 1920s, and publishers were quick to foster relationships with recording companies as well as singers. It is possible that many of the singers who recorded for Ajax (including Rosa Henderson, Edna Hicks, Hazel Meyers, Josie Miles, and Helen Gross) were under contract to Davis, although they may have been singers he employed on an occasional basis to sing songs he had in his catalog. These singers, while not particularly well known on stage, were apparently solid musicians with good diction (a vital characteristic) and quick studies, so they could be depended on to sing relatively unadorned versions of published songs with a certain measure of stylistic awareness.

Davis also maintained a side business "placing" singers with other recording companies to sing his compositions or other ones he published. This was a marketing strategy that required versatile singers whose enunciation and diction were particularly clear, in order to bring out the lyrics, and was certainly used by other record producers (especially Clarence Williams and Perry Bradford). In addition to this, Davis by the mid-1920s began buying up copyrights of older songs in order to have them republished and newly recorded, accounting for the reappearance of old material on recordings at this point (Bastin, 2012, 18–20, 43).

Paramount Records/J. Mayo "Ink" Williams

The Paramount record label was a subsidiary of the Wisconsin Chair Company and was active in the industry beginning just after World War I. Initially concentrating on White Broadway singers, the early 1920s found them close to bankruptcy. In an effort to stay afloat, the company leased masters from other companies (most notably Black Swan) and issued them under the Paramount label. By 1922, Paramount had reinvented itself as a "race" label, concentrating almost exclusively on African American artists. There is some disagreement as to who was responsible for this direction—the British executive Art Satherley (who supervised recording sessions in New York), sales manager Maurice Supper, or Chicago talent scout J. Mayo "Ink" Williams—although most of the records issued by Paramount until the middle of 1923 were recorded in New York.

Williams was an athlete who was one of the few Black students to attend Brown University in the late 1910s, and went on to play football professionally in Chicago in the 1920s. It was while doing this that he talked himself into a job as talent scout and manager with Paramount, which was looking to expand its operations in that city. From mid-1923 until 1928, most if not all the Black talent recorded by the company in its Chicago studios was engaged by Williams. Whether he in fact discovered them or not is less clear; Lovie Austin (the pianist for the Monogram Theater) accompanied many of the singers and also provided many of the songs they recorded and very likely brought entertainers who passed through her theater to Williams's attention. She was remembered with great affection by Alberta Hunter, Ida Cox, and others, who regarded her as a fair and supportive colleague, as well as an exceptional musician.

Williams, however, was the real power at Paramount in Chicago. As the first African American executive for a White recording company, he was an exemplar of the new generation of Black businessmen, although unlike most he was a fan of blues and Black vernacular music in general (Calt & Wardlow, part 2, 12–13). His financial arrangement with the company was unorthodox; he drew no regular salary and worked essentially on commission, getting a percentage of record royalties and having his name put on compositions he had recorded, assuring him of an income from Chicago Music Publishing, which handled the copyrights of Paramount artists.

Williams had an amazing degree of self-determination in his job, and his White corporate superiors clearly trusted him to the point that they largely left him alone to make decisions regarding talent. Given that he was responsible in some degree for bringing Ida Cox, Ma Rainey, Papa Charlie Jackson, and Blind Blake to Paramount, their trust was obviously well-founded. He did take advantage of the opportunity to claim much music as his and helped himself to percentages of royalties that kept him well-fixed for the rest of his life. Working with him as his stenographer and general factotum was pianist Aletha Dickerson.

Dickerson was a trained musician who was responsible for transcribing lyrics brought in by the artists and sending them to the Library of Congress for copyright. She was assisted in transcribing the songs by a stable of musicians who wrote, arranged, and occasionally played for the sessions; pianists Tiny Parham, Thomas A. Dorsey, and Austin were key elements in that part of the business. Dickerson's husband, Alex Robinson, was also active as a songwriter and pianist in the studio; as "Bob Robinson" he recorded accompaniments for singers, and also as part of the Hokum Boys, a group managed by the couple.

Williams did not use Vaudeville or Cabaret Singers very often in his recording sessions. Instead, he prioritized the material over the singer, with more rural or country singers taking precedence as entertainers popular with the target market for the records. By bringing in less professionally prominent singers such as Elzadie Robinson, who were less accomplished but much more inclined to use their own material, he could both subvert copyright payments and cut himself in on the proceeds of new compositions. Using more country-influenced singers such as Robinson to follow the example of Cox and Rainey led naturally to male rural singers like Blind Lemon Jefferson, Jackson, and Blake. Williams's system worked remarkably well, overcoming Paramount's budgetary constraints and poor recording and duplication processes to become arguably the most successful and prolific race records label in the country. Even more remarkable was the fact that they restricted their advertising to the Black newspaper, the *Chicago Defender*.

By 1928, the upper management of Paramount was changing, and Williams was feeling less freedom in his production projects. He founded a second label, Black Patti, in 1927, which he ran simultaneously with his work for Paramount and ultimately left in 1928 to work as a talent scout for Vocalion and later on Decca, producing many classic Chicago blues sessions in the 1930s and '40s. With his departure, Dickerson took on much of the responsibility of finding artists and running sessions, although the Depression greatly reduced the finances of the company, resulting in fewer and fewer sessions, leading to Dickerson's resignation in 1931.

Chapter 3

"Crazy Blues"

Cabaret Blues

The first African American singers to record blues came largely from the cabaret and nightclub scenes of New York or Chicago. These singers were well versed in the popular music of the time and were called on to sing a variety of current material as well as popular blues like the various compositions by W. C. Handy. As their records became more popular, the market for blues songs expanded as well, with publishers racing to bring out sheet music and stock arrangements of tunes with the word *blues* in the title and some measure of blues feeling or expression in the lyrics and melody.

At first these singers were largely dependent on the printed music; even though relatively few were musically literate, they learned by rehearsing with a pianist or music director as they would have in a cabaret or stage show. Record companies on the ground floor of this development such as Black Swan, OKeh, and Pathe employed staff arrangers to write band arrangements of the blues the singers would record. Many of these background charts were highly organized and sound today to be quite stiff, almost in a military-band style. This was not unusual for theater band orchestrations of the day, which were still using musicians who had been educated as ragtime and even classical players and who were not necessarily comfortable with improvisation or "faking" backgrounds.

Mamie Smith

Mamie Smith was born Mamie Robinson in Cincinnati, Ohio, in 1891. While documentation concerning her early years is both sparse and occasionally contradictory, she apparently began touring as a "pickaninny" with the "Four Dancing Mitchells" in vaudeville by the time she was old enough to comport herself on stage. At some point after 1910, she joined the much more prestigious Smart Set company, directed by comedian Salem Tutt Whitney, and toured African American theaters around the country, arriving in New York by 1913. At this point she married fellow entertainer William "Smitty" Smith and took his name (an earlier marriage to a different entertainer had not endured) and began to sing in various New York cabarets and Black entertainment theaters (Perry Bradford, 1965, 122).

As far as we know, Smith was employed primarily in theatrical venues rather than tent shows or circuses, and had evolved a stage presentation emphasizing her powerful yet flexible voice combined with good dramatic stage presence and the ability to put over a variety of musical material. It was this versatility that led songwriter and entrepreneur Perry Bradford to engage her to perform in a vaudeville sketch called *Sgt. Ham of the 13th District* in 1917, apparently assuming duties as her manager following that engagement. This led to a meatier role in the next Bradford production, a 1918 revue he named *Made in Harlem* (called *Maid of Harlem* in some sources) to feature a series of his own songs that were designed to appeal to African American audiences. Smith's performance of these songs encouraged Bradford to cast around for opportunities to record her singing his newly published tunes.

As mentioned earlier, Bradford lobbied recording companies incessantly until Fred Hager at OKeh finally gave him a chance to bring Smith into the studio to make records with a studio band. Identified as "Contralto, with Rega Orchestra," Smith's race was effectively obscured although her full name was prominently displayed on the label. This identification was enough for her many fans in Harlem to buy the record, and Bradford's ceaseless promotion brought it to the attention of African American audiences in areas such as Chicago and Philadelphia, where Smith was also a known commodity. The backup band has sometimes been referred to as a Black group, but in fact was a pseudonym combining the talents of Hagar (who had been a military band leader earlier in life) and his musical director, Justin Ring (aka Justin Ringelben, who had worked with Hagar for several different recording companies since the turn of the century; Baker, 2019). The record enjoyed respectable sales, despite the low level of promotion given to it by OKeh, and Hagar was very receptive to Bradford's new pitch to record Smith with a group of Black musicians playing his tune "Crazy Blues" (OKeh 4169) from *Made in Harlem.* Although the song was originally called "Harlem Blues," Hagar felt it was necessary to remove the specific regional mention for sales purposes, although the label described it as a "Popular Blue Song" performed by Mamie Smith and Her Jazz Hounds, a name apparently invented by Bradford to fool Hagar into thinking they had a regularly constituted band.

The band personnel is known primarily from accounts by Bradford and the great Harlem Stride pianist Willie "the Lion" Smith, who claimed he was part of the group and was tasked with assembling the group for its August 10, 1920 session by Smith's estranged husband, William "Smitty" Smith. His regular job at this point was in the African American club, Leroy's, where Mamie Smith occasionally sang as well. The band he brought in was composed of players from Leroy's (Bradford also said the band was recruited at Leroy's) and used the accepted instrumentation of the early jazz bands: cornet (Addington Major, although Bradford recalled Johnny Dunn, who did play with Mamie Smith's bands later), trombone (Dope Andrews), clarinet (Ernest Elliott), piano (Willie "the Lion" Smith"), and a violin (Leroy Parker) rather than drums (Smith, 1964 & Bradford, 1965). Truthfully, the sound of the acoustic recording is so murky that the clarinet and violin are occasionally indistinguishable and the piano is inaudible, but the music is definitely jazz, albeit in its earliest stages in New York.

The approach of this band and Smith's performance of the two tunes was considered revolutionary at the time, although the particular racial characteristics of the performance are difficult to appreciate today. A comparison of the accompaniment to Smith's first two OKeh sides (by the Rega Orchestra) and the next two shows that the first group was almost definitely reading from a printed score, sounding like a house orchestra for any mid-sized theater in New York at the time. It is difficult to separate the instruments in the mix, but at least one cornet, one or two clarinets, a trombone, tuba, saxophone, and possibly flute and piano are playing highly organized backgrounds with no evident improvisation and only a few instances of "tailgate" trombone evident on "You Can't Keep a Good Man Down" (OKeh 4113, February 14, 1920) to suggest the new jazz-influenced novelty effects.

On the other hand, the smaller group on the August session provides more sound definition, even considering the poor acoustic quality. Beginning with a four-bar introduction presumably improvised by the band, "Crazy Blues" (OKeh 4169, August 10, 1920) immediately promises something more energetic than that delivered by the first session. This group was, according to both Willie "the Lion" Smith and Perry Bradford, largely improvising its accompaniment and probably was working from a piano score rather than a stock orchestration (which the Rega Orchestra almost certainly used). The trombone takes on the role of both the tailgate style and the bass part in the absence of a tuba, while the cornet, clarinet, and violin are improvising fills and contrapuntal backgrounds throughout both performances. The style represented on "Crazy Blues" and "It's Right Here for You" is probably more consistent with the type of accompaniment African American singers might have had in smaller theaters and circus and tent shows. Mamie Smith's singing likewise demonstrates more flexibility and drive, which could be due to being more accustomed to the recording process, but may also be a response to the more energetic accompaniment.

The song itself is only partly in the form of a twelve-bar blues. Beginning with a sixteen-bar verse, it continues to a blues form chorus in which the second line is a continuation of the thought of the first line. This blues chorus is followed by a sixteen-bar refrain ("Now I've Got the Crazy Blues"), which is followed by two more blues choruses and then a second refrain.

> There's a change in the ocean, / change in the deep blue sea,
>   my baby
> I'll tell you folks, there ain't no change in me
> My love for that man will always be
> Now I can read his letters, / I sure can't read his mind
> I thought he's lovin' me, / he's leavin' all the time
> Now I see my poor love was blind
> I went to the railroad, / hang my head on the track
> Thought about my daddy, / I gladly snatched it back
> Now my babe's gone, / and gave me the sack

The language and phrasing of these lyrics is quite proper and even stiff compared to the records Bessie Smith and Ma Rainey would be making within three years.

The commercial success of this recording is difficult to gauge in the absence of organized charting of records, but by any standards it was a runaway hit, especially in African American communities like Harlem, which took pride in the success of one their favorite entertainers. One estimate was that 75,000 copies were sold in the first month in Harlem alone and that by the end of the year the sales might have approached a million. These were unprecedented figures, and the fact that an untried Black woman singer was the face of the concern (with Perry Bradford behind the scenes) made the success all the more remarkable, causing all other record labels to sit up and take notice. For her part Smith was able to capitalize on this success by taking her Jazz Hounds on the road (initially booked by Bradford) and commanding large fees. For the next three years she was probably the highest-paid African American entertainer in the United States, touring the country and conspicuously spending the money she made from personal appearances as well as frequent recording, until tapering off in the fall of 1923, when her popularity was overtaken by Bessie Smith and the more traditional-style blues singers. These singers obviously appealed more to Black audiences who had tired of the more dramatic presentations by Smith and her contemporaries. Bushell (1988, 22) points out that Mamie Smith "wasn't a real blues singer like Bessie Smith" and that she "was a bit higher cultured than a lot of the singers."

The remarkable thing about Mamie Smith's recorded legacy is that there are so few actual blues in her discography. From "Crazy Blues" through August 1923, there are no more than a half dozen pieces that are structural blues either in part or entirety. There are far more theatrical and novelty numbers, many composed by Bradford, Marion Dickerson (Bradford's wife), Clarence Williams, Spencer Williams, Maceo Pinkard, and Tim Brymm, a catalog of Black Tin Pan Alley composers of the late 1910s and 1920s. These songs were more suited to her voice and delivery than were the more direct blues repertoire of Bessie Smith or Ma Rainey. A comparison of Mamie Smith's recording of "Frankie Blues" (OKeh 4856, February 22, 1921) and the same tune done by Bessie Smith (Columbia 14023-D, April 8, 1924; see chapter 4) demonstrate vividly the difference in musical style between the two singers. Mamie Smith's Jazz Hounds is a full, jazzy group that bounces along supporting the singer's declaration of the lyrics, which follow melodically and lyrically the folk blues "Frankie and Johnny." Her performance was geared for a theater appearance (indeed this might have been one she featured on public engagements, possibly accompanied by this very band) while Bessie

Smith's is noticeably different. Another difference between the two is that Mamie Smith's recording is credited to Marion Dickerson and is told from the female perspective, while Bessie Smith's song is attributed to Perry Bradford (Dickerson's husband) and presented with a male protagonist.

Mamie Smith's relatively infrequent recording sessions from the fall of 1924 until February 1931, feature more blues (perhaps a nod to the current trend), but generally in the earlier style. A good example is "Kansas City Man Blues" from August 5, 1923 (OKeh 4926), accompanied by the Harlem Trio (Sidney Bechet on soprano sax, Clarence Williams on piano, and Buddy Christian on banjo). These three New Orleans musicians gave Smith a musical cushion her past (mostly northern-bred) musicians did not, and the results demonstrate a more elemental blues performance that, while closer to the authentic blues of Ma Rainey and Bessie Smith, still has the tinge of cabaret theatrics that was key to Mamie Smith's musical expression. Composed by Chicago pianist Clarence "Jelly" Johnson and Clarence Williams, "Kansas City Man Blues" (OKeh 4926, August 5, 1923) is a standard twelve-bar form with a verse featuring through-composed lyrics and a written countermelody, which occurs twice. Following this, the more familiar AAB lyrical pattern is established, allowing for improvised responses by Bechet and Williams to the vocal lines.

1. Kansas City, where I'd love to be [2x]
   Kansas City man is waiting there for me
2. He's got white teeth and two gold crowns [2x]
   He's got Poro hair and he's a copper-colored brown
3. Women all cryin', I ain't raised my hand [2x]
   It's all on account of me takin' one woman's man

These lyrics are more in the style of the traditional, "folk" blues that came from the South, rather than the theatrical blues composed by Bradford and the earthier, more blues-based accompaniment, and they demonstrate the change in style that was coming following the commercial success of Bessie Smith and Clara Smith. Blues using these traditional "floating" verses became much more popular as the decade went on. ("Poro" hair refers to a style worn imitating a smooth, leather look using a particular hair care product marketed to African Americans.)

After a few more recording sessions and a film appearance in 1929, Mamie Smith largely retired until beginning a second career in Black films in 1940. After a long period of ill health, she passed away in 1946.

Lucille Hegamin

The sudden and dramatic success of the first Mamie Smith recordings encouraged virtually every recording company in New York to audition African American female singers to cash in on the new fad. The second

Figure 3.1. Lucille Hegamin, ca. 1925. Courtesy David A. Jasen Collection. Photo. Public domain.

to appear on record was Lucille Hegamin, who began a long series of recordings for Arto (followed by Paramount and Cameo, as well as one-off records for others) in November 1920.

Born Lucille Nelson in 1894 in Macon, Georgia, she was touring Black theaters in the South by the time she was fifteen. The first press mention of her came in review of the Free-Harper-Muse Company at the Globe Theater in Jacksonville Florida in 1911 (*The Freeman*, June 24, 1911). Also included in the company was "Oscar Hegamin," who was billed as a pianist and female impersonator. Born in New Jersey, also in 1894, Bill Hegamin married Lucille in 1917, and he acted as her music director until they separated in 1923. During the mid-1910s, she sang in clubs and cabarets in Chicago (including the Panama Cafe with Florence Mills and Alberta Hunter), during which time she apparently introduced Handy's "St. Louis Blues."

Following their marriage, the Hegamins went on an extended tour, performing in clubs and theaters up and down the West Coast for two years. By 1919, they were in New York, performing primarily in cabarets and nightclubs before she began making the recordings that raised her professional profile to the point that she was engaged to tour with road companies of *Shuffle Along* (1922) and *Creole Follies* (1924). After her divorce, Hegamin continued to make recordings until early 1926 (with a single session in 1932 and a reunion album in 1962) and to perform regularly in the New York area in various shows until the mid-1930s.

At some point before 1930, she married George Allen, a Pullman Porter born in Virginia in 1898. The 1930 census has the Allen couple running what apparently was a rooming house in Harlem with numerous lodgers, including Lucille's mother, three siblings, and a niece. By 1940, Allen had died and his wife was listed as the head of the same household (still including her family as well as other boarders). Some sources suggest she became a nurse, although census records do not support that claim; it is more likely that her principal source of income was as a landlady, with occasional singing or acting jobs breaking the routine.

Hegamin's early recordings were made with formal orchestrations done, presumably, by her husband. For the first eight sessions (from November 1920 until January 1922) her group was called the Blue Flame Syncopators (what might have been the same band was called Harris' Blues and Jazz Seven on her first session) and included as many as eight or nine musicians who were clearly reading and not improvising. As with Mamie Smith, remarkably few of Hegamin's recordings were of twelve-bar blues—occasionally some (such as "Arkansas Blues") included a blues strain—but most of the tunes were either pop numbers or Tin Pan Alley fare. Her voice was quite light with superb diction, and the companies for which she recorded clearly prized these elements over any particular blues sensibility. Indeed, almost none of Hegamin's recordings over the course of her career include any overt blues expression: blue notes, bent notes, vocal coloration, and so on. One area beyond diction in which she clearly exceeded most of her contemporaries was in rhythmic assurance, which locates her more as a nascent jazz singer rather than a blues diva.

One song that clearly meant a great deal to her was Lem Fowler's "He May Be Your Man, but He Comes to See Me Sometimes," which she recorded three times over the course of eight months in 1922 (Arto 9129, January 1922; Paramount 20108, February 26, 1922; Cameo 287, October 1922). Apparently used as her theme song, all three records use more or less the same arrangement, which could have been either a specialty by Bill Hegamin or a published stock, but the use of an identical arrangement would suggest that she used the music in her live appearances as well. The storytelling nature of the song emphasizes the agency of the female protagonist who revels in her attraction—"I ain't no vampire, that is true / but I can certainly take your man from you / my wicked smile, my wicked walk / I've got the kind of eyes that seem to talk"—and doubtless led to much stage business in live dates.

While her 1925 and 1926 recordings seem to mine the repertoire that made her a competitor to White singers like Jane Green, Marion Harris, and Vaughn De Leath, Hegamin's last date before her 1962 comeback featured two of the "dirty" blues songs that had been popular a few years earlier. "Totem Pole" was about the most explicit of the whole genre—"I'll let you play upon my old tom-tom if you'll let me climb your totem pole . . . I know it's long and big, but I won't renege"—spares no offense, sexual, cultural, or ethnic. It is a remarkable irony that Hegamin's most uncompromising blues records were made accompanied by only a single pianist—the White composer J. Russell Robinson. "Downhearted Blues" in particular stands out among her discography as an actual twelve-bar blues cover of the Alberta Hunter and Bessie Smith records, and includes a wordless vocal chorus that is certainly not in the same class as songs with similar effects sung by Clara Smith and Ma Rainey, but nevertheless is a nod to more current trends in blues recordings (Cameo 381, June 1923). (From the same session came a cover of the frequently recorded Lovie Austin composition, "Bleeding Hearted Blues.")

Hegamin's last recordings were part of an album called *Songs We Taught Your Mother*, done for Riverside in 1962. Hegamin, along with Alberta Hunter and Victoria Spivey, was featured with an informal jazz band accompaniment doing songs they had performed four and five decades earlier. Hegamin demonstrated a remarkably youthful (if somewhat rusty) voice, singing "St. Louis Blues," "Arkansas Blues," and "Has Anybody Seen My Corrine" in a style much more jazzy than her two costars. She apparently was still living with her sister Minnie and her niece when she passed away after a long illness in 1970.

Mary Stafford

The first Black female singer to record for Columbia was Mary Stafford, who some sources say was born Annie Burns in Springfield, MO, although, if she was the sister of drummer George Stafford, the 1920 census has her born in 1889 in Delaware. In 1920 she was living with her mother, and brother in Atlantic City (where they were also mentioned in the 1900 census). George was listed as a drummer in a cabaret (he played for Charlie Johnson's Paradise Orchestra for much of the decade). Mary was listed as a hotel waitress, although she was known to have sung in clubs in the Atlantic City area at the time. Eubie Blake recalled accompanying her in local clubs as early as 1915 (Carlin & Bloom, 2020, 46).

By January 1921, she came to the notice of Columbia, who engaged her to be the first African American singer on their label, in direct competition with Mamie Smith. Her first release included Smith's signature "Crazy Blues" and the first recording of Clarence Williams and Spencer Williams's tune "Royal Garden Blues" (Cameo 381, June 1923). Generally singing popular material, Stafford's recording career lasted only through the year, although she returned for two more sides in 1926. Regular stage appearances through the 1920s (primarily in the Baltimore and Atlantic City areas) with Johnson's orchestra kept her in the public eye, although by the early 1930s she retired and apparently passed away in 1938.

Ethel Waters

One of the most consistently successful African American singers of the 1920s was Ethel Waters. Born in Chester, Pennsylvania in 1896 to a

Figure 3.2. Ethel Waters, 1939. Photo by Carl van Vechten. Library of Congress, Prints and Photographs Division. Public domain.

teenage mother as the result of a rape, Waters had an unsettled childhood and bounced between numerous relatives in Pennsylvania and Baltimore until she married Merritt Purnsley in 1909, when she was only thirteen. The marriage lasted only a year, but she took his name with her when she began her professional singing career, and it was as Ethel Purnsley that she appeared with the Hill Sisters trio in 1915 (Abbott & Seroff, 2017, 92). It was at this point that she became known as "Sweet Mama Stringbean," not solely because of her tall and lanky frame, but, as she recalled, in tribute the legendary Black comedian and singer, Butler "String Beans" May, who was headlining at the Dixie Theater in Richmond, Virginia (Waters & Samuels, 1951, 89). Waters, who could be fairly savage about other performers, was generous in her recollections of May (who died in 1917). She credited him and his wife with extreme generosity toward her in those early days.

It was as "Sweet Mama Stringbean" that Waters began singing blues songs, including Handy's "St. Louis Blues," to great acclaim, leading to her leave the Hill Sisters and go out on her own on the TOBA circuit by the late 1910s. While she found blues to be popular, Waters's repertoire included many other types of songs as well as a "shimmy" dance specialty, in which she vibrated while essentially standing still. She developed her repertoire while singing in Edmund's Cellar in Harlem beginning in 1919, and stretching off and on for several years. During that period she also began her recording career and almost launched her Broadway career as well.

Early in 1921, Waters made her first recording for the tiny Cardinal label, two sides of nonblues, dance music. Shortly after, either a talent agent (according to Waters), or Fletcher Henderson or Harry Pace (according to each of their own accounts), heard her either at Edmund's or in Atlantic City and arranged for her to make a record for Black Swan. Pace had cofounded the company with W. C. Handy and hired Henderson as his music director, so either story (or possibly a combination of the two) could be true. According to Waters, Henderson and Pace were initially unsure whether to record her singing blues or "cultural" numbers (which in this case likely meant show tunes). A compromise of sorts was reached by having her do the pop song "Oh, Daddy" and "Down Home Blues," composed by the Black songwriter Tom Delaney (Black Swan 2010, May 1921).

While she did not write the lyrics, her version of "Down Home Blues" became a runaway hit for Black Swan, generating revenue for Black Swan exceeding $100,000 within six months (Abbott & Seroff, 2017, 261). This success encouraged Black Swan to book a tour for Waters with an accompaniment by a band led by Henderson (his first important band leading experience). By late autumn of 1921, Ethel Swan and her Black Swan Troubadours were touring TOBA theaters from Washington, Baltimore, and Philadelphia through small-time venues in Pennsylvania and Ohio, before reaching Chicago in January 1922 (Bushell & Tucker, 1988, 31–39).

For the first few legs of the tour, the band was a large one, with a picture from its engagement at the Regent Theater in Baltimore showing a ten-piece band (unsigned article, *Afro-American,* December 2, 1921, 10). This was gradually pared down, until by the time it reached Chicago it consisted of only five pieces: trumpet, trombone, clarinet, piano, and drums (more like her recording groups). It was in Chicago that plans were announced to begin a tour through the South, which caused several of the musicians to quit because of the well-founded fear of racism and brutality familiar to Black entertainers of the time. With a new band, Waters embarked on a tour that lasted five months through Indiana, Arkansas, Tennessee, Oklahoma, and Texas, and included an extended stay at the Lyric Theater in New Orleans. During this stay she made one of the first radio broadcasts by an African American entertainer("Musicians Will Not Follow Star into Crackerland," 1922; the tour itinerary was described by Bo Lindstrum, 2018, 37). It was on this trip to New Orleans that Fletcher Henderson first heard Louis Armstrong, offering him a job, which he turned down. He was shortly to go to Chicago to join King Oliver's Creole Jazz Band.

By the summer of 1922, the tour had returned to New York, and Waters resumed her recording career for Black Swan, which stayed in business until the middle of 1923, when bankruptcy forced them to sell their masters to Paramount, which continued releasing earlier material. After this, Waters began recording occasional sessions for Vocalion before signing an exclusive ten-year contract with Columbia (practically unheard of for any singer, but unprecedented for an African American entertainer) in April 1925. Fletcher Henderson continued to be her musical director for most of her recordings until the end of 1925 (when his band had become a popular attraction at the Roseland Ballroom and on records of their own), after which Pearl Wright became Waters's primary accompanist for the rest of the decade.

During this period, Waters began to transition from vaudeville to the more "respectable" theatrical presentations that had Broadway as their aim. The Whitney brothers (Salem Tutt Whitney and J. Homer Tutt) were still producing all-Black shows in the 1920s, and their 1922 *Oh Joy!* was a revue in which Waters had a starring role. In Boston in October, just as Waters and dancer Ethel Williams (who was Waters's romantic partner at the time) were breaking in, they were involved in a car accident, which necessitated some time off. When she was ready to go back, Waters discovered the show was opening under a tent in New York City prior to its Broadway debut. She refused, saying working under a tent was in her past and left the show ("Ethel Waters Hurt," 1922). This aversion to the "under canvas" aspect of her vocation seems not to have come from any extensive experience in traveling carnivals or circuses; she may have instead been venting prejudice against what was considered a lower-class form of entertainment that she perceived as undignified.

Waters's independent streak was fortunately coupled with her superior singing abilities and a talent for acting and impersonation that made her a hit on stage in various revues and even book shows that made it to Broadway, including the *Plantation Club Revue* (1925, in which she replaced Florence Mills), *Africana* (1927, produced by Earl Dancer, who was sometimes identified as her husband), *Rhapsody in Black* (1931, produced by Lew Leslie), and her first film, *On with the Show* (1929, Warner Brothers). She also led her own unit on the otherwise White Keith-Albee vaudeville circuit in 1925. Not unimportant to her success was her gift of mimicry, especially well-preserved on two discs. On "Maybe Not at All" she interpolates a slow chorus before which she announces, "I'm gettin' ready for the Empress!" and then launches into a growly imitation of Bessie Smith (Cherry, in Springer, 2006, 269), as well as of Clara Smith (Columbia 14112, October 28, 1925). Her later version of "I Can't Give You Anything but Love" (with Duke Ellington and His Famous Orchestra) includes an astoundingly accurate imitation of Louis Armstrong's vocal on the same tune, growls and all (Brunswick 6517, December 22, 1932).

It is at this point that Waters began to focus more on "popular" material from her stage shows. Her October 1925 recording of "Dinah" became one of her biggest hits and a signature tune for the rest of her career. In a 1947 radio interview, Waters recalled that "Dinah" was written for the Plantation show that was an update of Gilbert and Sullivan's *The Mikado*, and was originally a hot dance number. When Waters was hired to replace Florence Mills in the summer of 1924, she was told to sing the song, which initially she didn't care for. After experimenting with it, she arrived at a ballad-like interpretation, which proved to be a show stopper, contributing her blues sensibility to an otherwise fairly nondescript pop song. (The interview and performance are on YouTube: *The Tex and Jinx Show* by Ethel Waters, August 4, 1947, accessed 10/12/21.) While she occasionally recorded blues-based material after this, her focus had shifted to theatrical and film presentations.

Given her talent for interpreting popular songs, it is particularly illustrative to compare Ethel Waters's initial recording of "Down Home Blues" (Black Swan 2010, April or May 1921) with a remake she did for Columbia (Columbia 14093, July 28, 1925). Both recordings feature a non-blues verse establishing the story of a missing lover. The chorus follows:

> Woke up this mornin', the day was dawnin'
> And I was feelin' all sad and blue
> I had nobody to tell my troubles to
> I felt so worried, I didn't know what to do
> But there's no use in grievin' because I'm leavin'
> I'm brokenhearted and Dixie bound
> I've been mistreated, ain't got no time to lose
> My train is waitin', I got the down home blues

After an instrumental chorus, Waters sings the same two blues choruses again. In her Columbia recording, she repeats the same verse, but then sings somewhat different lyrics, with the brighter tempo allowing for another chorus and then the original second chorus to finish.

1. Woke up this mornin', the day was dawnin'
   My lovin' daddy was not about
   And he's got that lovin' that always makes me shout
   And I hope he comes back before it all gives out

2. Now he was no true man, but then a new man
   could never tempt me or make me glad
   yet I need a good man, I need a good man bad
   'cause I ain't been gotten, that don't mean I can't be had

3. Why, some men like me 'cause I'm happy, / some because I'm snappy
   Some call me honey, / quite a few think I've got money
   Then again some tell me, / "Mama it looks like you built for speed"
   So if you put that all together / that makes me all a good man needs

4. But there's no use in grievin' because I'm leavin'
   I'm brokenhearted and Dixie bound
   I've been mistreated, ain't got no time to lose
   My train is waitin', I got the down home blues

Of interest is the third chorus, which was taken over almost verbatim by Billie Holiday on her 1936 recording of "Billie's Blues," credited to Holiday.

While the lyrics show a development of over four and a half years of performance, it is the accompaniment that demonstrates the greatest illustration of stylistic evolution. In the Black Swan recording, the band (probably a Fletcher Henderson unit including a number of New York–based Black dance band musicians of the day), is playing an obviously written-out chart that is not far removed from a Sousa arrangement and was obviously designed for stage use. Garvin Bushell remembered that on recording dates, when he was backing singers during this period, the band often played from individual instrumental parts (presumably published stock orchestrations) (Bushell & Tucker, 1988, 32). The stiffly played parts reflect a prejazz approach to phrasing and would possibly have been viewed as stiff by contemporary Black musicians and singers on the tent show circuit as well. Waters is remarkably able to overcome the inflexible accompaniment to produce an elastic performance, which actually manages to swing, supporting Bushell's claim that she was really the first jazz singer.

The Columbia recording is much more freewheeling. She rerecorded several of her Black Swan "hits" for release on her new label. With the accompaniment being limited to cornet, piano, and tuba, Waters has room to sing more verses and to explore more melodic variations, which do not clash with the stolid arrangement of the earlier recording. The improved recording quality also highlights the remarkably varied colors of her voice and the pitch control for which she was renowned. Using a catalog of growls, trills, and leaps into her high register, Waters demonstrates a remarkable improvisational skill that was not part of the lexicon of most of the later "Downhome Blues" singers. Her October 20, 1925 session featured her singing two popular tunes from the revue—"Dinah," and "Sweet Man"—which was her first coupling of two pop tunes, significantly not released on the Columbia 14000 race series.

Ethel Waters's career, from the late 1920s until she died in 1977, continued the trajectory of refinement, moving from revues and "high-class" vaudeville to Broadway, films, radio, and television, and finally as a singer for the Billy Graham crusades, all the while building on her early experiences in African American music on the TOBA circuit as well as the speakeasies and dives of early 1920s New York.

Alberta Hunter

One of the most driven personalities among all the female African American singers of the 1920s was Alberta Hunter. Born in Memphis in 1895, Hunter had left a difficult home life by the time she was twelve, taking a train to Chicago and supporting herself doing menial work for several years while taking any opportunity she could to sing and listen to other singers.

By 1912, Hunter was singing at "Dago Franks"—a bordello catering to a White clientele—a job that continued through the summer of 1913. Following that, she went to Hugh Hoskins's Iowa Club—a Black club at which she sang for about a year, garnering her first press mention (Russell, May 19, 1914, 4). A short stint at the Elite No. 1 (where she worked with legendary New Orleans pianist Tony Jackson) brought her to the Panama Cafe, where she performed upstairs with the more earthy, bluesy entertainers rather than the higher-class downstairs room where Ada "Bricktop" Smith, Glover Compton, and Florence Mills held forth (Taylor, 46). Hunter began singing with some of the New Orleans musicians who had moved to Chicago in the late 1910s, first at the DeLuxe Café (with Jimmie Noone and Freddie Keppard) and then at the Dreamland Ballroom with King Oliver's band, where she was featured until 1923, with time off for touring.

Following a short marriage in 1919 to a returning soldier named Willard Saxby (they separated not long after the wedding and were divorced officially in 1923), Hunter began frequent trips to New York to explore professional opportunities, as well as pursuing a romantic relationship with Lottie Taylor, the niece of Bert Williams. Hunter was one of the many Black women singers of this period who privately identified as either as lesbian or bisexual, but she was only one of the few who maintained long-term relationships with women at different points in her life.

For most of the 1920s, Hunter shuttled between New York and Chicago, depending on performance possibilities. Beginning in 1920, she appeared in a series of short-run shows by the Black composer and entertainer Shelton Brooks, which also took her to Connecticut and

Philadelphia, although she was mainly known as a Cabaret Singer, as she had been in Chicago (Taylor, 68–70). In May 1921, she came to New York specifically to make her first recordings, for Black Swan. On this trip she also apparently auditioned (and was rejected) for the soon to be hit show, *Shuffle Along* (Taylor, 75). A series of reasonably popular recordings resulted, although Hunter was unhappy with the promotion the company gave her in the Black press, compared with the much more aggressive marketing campaign for Ethel Waters. This resulted in her leaving Black Swan and signing a contract with Paramount: an unusual move in that most of her recordings took place in New York, while most of Paramount's blues records were done in Chicago. The inferior sound quality of the Paramount discs also covers up a significant amount of Hunter's vocal quality, although enough comes through to demonstrate her consistent success on record and particularly on stage.

After a short return to the Dreamland in Chicago, Hunter came to New York to perform in comedian Eddie Hunter's show *How Come?* a week or so after its Broadway opening on April 16, 1923. The show had been "trying out" in Washington, DC and Philadelphia for the first four months of 1923, using various Black singers including Ethel Waters, Trixie Smith, and Bessie Smith (who was brought from the show to do her first recordings). Hunter received rave reviews for her featured numbers in what was essentially a revue that also included New Orleans clarinetist Sidney Bechet at various times, and remained until the Broadway closing on May 19, touring with it throughout the mid-Atlantic states through October. A review near the end of the Broadway run stated that "Alberta Hunter has reached stardom" (Jackson, 1923), and a profile in November asserted that she had been strictly a Cabaret Singer until she began performing in *How Come?*, although it also mentioned she had done some limited stage work before that (Ready, 1923).

The success and recognition that Hunter received due to her initial Broadway experience generated more opportunities in theatrical shows and vaudeville. For several years until 1927, Hunter was a regular performer on the White Keith-Albee circuit, often touring with Sam Bailey as her foil in a show that was probably similar to the "battle of the sexes" comedy of performers such as Butterbeans and Susie, as well as Liston and Gray (Taylor, 1987, 126). This success in White vaudeville had an unintended negative effect, with the Black press largely ignoring her during this period, although she continued making records that sold reasonably well. Nevertheless, Hunter usually avoided work on the Black

TOBA circuit, suggesting that her singing style was more appealing to White and northern Black audiences.

In August 1927, Hunter embarked on an almost two-year trip to Europe, which found her singing in clubs in Paris as well as participating in the London version of Jerome Kern's *Showboat* with Paul Robeson. On her return in the spring of 1929, she found that her style of singing was not especially popular in New York, so she went back to Chicago once again. By 1933, she had returned to England and was featured at the Dorchester Hotel, making a series of records of popular songs. After returning to New York in the late 1930s, Hunter continued frequent stage appearances and USO tours, as well as occasional recordings of her earlier blues songs before retiring from show business in 1957 to embark on a career as a nurse. Following her retirement from nursing in 1977 (her employer thought she was seventy, when she was in fact eighty-two), she returned to professional singing, making several albums and touring extensively until her death in 1984.

Hunter's recordings in the 1920s run the gamut from vaudeville blues through sophisticated pop tunes to blues songs she composed. Her most recognized composition was "Downhearted Blues," which she recorded for Paramount in July, 1922, and which was Bessie Smith's first released recording for Columbia in 1923, generating sizable sales (see Clark, 2017, 13–14). Hunter's first recording was "He's a Darned Good Man to Have Hanging 'Round," (Black Swan 2019, May 1921), which demonstrates the projection and personality she had been developing in Chicago cabarets for over five years. The wooden accompaniment is representative of a standard theater band of the time, although Hunter for the most part had been singing only with a piano in her club appearances, aside from occasional guest shots at the Dreamland and the Deluxe. Probably more representative of her nightclub repertoire was "I'm Going Away Just to Wear You off My Mind," with Eubie Blake's piano being the sole accompaniment (Paramount 12006, July 1922). Blake's midpoint representation between ragtime and jazz matches Hunter's declarative singing in the same way that her accompanists must have done in the Chicago cabarets from half a decade previously.

While Hunter did not really consider herself a blues singer, she wrote several compositions based on the blues form either entirely or in part and could sing such material convincingly. The impression from hearing her records is that she was probably approaching the blues from the point of view of an imitator rather than as an authentic interpreter.

Her appearances on stage as well as the bulk of her recordings up to 1939 show her to be an exceptionally gifted popular-song singer, with a taste for sophisticated material that required a significant degree of theatrical skill to pull off. This was doubtless part of the reason that she was never a popular attraction in the South, or for the most part with Black audiences, although one gets the feeling that her focus was, as with most things in her life, a result of deliberate choice.

Edith Wilson

Edith Wilson was a singer with an impressively long and varied career. She could be included in either the section on Cabaret or Vaudeville Singers because of her recording career in both styles, although stylistically she is probably more in line with the former group. One of the many singers from the fertile Black entertainment center of Louisville,

Figure 3.3. Edith Wilson and Her Jazz Hounds, ca. 1925. Courtesy David A. Jasen Collection. Public domain.

Kentucky, Edith Goodall was born in 1896, and was touring vaudeville by the mid-1910s. She had joined Danny and Lena Wilson, a sibling act, by 1919, and shortly thereafter married Danny, an accomplished pianist and music director.

By 1920 she was in New York, and by late 1921 was featured in Irvin Miller's *Put and Take* (replacing Mamie Smith) and getting very positive reviews (Abbott & Seroff 2017, 254). According to Wilson, it was her association with Perry Bradford that was responsible both for getting her into that show and the Columbia studios in September 1921. to record two of the tunes she had been singing in the show (both by Bradford). Wilson was unique among singers of this period in that her recording career was closely attached to her accompanying band, Johnny Dunn and His Jazz Hounds. This group was the most extensively recorded Black jazz group of the early 1920s, and featured cornetist Dunn, who was considered to be the foremost jazz instrumentalist in New York before Louis Armstrong arrived in 1924.

Wilson was accompanied by various Dunn-led groups for the first year of her recording career, producing about twenty issued sides for Columbia, most of which were either composed or published by Bradford. "Nervous Blues" (Columbia A-3479, September 15, 1921), from her first session, gives a good picture of a popular stage blues of the period.

> Gee I'm blue, downhearted too, feeling forlorn, my man is gone
> Crying' for him, whinin' for him, I'm sighin' for him, cryin' for him
> I want to know why everybody treats me mean

Singing in a vigorous style, Wilson benefits from what was at the time the cutting edge of jazz players doing an apparently improvised accompaniment. Her careful articulation does not impede the flow of the performance, which is unusual for the time. In this, she is very similar to Ethel Waters, whose career trajectory in the 1920s Wilson mirrored to a certain degree.

After a hiatus of slightly more than a year, Wilson returned to Columbia studios for four sessions over the course of about a year, backed by two jazz bands, a solo guitar, and in a crosstalk duo with comic Doc Straine. These records obviously were not successful and Columbia did not use her again; this worked well with her touring schedule, which took her to England in 1926 and 1927 and Germany in 1928, appearing with the legendary Florence Mills in *Blackbirds of 1926* in Paris, London, and Belgium. By 1929 she was back in New York and starring in *Connie's Hot Chocolates*, where she, Fats Waller, and Louis Armstrong were billed as "A Thousand Pounds of Joy," and she premiered the Waller/Andy Razaf tune "Black and Blue," which she recorded for Victor during a brief resumption of her recording career.

These 1929 and 1930 recordings (done with either theater bands or Bubber Miley's jazz group) presented Wilson in a theatrical vein similar to the way Ethel Waters was being used by Columbia at the same time (even doing two different versions of Waters's hit "My Handy Man Ain't Handy No More" (Victor V-38624, October 6, 1930, and a different version released under the same matrix number, but recorded on October 28, 1930). While Wilson's voice was not in Waters's class, she was clearly an experienced actress and was well regarded in that field. In the 1930s she did extensive work on radio and film as well as on stage, but her most visible (and notorious) role was as the face of "Aunt Jemima" from the late 1940s until the mid-1960s, a character that did not sit well in the civil rights era, but one that she defended as a dignified and positive portrayal. By the late 1960s, she was active in various performers' unions and began singing again, making records with jazz and blues players (including her elder, pianist Eubie Blake) until her death in 1981.

Esther Bigeou

"The Girl with the Million Dollar Smile" is how Esther Bigeou was billed in numerous trade paper accounts and for personal appearances in the 1920s. Born in New Orleans, apparently to a Creole family in 1895 or thereabouts, her name appears in later census records as "Hester Bijou" and other variants. Her father's mother was apparently the grandmother of drummer Paul Barbarin and the great-grandmother of guitarist Danny Barker, locating her in that musical family's lineage. By 1912 she was prominent enough in local entertainment circuits to be reviewed by the *Freeman*, which gave a positive account of her performance at the Temple Theater in an Irvin C. Miller show, singing "Undertaker Man" ("Temple Theater in New Orleans . . . ," *The Freeman*, November 2, 1912, n.p.).

Miller was the eldest of three brothers, the most famous of whom was Flournoy, who teamed with Aubrey Lyles as a comic duo in numerous shows during the 1910s and '20s, peaking with the unprecedented success of *Shuffle Along* in 1921. Bigeou toured with various Miller shows until about 1918, and was possibly married to him during that period, although evidence is scarce. Shows starring both (with Bigeou being cited for her comedic abilities as much as for her singing) toured the Black vaudeville circuit consistently during the period.

Following the couple's parting, Bigeou began touring with other companies, including Perrin and Henderson and under her own name. There are very few mentions of her in the Black trade press from 1918 until 1921, when she apparently landed in New York to make recordings for OKeh.

How she came to be contracted to OKeh is a mystery, but her first five releases show that she was seen as a blues singer, with the initial coupling being W. C. Handy's most famous pieces "Memphis Blues" and "St. Louis Blues" (OKeh 8026, October 5, 1921). Accompanied by an unknown group, obviously reading an arrangement, these records demonstrate both her strengths and weaknesses as a singer. A clear voice and good articulation is undermined to a degree by a twittery and clipped delivery. Her cover of "Gulf Coast Blues" (OKeh 8056, March 20, 1923) was done six weeks after Bessie Smith's hit record and seems to be a conscious imitation of Smith's delivery, even down to the cadential thirds that were apparently seen as one of the stylistic traits in her early records. Ultimately the attempt is unconvincing, due to the lightness of Bigeou's voice and clipped phrase endings.

Bigeou did not make any records between November 1921 and March 1923 (presumably because of touring), and after her initial return with Bob Ricketts's band (and, presumably his arrangements) she was accompanied only by her hometown friend Clarence Williams on piano. He remained her only accompanist except for her final recording in December of that year, when she made a guest appearance with Armand Piron's New Orleans Orchestra. This group was doing a residency at the Roseland Ballroom in New York and was about to return home, where they were considered one of the top society bands in the city. Bigeou, as part of the Creole culture of New Orleans would doubtless have been familiar with them, making the collaboration a sensible one. "West Indies Blues" (OKeh 8118, December 14, 1923) by Edgar Dowell, Clarence Williams, and Spencer Williams was a tribute to the Caribbean heritage of many African Americans in New York at the time, and was recorded by numerous other singers, including Clara Smith and Rosa Henderson.

During the 1920s, Bigeou toured in various shows, at least some of which she headlined (possibly as a result of her recorded fame), although her chief claim to fame during the decade seems to have been her endorsement of Hi-Ja beauty products, which appear dozens of times in the local Black press. In 1925, she toured with Willie Eldridge as "Eldridge and Bigeou's Foot Lite Follies," and the following year in a similar show with Earl Evans. She apparently visited her home town for an extended stay in 1925, and then again in the early 1930s, dying there in 1934. The census of 1930 has her living with her mother and her brother, Louis Bijou, and gives her occupation as "seamstress." After her death, Louis apparently named his daughter for her.

Trixie Smith

Trixie Smith was born in or near Atlanta, Georgia, probably in 1888, although various documents have 1895 and even 1900. The 1940 census has her (using her married name of Trixie Muse) as a fifty-two-year-old widow living with her son, daughter, and two grandchildren. Some sources cite a middle-class upbringing in an Atlanta suburb and a period of study at Selma University in Alabama, but the original source of these claims is unclear ("Champion Blues Singer Here," 1924; the college connection is mentioned in this interview in passing, and the implication is that Smith was a fairly well-bred person, although the article is a typical puff piece publicizing an upcoming appearance, so should be treated with some skepticism). What is clear is that she was on stage by 1911, when she was referred to as "a little soubrette" performing with F. A. Barasso's Strollers in Mobile, Alabama ("F. A. Barrasso," *The Freeman*, February 11, 1911, n.p.). For the rest of that year she toured with either that group or the Brooks-Smith Players, with whom she appeared for three years and with which she was described as a "coon shouter" ("Crown Garden Opens . . . ," *The Freeman*, December 9, 1911, 5).

By the fall of 1914, she was touring as a single in vaudeville, doing a blackface comedy act with singing. For the rest of the 1920s, Trixie Smith was credited as a comedienne at least as often as a singer and her renown was equally due to both. Touted as "the girl who sings her own blues" ("Crown Garden Opens . . . ," *The Freeman*, December 9, 1911, 5) and "one of the race's greatest black face comediennes" (Columbus Bragg, "On and Off the Stroll," *Chicago Defender*, November 7, 1914, 6), Smith developed a reputation as a headlining act. It was probably because of that that she was engaged to tour with the Alexander Tolliver Circus in the fall of 1915, along with Ma and Pa Rainey and Jodie Edwards, among many others. A short tour with them sent Smith back into vaudeville by early 1916, which continued with a few interruptions until the early 1920s.

In April 1918, she met and wed a man named Comanche (or Carnache) Muse, with a daughter following soon after. That child died of meningitis in 1919, but a second daughter (Madeline) was born in 1920. Comanche was apparently still alive in 1936 when Madeline married but had died by the 1940 census (which lists Madeline's two children but not her husband). It is unclear if Comanche was involved in the entertainment industry, but apparently their domestic arrangement continued, with their son Edward being born in 1925. In 1926 Smith was apparently forced to cancel several weeks of engagements because she had to take care of her daughter, who was recuperating from an illness at a relative's home in Detroit.

By 1921 she was in New York and making the rounds of local theaters, although apparently without a great deal of success. An opportunity presented itself in January of 1922, when she was invited to compete in a "blues competition" put on by the Fifteenth Regiment at the Manhattan Casino on January 20. The honorarium of $20 was something she apparently needed and was her main motivation for participating. By her own account,

> Arriving, I was slightly embarrassed to hear several of the contestants refer to me as "The Black Gal," and I seemed to be affording considerable amusement by entering. A performer, who today is an international figure, assisted the rest to the stand to sing their numbers, but let Old Black Trixie [*sic*] struggle along as best she could. . . . I went up to get that twenty and get out. I sang my own number, "Trixie Blues" and came very near fainting when the judges awarded me the cup. ("Champion Blues Singer Here," *African-American*, April 11, 1924)

The "international figure" in question was likely Noble Sissle, who was the emcee for the event and who was accused by other singers (including Josephine Baker) of being prejudiced against darker-skinned Blacks. Smith won over much better known (and already recorded) singers Lucille Hegamin, Daisy Martin, and Alice Leslie Carter and was awarded $1,000 in addition to the cup, and the victory apparently led to a recording contract with Black Swan ("Trixie Smith Wins Big Blues Contest," February 9, 1922). The article says Smith picked Black Swan over other options due to its "bright future" and the fact that it was an all-Black company.

This contest victory proved a major feather in Trixie Smith's cap, and she was identified as its winner in publicity for the rest of the decade. Her first issue on Black Swan, "Desperate Blues/Trixie Blues" carried the legend "Winner of the 15th Regiment Blues Contest" and was a significant seller for the company (Black Swan 2039, February 1922). "Trixie Blues" was Smith's own composition and became popular enough to be covered by Lizzie Miles a year later for OKeh. In many ways Smith was a transitional figure between the cabaret and vaudeville styles; her first records (generated by the contest win) were solidly in the early style, but her extensive vaudeville experience made her comfortable in the later style as well.

The recognition Smith received from her win brought her to the attention of not only recording companies, but also show producers and theater managers. In the spring of 1923, she was an added attraction to the show *Seven Eleven* at the Lafayette Theater in Harlem. The first half of 1924 found her doing a vaudeville tour in the South with an extended stay in Florida. Press accounts of this tour said that she would be touring with a jazz band in the following season ("Trixie Smith," *Afro-American*, August 1, 1924, 10). The end of the year found her singing with a Sissle and Blake review in New York (despite her contentious encounter with Sissle at the contest) ("Billboardings," *Chicago Defender*, January 3, 1925, 7).

It is perhaps not fair to suggest that Smith was primarily an actress/comedian with no evidence of her talents in that direction, but the Black press clearly saw her acting and blackface performances as at least coequal with her singing. The fact that she was given the opportunity to make recordings fairly early in the blues era clearly positioned her as a singer in the ears of the public. As Daphne Duval Harrison points out, her voice was light and lacking in character (Harrison, 1988, 245) and the charm of the performances come as much from the accompaniment as the singer. After Black Swan folded and she began recording for Paramount, her accompanying groups became quite impressive, with most of them being members of the Fletcher Henderson Orchestra, including Louis Armstrong, Joe Smith, Charlie Green, and Buster Bailey.

Smith composed "Railroad Blues" as well as "Trixie Blues," and these constitute her most impressive singing on records. Her earlier reputation as a "coon shouter" and "blues singer" in vaudeville clearly prepared her for impressive blues expression, even if it wasn't necessarily her forte. Her cover of Bessie Smith's "Sorrowful Blues" is also interesting, although it is unlike her other blues singing. Here, she in effect is doing a Bessie Smith imitation, replete with a hovering dependence on the phrase ending third, which was an important part of the better-known singer's style.

"Railroad Blues" is a fairly typical blues narrative involving the desire for travel to escape.

1. Now if the train stays on the track, I'm Alabama bound [2x]
   Don't you hear that train coming, I'm Alabama bound
2. Now the train went by with my papa on the inside [2x]
   Lord, I couldn't do nothin' but hang my head and cry
3. Did you ever take a trip on the Seaboard and Air Line? [2x]
   'Cause if you ride that train, it will satisfy your mind
4. I got the railroad blues, I wanna see my hometown [2x]
   And if the Seaboard don't wreck, I'm Alabama bound

A driving performance featured contributions from trombonist Green, clarinetist Bailey, but most notably a full chorus by Armstrong, which must be ranked as one of his best solos from his New York period. For her part, Smith delivered some truly impassioned singing not surpassed on any of her other recordings; one suspects she was deeply inspired by the accompaniment, which represented the best jazz players in New York at the time (Paramount 12262, March 16, 1925).

After a remarkable incident in December 1925, in which she made the papers for having been arrested on a fabricated charge of prostitution ("Race Actresses Said Framed by Police," December 26, 1925, 10; the paper later published an op-ed exonerating her and essentially blaming an associate of hers for setting her up), Smith toured theaters up and down the Eastern seaboard and as far west as Detroit and Chicago (where she made her last recording date until the late 1930s). A succession of moderately successful shows followed: *Syncopated Sue* (1927), *Gettin' Hot* (1929), and others featured her singing, but by 1930 she was appearing as a supporting actress in numerous shows and theater reviews. An appearance in a film—*Black King*—in 1932 essentially ended her active career for the decade. The 1940 census lists her as having been unemployed for

438(!) weeks, although she certainly had occasional work, including at least two recording dates, so that number must have referred to full-time employment. She apparently ended her performing life singing occasional gigs at a club in Maine shortly before she passed away in September 1943.

Lizzie Miles

One of the most interesting singers of the 1920s, as well as one of those with the longest careers, was Lizzie Miles (Interview with Lizzie Miles, Hogan Jazz Archives, 1951). Born in New Orleans on March 31, 1895, as Elizabeth Mary Landreaux, Miles grew up in a Creole-speaking household and benefited from a good education as well as musical training in her church and exposure to a wide variety of music. After appearing locally in children's concerts she began singing with various bands, including those led by Armand J. Piron, Manuel Manetta, and King Oliver and making a name for herself as a popular singer. Inspired by hearing Sophie Tucker at the Palace Theater, she began to consider making the stage a career and started singing in theaters in the area.

By 1912 she had married August Pajeaud and began touring the South in minstrel and tent shows, although her primary employment until the World War I years was with the Jones Brothers and Wilson Circus, and then the Cole Brothers Circus, where she sang in the side show and with the band in the main tent as well as riding the elephants in the parade! Apparently, her marriage to Pajeaud did not last, as she married musician John C. Miles in 1914. (In a later interview, she said her stage name of Miles came from the billing "Miles of Smiles with Lizzie Miles," with no mention of her husband; see Miles interview, Hogan Jazz Archives, 1951.) Miles was the bandleader for the Jones and Cole Brothers circuses and he and his wife toured with them as far north as Vermont and west to Arkansas and Texas, apparently appearing in a silent film in 1917—*The Sawdust Ring* (Triangle, starring Bessie Love)—indicating that they got as far as California. J. C. and Lizzie Miles both contracted flu during the Spanish Influenza pandemic in November, 1919. J.C. died shortly after, although Lizzie recovered, but temporarily stopped singing and returned to New Orleans (Abbott & Seroff, 2007, 178–83). After a year recuperating at home, she went to Chicago (which she may have visited during the previous decade) and sang occasionally with her hometown friends King Oliver and Freddie Keppard. After touring with a cabaret

Figure 3.4. Lizzie Miles, ca. 1925. Courtesy David A. Jasen Collection. Public domain.

show, she met with the songwriter Spencer Williams, who recommended her for a recording contract in New York. Following her first recording in February 1922, New York was to remain her base until she left in November 1924 for a European trip, singing at a series of places in Paris until returning in early 1927.

Following a series of New York club engagements and an appearance in the 1932 Vitaphone short film *Tip Tap Toe*, in which she sang "Three's a Crowd," Miles returned to Chicago in 1939 for one final recording date before returning to New Orleans to take care of her mother. After her mother's death she resumed her career, singing with a variety of New Orleans and Traditional jazz bands from 1950 until about 1957, when she went on an extended tour to California and Las Vegas. By the end of the decade she had returned to New Orleans, devoting her last years to gospel music and church work until her death in 1963.

Miles's half-sister was singer Edna Landreaux, who sang under the name of Edna Hicks. Slightly older than Miles, Hicks and her first husband, Will Benbow, toured with Benbow's Chocolate Drops company, taking the teenaged Miles with them. In her recollections of this period, Miles referred to Hicks as a "coon shouter," implying she featured more bluesy and folk-based material. She, on the other hand, rejected the term "blues singer" in reference to herself, feeling that her repertoire was far more extensive and her performing style more refined.

Miles recalled the pianist and songwriter Bob Ricketts doing arrangements for her early OKeh records, which were accompanied by a White band that did not improvise. Ricketts is credited as the leader of "Ricketts' Stars," who accompanied her on her January 1923 session, suggesting it might be drawn from the group of Black musicians, including cornetist Thomas Morris, trombonist Charlie Irvis, and reed players Ernest Elliot and Bob Fuller, who Ricketts used backing other singers during this period. The sound of the band is not remarkably different from that of the first five sessions backed by an otherwise anonymous group that fits the profile of a studio group reading arrangements.

As Daphne Duval Harrison pointed out, Miles's recordings are "topnotch" (Harrison, 1988, 236). Her decade of performance across a broad spectrum of the entertainment industry translated into a confident delivery and a faultless rhythmic sense, coupled with excellent pitch and diction. Her first record, "Muscle Shoals Blues," composed by George Thomas the year before, was one of her only straight twelve-bar blues during this part of her recorded career (OKeh 8031, February 24, 1922).

One other example was "Yellow Dog Blues" from the Ricketts' Stars session, perhaps demonstrating how Miles might have sounded singing that song on the tent show circuit or with circus bands (OKeh 8052, January 1923). Other songs recorded from the beginning of 1922 to 1923 demonstrate her versatility: pop songs like "Hot Lips" and "You've Got to See Mama Every Night" (associated with Sophie Tucker), stage blues, and novelty numbers, as well as a cover of Trixie Smith's "Trixie Blues."

Beginning with her February 1923 session, Miles was accompanied by only a pianist, most often the Chicago-based piano player Clarence Johnson. Her OKeh contract had apparently been for only a year and her recordings for the rest of her career were done as contract work for Emerson, Victor, Columbia, Banner, and Brunswick. "Sweet Smellin' Mama" (Columbia A-3897, April 26, 1923) is subtitled "Poro Blues," and represents another element of humor in the blues that was a key component of Miles's style on stage and, presumably, from her days in the circus sideshow.

> Sweet, oh sweet smelling mama
> Poro, is stamped all over you
> Poro, look what you've done, made this fat papa run
> I used to tell, how sweet you'd smell, / like a ten-cent bar of soap

Mamie Smith and Ma Rainey also made reference to Poro, a popular brand of soap and cleansing products in the early years of the twentieth century. The song was composed by Bob Miller, a White composer of Tin Pan Alley songs as well as hillbilly material.

In her interview with Richard Allen, Miles pointed out that she had little or no say in who would accompany her on record, although she seemed to have better luck in this regard than many of her contemporaries. This was especially true after her return from Europe, when she appeared with established jazz instrumentalists (and friends from early New Orleans days) King Oliver, Pops Foster, and Jelly Roll Morton, as well as New York dance band players such as Bob Fuller and Albert Socarras. She even appeared with a band billed as "Jasper Davis and His Orchestra," which was the group banjo player Elmer Snowden was leading at the Nest Club in 1929, featuring several members of the Luis Russell Orchestra. The number of twelve-bar blues in her discography also increases toward the end of the decade, reflecting both the vogue for double-entendre pieces such as "Electrician Blues" and "My Man O'War," which is somewhat unique as an example of a comic number in a minor key and using military imagery (Victor 23281, January 27, 1930).

Miles's later career is sporadically documented on disc, with a single session done for Lester Melrose in Chicago in 1939, exploring the party music, early rhythm, and blues style, and then several later albums and appearances with traditional jazz musicians such as Bob Scobey and Sharkey Bonano. A television appearance in 1957 gives a good idea of her stage presence and generally acknowledged charisma on stage; her gestures, vocal quality, and theatrical presentation seem very much in keeping with her early influence, Sophie Tucker.

Other Singers

Flo Bert was the second African American woman to record, making six records for Paramount in December 1920. She sounded very much like a White musical comedy actress, even to the point of sounding like a female version of Al Jolson on "Whistle and I'll Come to Meet You," (Paramount 20023, December 1920), which was released in the general catalog, rather than on the race records list.

By the spring of 1921, every record company was trying to engage Black female singers to capitalize on the craze started by Mamie Smith; Katie Crippen and Lulu Whidby (Black Swan), Lavinia Turner (Pathe), Lillyn Brown (Emerson), Alice Leslie Carter (Arto), and Gertrude Saunders (Columbia) all made a handful of recordings each but never caught on with the public.

Somewhat more commercially successful was Daisy Martin. She recorded about a dozen sides, mostly in 1921 for OKeh. On the basis of these sides, one must conclude that she was a terrible singer—shrill, dramatic, and out of tune. For most of her recording she was accompanied by a White band (the Tampa Blue Jazz Band) and her final two were with a group called her Royal Tigers, which might have been a version of the Original Memphis Five and represented a significant improvement over the earlier ones. The same Tampa Blue Jazz Band accompanied Josephine Carter for OKeh in the fall of 1921, on performances that seem closer to operetta than blues. (This group seems to have been a house band for OKeh during 1921. It probably included musicians drawn from society orchestras led by Joseph Samuels and Sam Lanin and was led by cornetist Jules Levy Jr.)

Another singer popular enough to last into the next stage of singing was Lena Wilson. She was the sister-in-law of Edith Wilson, and they toured along with Edith's husband Danny (Lena's brother) for several years in the late 1910s. She was born around 1898 in North Carolina, and worked in several major Black shows, as well as in the cabaret the Shuffle Inn. A short recording career (1922–1924 and 1930) produced about thirty sides that cast her clearly as a Cabaret Singer who went on to do quite a bit of acting. By the early 1930s, she had married Ralph "Shrimp" Jones—a violinist in the Plantation Club Orchestra, although she was reported to have died in 1939.

Wilson's recording career began at Black Swan, where she recorded only two sides, suggesting the results were not to the company's liking. She seems never to have had a contract with any single company, having records issued on no fewer than nine companies between 1922 and 1924, with a short curtain call in 1930. In general, she presents a professional, musical approach to the vaudeville songs and few blues she was called on to record, emphasizing the idea that many of these singers were viewed (and viewed themselves) as dependable pros who were called on to do a job.

There were many others who somehow earned the right to record, some based on musical ability, some for other unrecoverable talents. Nettie Gray made several sides for Black Swan, although she was very much in the classical style (as was male singer Eddie Gray). Two singers who did not record until a year or two after the cabaret period were Mattie Hite (for Pathe) and Marjorie Royce (OKeh), both of whom were obviously cabaret-style singers using very elaborate background arrangements and a dramatic style.

Leona Williams made sixteen recordings for Columbia, many of Clarence Williams tunes, all backed by Original Memphis Five. She apparently had a one-year contract from January 1922 to January 1923, and it is not difficult to imagine that her option was not picked up because of Bessie Smith's signing and instant success, thus signaling the change to the next style of "blues" singing.

Chapter 4

"Lost Your Head Blues"

Vaudeville Blues

> The pioneer recordings of northern blues women reflect the more urbane tastes of metropolitan theatergoers and the cultural context of the Harlem Renaissance. Typically, their singing is more self-conscious than the southern blues shouters, smoothing over the rough edges in the manner of "light entertainment." The resonance of folk style is stronger in the recordings of southern singers, as are patterns of black vernacular speech and phraseology. Blues sentiments may be universal, but they are conveyed more convincingly by a singer with a southern accent.
>
> —Abbott and Seroff, 2017

The development of "Vaudeville Blues" occurred throughout the 1910s, with repertoire, performance practice, and individual style being incubated on stages of venues catering primarily to African American audiences. When performers in this style finally began recording in 1923, they brought to the studio a southern background and a history of professional experience that in some cases went back more than two decades. While in some senses they sounded more coarse and rural than their cabaret-singing counterparts, they often had longer professional pedigrees and were called on to perform a wider range of material within the blues idiom. In addition, their training in large performance venues had developed within them a comfort with communicating feeling and emotions on a much more dramatic scale than was the case with the earlier performers.

Eva Taylor

One of the most prolifically recorded vocalists of the 1920s was Eva Taylor. Born Irene Gibbons in St. Louis in 1895, she was one of twelve children whose father died when she was fifteen months old (biographical information from "Looking Back with Eva, Parts I and II," *Storyville* 14, December 1967–January 1968; 15, February–March 1968). Financial need compelled her mother to commit the girl to employment on the stage when she was just three years old, going on tours with Josephine Gassman and Her Pickaninnies, which took her as far afield as Australia, New Zealand, England, France, and Germany by the time she was a teenager. During this period she appeared on bills with Bert Williams, Nora Bayes, Sophie Tucker, and Ethel Barrymore, as well as many other lesser lights. This incredible early training served her in good stead for the rest of her life; she was a quick study learning music and had a well-rounded, if small, voice that she could project well, as well as pitch

Figure 4.1. Clarence Williams and Eva Taylor, ca. 1925. Courtesy David A. Jasen Collection. Public domain.

control and enunciation that occasionally made her sound as if she had classical training.

During an appearance in Chicago in the late 1910s, she met her future husband, New Orleans pianist, composer, and entrepreneur Clarence Williams, who was operating a publishing company and appearing as a singer and dancer in vaudeville at the time. By 1921 Taylor (who had taken her stage name from a family she had stayed with in New York during her early tours) was in New York, performing in *Shuffle Along* and had married Williams, to whom her subsequent career was completely bound. Taylor's early recordings tended to be more jazz- and blues-oriented, with her vocal choruses on Williams's band recordings being no letdown after the instrumental portions. During the first year or so of her recording career, she also covered a number of successful blues compositions by other singers.

Taylor and Williams were known in the African American music scene in New York during this period for breaking down numerous barriers; they had a regular radio show at the end of the 1920s, put on a Broadway show (*Bottomland*) in 1927 that lasted for nineteen performances, and made a long series of recordings, primarily for OKeh, but branching out to other companies as well using different names. While Williams recorded with virtually every Black singer in New York during this period as part of his various business ventures, Taylor was his most frequent partner in the studios and her musical flexibility was key to the success of many of his publications (which were often driven by recordings).

For her part, Taylor premiered many of the tunes either credited to or published by her husband in styles that ranged from traditional blues to Tin Pan Alley numbers to pseudo-classical numbers, such as her duets with baritone Lawrence Lomax in November 1923, or her later recordings of waltzes (released as by "Irene Gibbons"). In addition to almost eighty sides released under her name, she contributed vocals to dozens of other records run by Williams and continued to record with him into the early 1940s, when she retired to raise their children and grandchildren. After her husband's death in 1965, she resumed singing publicly, even touring and recording until her death in 1977.

Eva Taylor's career during the 1920s was so bound up with the interests of Clarence Williams and his publishing company that she really needs to be considered outside the mainstream of African American singers of the period. In more modern times she might have been called a "demo" singer, albeit one whose demos were released to the public for general consumption. Alan Balfour points out that she, in later interviews, said that her recordings were almost entirely decided on and organized by her husband, who clearly valued her abilities to present songs in a clear, musical fashion that could be depended on to advance sales (Balfour, 1995). Her abilities in that regard were further highlighted by the fact that she was one of the very few African American singers to record with White groups, as she did in the late 1920s with the Charleston Chasers and the Knickerbockers (in a rare professional opportunity away from Clarence Williams).

Monette Moore

Born in Gainesville, Texas, in 1902, Moore was raised in Kansas City, making her way to Chicago by the early 1920s. It was there that she began her singing career, recording for Paramount during a trip to New York in January 1923. For the next year she apparently used Chicago as a base, recording a few sides there before returning to New York, which she made her home, appearing in theaters and occasional shows and even recording with the popular Paradise Orchestra led by Charlie Johnson in 1928. From October 1924 to the following March she was contracted to Ajax and was billed as "Susie Smith." After initially making cover versions of several Bessie Smith songs, she began recording with the Choo Choo Jazzers and doing duets with comic Billy Higgins (much as Josie Miles was doing at the same time). Following Ajax's demise in early 1925, Moore recorded several sides for Columbia and Victor over the next three years, but apparently was not very active in the entertainment industry.

Moore must have had some background in blues singing; her first recording was a cover of the popular Clarence Williams tune "Sugar Blues" (Paramount 12015, January 1923), which had also been Sara Martin's first recording three months earlier. Later that same month, she recorded "Gulf Coast Blues" and "Downhearted Blues" (Paramount 10230, January 1923), beating Bessie Smith by at least two weeks and demonstrating that the recording executives obviously identified her as a blues singer. Moore's recordings with just piano are impressive, but her later records with bands give another level of energy. On Jimmy Blythe's "I'll Go to My Grave with the Blues," (Paramount 12046, June 1923), she is accompanied by a trio of Chicago mainstays—New Orleans cornetist Tommy Ladnier, clarinetist Jimmy O'Bryant, and pianist Clarence Jones—and creates a storming performance in which she holds her own in the ensemble.

Figure 4.2. Monette Moore, ca. 1925. Courtesy David A. Jasen Collection. Public domain.

On the Ajax recordings, Moore is the beneficiary of a well-integrated (if shifting) group that had backed up numerous singers under the direction of pianist Louis Hooper, and included brass players Bubber Miley, Rex Stewart, and Jake Frazier; reed players Bob Fuller, Ernest Elliott, and sometimes Elmer Snowden, who also played banjo. Initially, it was obviously the duty of "Susie Smith" to provide Ajax with versions of Bessie Smith's current hits on Columbia; at least six of Bessie's tunes were covered in her first four sessions with the label. More space is left for individual solos or group improvisation than was the case on the Bessie Smith records, suggesting that the label recognized both the importance and the abilities of their house band.

Even after making several years' worth of recordings, Moore was not identified as a recording artist in reviews of her show performances during the 1920s. A review of her popular appearance in the 1933 show *Flying Colors* takes the "rags to riches" approach, saying that even as recently as 1928, when she was a part of the Broadway show *Messin' Around* she had been supporting herself in part by scrubbing floors (Calvin, 1933). The 1930s and '40s saw Moore active in films, radio and even television, where she appeared with Hattie McDaniel on *Beulah* in 1949. She relocated to Los Angeles during the 1940s and continued to perform as a singer until she died just before a regular performance with the Young Men of New Orleans at Disneyland in 1962.

Bessie Smith

Bessie Smith is by far the most written about figure of the blues or jazz period of the 1920s, with the exception of Louis Armstrong. Several full-length biographies, numerous articles, book chapters, and at least four collections of her complete recordings have appeared since 1970, many attempting to counter the sizable number of anecdotes and legends that appeared both during her lifetime and following her controversial death in 1937.

Smith was the most prolifically recorded singer of the 1920s and it was said that the success of her records lifted Columbia out of bankruptcy, as well as encouraged them to start their "race series" (the 14000 numbers that were soon followed by the 15000 series devoted to "hillbilly" music). She was in fact a bankable star who led shows and was featured in other revues well before she began recording and had actually made rejected test records for several companies, including for Harry Pace at

Black Swan, who apparently felt her voice and approach was too rough for his preferred clientele.

By the time Bessie Smith and Ma Rainey began their recording careers in 1923, each had been an established star in her own right for years: Smith for almost fifteen years and Rainey for nearly twenty-five. Many of the common assumptions about the period are that they were somehow only popular in the rural backwaters of the South and were brought into the light after the public tired of the big stage stars such as Mamie Smith, Lucille Hegamin, Ethel Waters, and Alberta Hunter.

Actually, the reverse was closer to the truth. The first African American female recording stars were for the most part either minor stage personalities or, like Waters and Hunter, Cabaret Singers (who in any event had continued popularity through the decade). Smith and Rainey were essentially the superstars of the era of Black entertainment following the deaths and retirements of George Walker, Ernest Hogan, Billy Kersands, Aida Overton Walker, String Beans May, and Baby Seals. From that generation, only Bert Williams survived and he would be dead before he could resume his recording career.

Bessie Smith was born in 1894 in Chattanooga, Tennessee, to a poor family, and by the age of nine had lost both her parents. Raised in very slim circumstances by her older sisters and brothers, Smith began singing and dancing on street corners for spare change while quite young. Her brother Clarence is often given credit for taking her out on the road in 1912, with a tent show that included Ma (then Gertrude) Rainey, but she was receiving notices as early as 1910 about her performances ("Savoy Theater," *The Freeman*, October 22, 1910, n.p.). By 1911, she was touring with F. A. Barrasso's Strollers, Benbow's Alabama Chocolate Drops, and a trio of performers called Fulk, Smith, and Levi. These were primarily stage shows in vaudeville theaters and she was known as a "coon shouter" as well as a dancer and comedienne ("F. A. Barrasso," *The Freeman*, February 11, 1911).

By 1916 she was identified as a blues singer who also danced. "St. Louis Blues," "Yellow Dog Blues," and "Hesitation Blues" were all numbers mentioned as being part of her stage act at the time, and the composer of all three, W. C. Handy, was a devoted supporter of her for the rest of her career ("Notes from Florida," *The Freeman*, January 1, 1916, n.p.). For the rest of the decade she was maintaining a schedule of tent shows in the spring and summer, followed by a vaudeville tour in the fall, usually as part of a duo with either Wayne "Buzzin'" Burton or Hazel Green.

At some point around 1920 or 1921, she established a home base in Philadelphia, bringing her extended family to keep house. For the next ten years she performed in the area, including Atlantic City, while home while still touring the South in the spring and fall. She also used her proximity to New York City to begin appearing in some of the Black theaters in Harlem and becoming familiar with northern audiences. In 1923, she appeared briefly in a revue called *How Come?*, later being replaced by Alberta Hunter. It was during this run that she was brought to the Columbia studios in January by Clarence Williams to make a test record. The success of that test encouraged recording director Frank Walker to bring her back in February to make her first released record: "Downhearted Blues" and "Gulf Coast Blues" (Columbia A3844, February 16, 1923). This record became practically an overnight success, perhaps not surprising given Smith's fame with African American audiences and Columbia signed her to a year's contract (which was to be renewed several times) following her third session (Clark, 2017).

"Downhearted Blues" is often cited as one of Smith's greatest records, but "Gulf Coast Blues" is an even better example of her style. Using just an octave range, Smith creates a palette of emotional intensity that nevertheless maintains a musical architecture over the course of the three-chorus vocal. The first and second phrases of each chorus also cadence upward to the third, a stylistic device that was obviously associated with Smith, if cover versions of this and several other tunes are any indication. An even more vivid example of this is Perry Bradford's "Frankie Blues" (Columbia 14023-D, April 8, 1924), which is a complicated structure of a twelve-bar modified blues verse, four-bar bridge, one blues chorus, and a key change to a twenty-bar trio with a reprise of the last twelve bars of the trio to finish. The blues chorus utilizes the "third-seeker" (Brooks, 1982, 7, 25) cadence on the third on each of the first two phrases (with the second repeated twice).

Another element of this performance is the inclusion of violinist Robert Robbins, imparting a definite "country" air to the sound. This was an obvious attempt to capitalize on the success of the Sara Martin and Sylvester Weaver recordings of the previous October, which are considered to be some of the first country blues discs.

1923–1924 was a banner period for Bessie Smith. The runaway success of her recordings allowed her to tour better theaters and to make more money (including selling records at her appearances). While doing much of her stage work in Philadelphia, New York, and Chicago, she toured up and down the East Coast as well as the southern theaters she

Frankie Blues

2nd Strain

Perry Bradford

had been working in for a decade. She also married Jack Gee at this time which, initially, was a positive association. Beginning in 1925, she began starring in her own show, *The Harlem Frolics*, which included a full jazz band, comics, dancers, and even other singers—a presentation large enough to justify buying her own railroad car. These tours continued alternating between tent shows and theater tours for several years.

Beginning in the fall of 1925, Smith began to be accompanied on record by larger groups, often subsets of the Fletcher Henderson band, including Louis Armstrong, Joe Smith, Charlie Green, and Buster Bailey. The interaction between singer and instrumentalists came to be a prime component of her records for the rest of her career. Virtually none of the earlier singers and very few of the subsequent ones in the 1920s responded to instrumental stimuli the way she did; in that way, she was clearly more of a jazz singer than most and much of her subsequent fame has been based on that.

While the collaborations between Armstrong and Smith are rightfully regarded as some of the highpoints of 1920s jazz, she reportedly preferred the more measured cornet sound of Joe Smith, who clearly viewed himself as an accompanist rather than as an equal partner (as did Armstrong). The following example is of the fourth and fifth choruses of her own "Lost Your Head Blues" (Columbia 14158, May 4, 1926), with the two Smiths and Fletcher Henderson creating a three-way dialogue, the vocal part being preeminent.

This demonstrates how a superior accompanist could support yet not overpower a vocal line while simultaneously inspiring the singer.

Occasionally when Smith had no other horn player to dialogue with, she would supply her own answering phrases. On "Jailhouse Blues" (Columbia A-4001, September 21, 1923) she realized Irving Johns was not

Chorus 5
11
tell you the rea son why
Days
are lone ne
Ab7
Eb
Eb
Bb7
Eb
15
some
nights
are
long
days
are lone some
Eb
Eb
Eb7
Ab
19
nights
are
so
long
I'm a
good old
gal
but I've
Ab
Eb
Eb
Bb7
23
just
been
treat ed
wrong
Ab7
Eb
Eb

up to the task of filling in the ends of phrases in any way she wanted, so she simply extended her lines and did earlier pickups to the next phrase, as comparison with the original sheet music demonstrates.

By the end of the 1920s, the vogue for Vaudeville Blues had waned considerably and the onset of the Depression put another nail in its coffin. Smith, however, remained popular and well employed on the stage. May 1929 found her to be the only positively reviewed element of the Maceo Pinkard Broadway show *Pansy*, which closed in plenty of time for her to film the two-reel *St. Louis Blues*—the only existing film appearance of a Classic Blues singer in something like her native professional element. Unfortunately, the film was not a success, but Smith continued to tour with shows like the *Midnight Steppers* and *Happy Times* in 1930, with smaller shows and reviews occupying the rest of the decade. She made her final recording session in 1933, and seemed poised to have something of a renaissance in the swing era, with bookings at the Apollo Theater and Connie's Inn in New York in 1936, but she was killed in a car accident while on tour with a tent show, *Broadway Rastus*, in September 1937.

Bessie Smith was by far the best of the generation of singers who made their names on records in the 1920s, but her artistry both in terms of music and stagecraft was developed over the fifteen years preceding her first recording. She, along with Ma Rainey, represented both the midpoint of the recording history of the genre and the summit of the profession.

Viola McCoy

For a singer as prolifically recorded as Viola McCoy was, little or no information is known about her upbringing or even her birth. Her birth date is often given as 1900, but a notification in *The Freeman* in 1910 mentions someone by that name singing with the Palace Stock Company at the Palace Theater in Houston, which would obviously suggest a birth date of at least five or six years earlier ("The Palace Theater at Houston, Texas," April 2, 1910).

The early 1910s found McCoy touring with southern minstrel shows, featured as a singer. By 1916 McCoy was singing professionally with Stark's Minstrel company in New York, being featured on "Scaddle De Mooch" and "Daddy" ("Spark's Minstrel," *The Freeman*, May 27, 1916), shortly thereafter doing a tour with the Smart Set company before settling in New York permanently around 1920. From that point she was primarily employed at high-end supper clubs and cabarets, as well as resorts. McCoy played regularly at Saratoga Springs during the summer seasons in the 1920s. The band she had with her during the summer of 1924 had a strong front line—June Clark on cornet, Jimmy Harrison on trombone, and Benny Carter on saxophone—all at the very beginning of their careers ("Viola at It," *Chicago Defender*, August 2, 1924).

McCoy's stage training is immediately apparent from her first recordings in 1923, which display excellent diction, projection, and solid

Figure 4.3. Viola McCoy, ca. 1925. Courtesy David A. Jasen Collection. Public domain.

rhythmic concept, but not a great deal of blues feeling. Oddly, her first year's recordings are heavily slanted toward blues tunes, many of which were composed by Porter Grainger, who accompanied her on most of her early sessions. She, in fact, might have been working for Grainger and his partner Bob Ricketts (who also accompanied her on two sessions), publicizing their songs, as her records were initially done for Gennett, Vocalion, and Columbia (as by Amanda Brown), so she did not have a regular label association until 1926, when she started working for Cameo, replacing Lucille Hegamin.

McCoy's early recordings included two versions of the novelty oriented "Laughin' Cryin' Blues" (a bigger hit for Sara Martin and composed by Ricketts and Grainger) accompanied by Grainger (Gennett 5108, March 7, 1923 and Columbia A3867, recorded March 27, 1923) and Clarence Williams's "Gulf Coast Blues" (Gennett 5151, April 26, 1923), accompanied by a jazz group led by Ricketts. These demonstrate a familiarity with blues style, but a stylized and highly mannered approach using vocal catches and mordents in place of blue notes. By the time she recorded "Bama Bound Blues" (Silvertone 3007, August 7, 1923), she had developed a much more convincing style with authentic touches of bent notes and even moaning.

For the second half of her recording career, McCoy did much more work as a jazz and popular singer, with accompanists including soon to be famous musicians like Bubber Miley, Rex Stewart, Louis Metcalf, Cliff Jackson, and Elmer Snowden. Her abilities to negotiate up-tempo dance numbers (such as "If Your Good Man Quits You, Don't Wear No Black" Brunswick 2591, March 11, 1924) set her apart from the majority of singers recording at this period who favored slower tunes, even novelty numbers.

By the early 1930s McCoy had pretty much retired from show business and lived in the Albany area, where she apparently died in the mid-1950s.

Edna Hicks

Edna Hicks was part of the Landry (or Landrieux) family of New Orleans, which also produced singer Lizzie Miles (Edna's younger half-sister) and the trumpeter Herb Morand. Born in the early 1890s, Hicks had left home by the early 1910s, and was appearing in Will Benbow's *Choc-*

olate Drops company when she married the boss in 1912. They toured together for a few years until the marriage dissolved, pushing her into a vaudeville career, which continued for the next decade and brought her to the attention of various recording directors who used her frequently during her single year in the studios.

Hicks made about thirty recordings for a multitude of companies over the period of exactly a year, beginning in March, 1923. She seems not to have had any contract with a single company until the last three sessions of her career (with Paramount), instead being engaged for numerous one-shot sessions, often accompanied by either Lem Fowler or Porter Grainger, who provided at least some of the tunes. With a repertoire overwhelmingly slanted to twelve-bar blues, Hicks must have been considered a specialist in that area, possibly due to her New Orleans heritage and relation to Lizzie Miles. The evidence on the discs suggests that this trust was seriously misplaced; her singing is rhythmically stilted and her voice is harsh and reedy. Her covers of "Downhearted Blues" and "Gulf Coast Blues" demonstrate a familiarity with the Bessie Smith records but nothing of Smith's conviction or dramatic presentation (Brunswick 2463, June 18, 1923).

She is somewhat better on her own tune (composed with J. Meller) "No Name Blues," which she recorded twice (Gennett 5252, early September 1923, and Columbia 14001, September 24, 1923, which was her only release for that label, suggesting it was an unsuccessful audition). On these she sings with more energy and involvement than on virtually any of her other records, suggesting that it might have been part of her regular repertoire rather than something she had to learn for the recording session. Her last recordings in New York, recorded with small groups led by Grainger and Fletcher Henderson and in feature some of her own tunes, which are better than her earlier efforts. By the beginning of 1924, she had relocated to Chicago and her last records were made there in March for Paramount, accompanied by Love Austin.

Hicks's career and life came to a premature end. While in Chicago in August 1925, she was helping her husband John Hicks fix an automobile in their driveway and was killed when a lighted candle ignited some gasoline.

Rosa Henderson

Information on the life of Rosa Henderson is remarkably scanty. Born Rosa Deschamps in Hendersonville, Kentucky in 1896, she left home

Figure 4.4. Rosa Henderson, ca. 1925. Courtesy David A. Jasen Collection. Public domain.

early, apparently touring with a circus as a teenager. She married fellow entertainer Douglas "Slim" Henderson in 1912, giving birth to her daughter Marie in 1913, apparently while on the road in Arizona, followed by Minty in 1916. In the 1930 census, Rosa Henderson was listed as having been married at fourteen with one child (Marie had died in July, 1929). The 1920 census record has the four Hendersons living in Terrebone, Louisiana, with his parents. Rosa and her daughters are listed as "mulatto," which makes her early years more intriguing, while Rosa and Douglas were cited as "vaudeville entertainers." Minty later went into show business as a chorus girl.

After several years working under canvas (much of it in Texas, where she said she claimed she sang primarily blues), the Hendersons began appearing in vaudeville in New Orleans and then moving out to tour for most of the 1910s in the Mason-Henderson Show (Kunstadt, *Record Research 75*, April 1966). In 1920, the popular duo was appearing at the Lyric Theater in New Orleans in the show *Show Folks*, credited to Perin and Henderson (Joe Loomis, *Chicago Defender*, May 29, 1920, 4). Tours with numerous shows and as a single act on the TOBAbrought the Hendersons around the circuit and eventually to New York, where Rosa was given auditions for numerous record companies, beginning with Paramount and Victor in May 1923.

During the first twelve months of her recording career, Rosa Henderson made recordings for no fewer than eight different companies. The lack of a consistent professional association surely hurt her chances for popular success, although the fact that she ultimately made at least ninety records (some under pseudonyms) demonstrates her dependability as well as what must have been at least a reasonable sales potential. Henderson's versatility is also remarkable; she recorded a variety of material comparable in some ways to the more "sophisticated" singers of the day, such as Alberta Hunter and Ethel Waters, although she clearly had more of a traditional blues perspective as well as pedigree.

The press notices about her recordings must surely have helped her (and her husband) secure higher profile engagements in New York and down the East Coast. They participated in *Sheik of Harlem* (Irvin Miller, fall 1923), *Miss Dinah of 1926* (Miller and Slayter, fall 1926), *The Dixie Brevities* (later fall 1926), *The Dixie Dandies* and *Chocolate Scandals* (spring 1927), *The Harlem Rounders* (fall 1927), and *Brunettes Preferred* (later fall 1927). By early 1928, the duo had reunited with their former partner John Mason and they were performing in a variety show at the Lincoln

Theater in New York, but Slim Henderson would die suddenly in early May of that year ("Slim Henderson Dead," 1928).

Several accounts state that Rosa Henderson was so devastated by the loss of her husband that she lost interest in performing professionally. This is certainly discounted by the fact that she appeared in numerous shows following his death until at least 1932, although except for one recording session in 1931, her career on records ended shortly before her husband died. One can imagine that the death of her eldest daughter in 1929, as well as the onset of the Depression must have had a significant impact on both her enthusiasm and performing opportunities. That, coupled with the need to be the sole provider for her other daughter apparently caused her to try domestic service (the 1930 census lists her as a maid for a private family) and then to work for years in a department store. She apparently did consent to sing now and then and remained in New York until her death in 1968 (Stewart-Baxter, 1968).

A survey of Henderson's recordings during the 1920s shows her to be a versatile professional able to handle a wide variety of material, much of which was presumably new to her. In an interview at the end of her life, she recalled "rehearsals" with her most frequent accompanist, Fletcher Henderson, on the subway on the way to the recording sessions! One is also struck with the consistently high level of singing on her recordings; clearly, she was a superior singer who might have had some musical training. In his entry for Henderson, Rust (1973) suggests that she accompanies herself on piano on her first recording session and the test session for Victor that followed. In terms of vocal equipment, she had a centered and very confident sense of pitch which, combined with a significant vocal range and a remarkable rhythmic sure-footedness. This combination of talents separated her from most of her contemporaries, although she composed little or nothing of the repertoire she recorded. She also profited by consistently effective accompanists—whether solo pianists or small bands—that overall were better than those behind even Bessie Smith and Ma Rainey.

Why was this the case? Henderson did not have any long-term affiliations with any record companies, but she had what must have been long-term professional relationships with both Fletcher Henderson and some other Harlem musicians. As mentioned earlier, for the first year of her recording career, Henderson recorded for as many as eight different New York–based companies, large and small. The common denominator for almost all these sessions was the presence of Fletcher Henderson. At the time, Henderson did not have a touring band, so he was available more or less consistently in New York, and backed up many singers, cementing his reputation as a strong musician who could be depended on to shepherd singers of wide-ranging abilities through the recording process.

With Rosa Henderson, Henderson had a singer who was obviously capable of singing fairly complicated material and holding her own with ensembles from a solo piano to a six-piece band. Indeed, the pianist shows up on her recordings in a much more favorable light than was the case with other singers; on a song like "Got the World in a Jug" (Ajax 17021, December 1923) the singer and the pianist roar through the composition (which takes its title from some lyrics in the Alberta Hunter song "Downhearted Blues," but is not a blues in form) with one of Fletcher Henderson's best piano solos from the period. Likewise, the swing of "Fletcher Henderson's Jazz Five" backing "Clearing House Blues" and "West Indies Blues" (Brunswick 2612, April 10, 1924) is some of that group's hottest playing prior to Louis Armstrong's appearance six months later, suggesting that the singer may have been the inspiration for the rhythmic drive of the performance, similar to the way Armstrong ignited performances of the full group during his year with the band. "West Indies Blues" was one of several tunes she recorded that referenced the popular "Back to Africa" movement of Marcus Garvey, as did "Barbados Blues" and "Black Star Line." What connection, if any, she had with Garvey (or the West Indies for that matter) is unknown. "Papa Will Be Gone" (sung as "Sweet Mama Will Be Gone" Brunswick 2589, February 13, 1924) recorded with the same group has a similar fire and also introduces two tempo changes, going into half time with the return of the vocal following the ensemble interlude and then doubling up again at the end, a highly unusual and complex routine for blues recordings of the period.

More remarkable is a one-off performance of "Struttin' Blues" with the Virginians (Victor 19157, September 25, 1923). Directed by reed player Ross Gorman, the Virginians was an offshoot of the enormously popular orchestra led by Paul Whiteman. Later dubbed "The King of Jazz," Whiteman included effective jazz players in his bands throughout his career and occasionally, as with the case of the Virginians, allowed them to make records outside the contract of the full group. This unit was a standard dance band (minus drums) playing from what sounds to be a publisher's stock arrangement of a new tune by the Black bandleader Tim Brymm, with Chris Smith and Al Siegel. Why a Black singer was engaged to record with a White band is difficult to fathom at this point (although there were other examples from this period), but Henderson's technical abilities and presumably her ability to read music (a talent shared by few of her contemporaries) and stage experience must have played into the decision. Her performance of this tune is remarkably confident and highly musical, making one regret that she did not have other opportunities.

Rosa Henderson recorded remarkably few blues or blues-based compositions during the first year of so of her recording career. Clearly, she was regarded as a popular singer, although her credentials as a blues singer were much more convincing than those of more widely recorded contemporaries like Ethel Waters or Alberta Hunter. "Down South Blues" (by Waters and Fletcher Henderson) (Vocalion 14635, June or July 1923) and "Chicago Monkey Man Blues" (by Lovie Austin) (Vocalion 14832, May 23, 1924) are performances of very different types of blues—both very convincing in the vocal delivery, which avoids the chirpy, optimistic tone of some of the cabaret and theater singers who were treating the blues as a style, rather than an expression of emotion.

More traditional is "Barrelhouse Blues," which was one of the few tunes Henderson recorded twice (Vocalion 14831, May 24, 1924 with Fletcher Henderson and Banner 1394, July, 1924 with Edgar Dowell), although the lyrics are completely different (throwing the composer into doubt, although the second version bears similarities to the tune of the same name recorded by Ma Rainey). The earlier version laments a lost lover with relatively little to do with the title of the song until the end, when the singer says she will give up drinking when her man comes home, while the second version uses traditional blues lyrics referencing the theme of a barrelhouse to evaluate marital relations.

> Papa likes his whiskey, mama likes her gin [2x]
> Papa likes the women, mama likes her men

Rosa Henderson's farewell to her collaboration with Fletcher Henderson was "Do That Thing," billed as with Fletcher Henderson and His Club Alabam Orchestra (Vocalion 14838, May 28, 1924), and was her only recording with the full ten-piece Henderson band, which apparently was about to embark on a summer tour in New England before beginning a ten-year residence at the Roseland Ballroom in the fall. A full-band arrangement introduces the singer as an added attraction, given away by the sudden key change after the first chorus and the singer being accompanied by only piano and some apparently faked horn backgrounds. An improvised clarinet break and an exhortation from the singer "Come on Fletcher, do that thing!" leads into a band chorus featuring Coleman Hawkins on tenor sax in a new key. That he (or his music director, Don Redman) would adapt what must have been either a new publisher's stock or possibly a number the band had been playing as an instrumental at the Alabam demonstrates his high regard for the singer's abilities. At the end of his life, Henderson recalled Rosa Henderson with great fondness and a high professional regard (Kunstadt, 1963).

The rest of Henderson's recording career (until 1931) produced slightly more issued recordings than did her first twelve months in the studio. Although many fine Harlem musicians, including Bubber Miley, Louis Metcalf, Cliff Jackson, Fats Waller, Louis Hooper, Rex Stewart, James P. Johnson, and Bob Fuller, participated on one or more records, the quality of the accompaniments was not as consistent as it had been, although the singing remained of a high caliber. The proportion of her blues performances was significantly increased, perhaps in response to her identification as a "blues singer" in the various reviews and shows she did from that point. This might also have been due in part to the greater diffusion of her recordings through pseudonyms and for smaller labels that didn't have the budget for much preparation or higher-priced musical talent.

While Rosa Henderson was known on the various Black entertainment circuits as half of a comic duet with her husband, Slim, she also sang solo numbers and was often credited for her vocal performances in the Black press. As late as 1927, she was noticed singing both "St. Louis Blues" and the relatively new Tin Pan Alley tune "After You've Gone," demonstrating her versatility and the wide appeal she had been building since her early days on the TOBA. It is fortunate for our understanding of the era and the variety of characters and participants that Rosa Henderson as able to record as much as she did; her dependability and overall musicality ensured her frequent presence in the recording studios all through the 1920s, preserving a good sample of a superior singer and entertainer who was never able to crack the upper reaches of commercial success.

Clara Smith

One of the drawbacks of being dependable and uncontroversial is that you are often overlooked by history. Such is the case with Clara Smith, who was second only to Bessie Smith in terms of recorded legacy during the 1920s, and who seems to have been able to work consistently, even during the early years of the Depression.

Born in Spartanburg, South Carolina, in September 1892, Smith's early years are an almost complete blank. She may have been an only child—what became of her parents and how and when she entered show business is a mystery—although she may have begun singing in church (she later made several recordings of gospel tunes) and from there joined a traveling tent show as an escape from the menial lot of most African American women in the South during this period (Rimmer, 2018).

The first mention of her in the Black press comes from the early 1910s; she was touring in vaudeville shows (primarily in the Carolinas, Georgia, and Florida) by 1911, both as a single and with larger companies. In C. W. Park's *Musical Comedy Company* in 1914, she was paired with a fellow named Jones in a team known as "Jones and Jones," from which she received her first significant press notice, calling her "Miss Blue" and "Queen of the Blues" but crediting her equally for her monologues and humorous interaction with the audience (Abbott & Seroff, 2007, 126). Abbott & Seroff also point out that this press acknowledgment of an African American performer as a blues singer rather than a "coon shouter" was a significant, and possibly unprecedented, development signaling a move away from the minstrel-derived, nineteenth-century view of Black entertainers. From 1915 until the early 1920s, she seems to have alternated between the higher-class tented minstrel shows such as Tolliver's *Big Show* (1915–1917), Wooden's *Bon Tons* (1917), Al Wells's *Smart Set* (1920), and an E. B. Dudley show (early 1923, as part of "Smith and Graham"), and appearances in vaudeville, including short tours in "sister acts" with Leola Grant (fall 1915) and Bessie Smith (fall 1918), as well as Smith and Graham in 1923 (see Abbott & Seroff, 2007, 130, and *Chicago Defender*, January 27, 1923 and March 17, 1923).

At some point late in 1920 through the summer of 1921, Smith headlined a vaudeville show for the promoter Bob Russell that toured the TOBA circuit with extended stays in St. Louis, Memphis, and New Orleans. It was in St. Louis that she became acquainted as well as enamored with a fourteen-year-old aspiring singer and dancer named Josephine Baker. Several accounts describe a possible love affair, although the more measured reflections of dancer Maude Russell recalled that female performers of the time often clung to each other socially, romantically, and physically to protect each other from abusive men and deal with the loneliness of touring as much as for relationships' sake (Baker, 1993, 37–39, 64). Rimmer (2018) positions Smith as an avatar of gay culture in New York during the late 1920s, producing shows and revues directly aimed at that population, apparently based on their titles; however, I can find nothing in the literature or press releases to support this). What is likely is that the attention paid to her by the older singer certainly influenced both the stage presence and future direction of Baker's career.

It is unknown how Clara Smith came to the attention of the recording executives at Columbia, but it is intriguing to think that perhaps Bessie Smith had something to do with it. The two Smiths had been friends as they toured the TOBA circuit and apparently maintained at least a cordial relationship into the mid-1920s. Bessie Smith had beaten Clara into the Columbia studios by three months (following a series of aborted test recordings), but by Clara's first successful date in June 1923, the first Bessie Smith records had been enormous sellers and the company would naturally have wanted to capitalize on her success. Even though they shared a surname and a general pattern to their careers, the two Smiths were very different singers; Bessie Smith was clearly the more "southern" of the two, with a particular affinity to the blues that led her to be a headliner in tented minstrel shows touring the rural South as well as vaudeville theaters. Clara Smith, on the other hand, had a much lighter voice that lent itself to more popular material. While she toured in the South with larger shows, she was apparently never a headliner and found much more consistent success in vaudeville theaters where she was often celebrated for her comedic abilities.

As the press notices show, Clara Smith had been traveling as part of Smith and Graham in vaudeville and with E. B. Dudley in New Orleans and Detroit during the first three or four months of 1923. Presumably, she would have been brought to New York during an off period to make her first records. After a summer in which she visited the Columbia studios on at least eight different occasions and presumably worked in theaters in the New York area, Clara Smith began a fall vaudeville tour through Nashville, Detroit, and eventually to Chicago, leading her own troupe with pianist Stanley Miller as her primary accompanist.

The commercial success of her records allowed Smith a great deal more leeway in her tours. Bessie Smith and Ma Rainey were established headliners by the time they began their recording career, so their appearances were often used to publicize their records. Because her success on recording came before she was acknowledged as a headliner, Clara Smith followed the trajectory of the first wave of blues singers, although she was clearly more located in the southern folk tradition. Instead of having to barnstorm through the rural South, she could make a reasonable living leading shows, including as many as twenty or thirty other performers in "high-class vaudeville," which was on the TOBA circuit through the South, Midwest and eastern Atlantic states (Bob Hayes, *Chicago Defender*, February 23, 1924, 6). This was largely the pattern of the rest of her career, with short stints on Broadway—she appeared in *Sweet Chariot* (October 1930 for three performances), and possibly others as well—and occasional appearances outside of the main circuit.

As mentioned earlier, Clara Smith's voice was significantly lighter and more flexible than that of some of her contemporary southern singers, most notably Bessie Smith and Ma Rainey. While this might have been a handicap on stage in tent shows, it proved to be an asset in the recording studio and for the new style of more intimate singing, encouraged by the use of microphone following the adoption of the electric recording process by Columbia in 1925. Two recordings, "Chicago Blues" and "Thirty-First Street Blues" (Columbia 14009, January 31, 1924), accompanied by a small group of dance-band musicians led by Fletcher Henderson prove that she was far more comfortable singing in a rhythmic, "jazzy" style than were some of her contemporaries. By the late 1920s, she had begun to evolve a much more subtle style similar to that of her contemporary Lizzie Miles and looking forward to the 1930s singing of Mildred Bailey.

During the 1920s, the Black press frequently reviewed Smith's performances, and in general they were quite enthusiastic about her contributions and the general reception of her shows. As often as she was celebrated for her singing, it was her interaction with the audience and her comic asides and "lectures" that received the most mention. For example, she was specifically cited for her talking and singing about "marital relations" and "advice about holding sweethearts" (*Afro American*, May 15, 1926), as well as causing the audience "to ache from laughter" by her "facial expressions, combined with a distinct personality" (*Chicago Defender*, February 27, 1926).

Smith was responsible for writing relatively few of her own songs, but she clearly had a hand in picking her repertoire and quite possibly in what she recorded as well. One early example from her discography is "Don't Advertise Your Man," credited to Jimmy Foster (who also composed several other songs recorded by Smith), recorded on April 23, 1924 (Columbia 14026 D; this song was also covered later in the year by Rosa Henderson and in 1931 by Mamie Smith. Sippie Wallace later adapted it into her signature song, "Women Be Wise," in the 1960s).

Open your eyes, women be wise,
Don't advertise your man
It's all right to have a little bird in the bush
But it ain't like the one you've got in your hand
Your head will hang low and your heart will ache
You're fattening a frog for a vampin' snake
So take a tip and hold your lip
And don't advertise your man

While no mention of "Don't Advertise Your Man" is found in contemporary reviews, it is obvious that this is the sort of song she was known for in her stage performances (and one which could have been extended indefinitely with comic lyrics).

More interesting in a blues sense is "Sobbin' Sister Blues," from May 23, 1928 (Columbia 14344 D). Composed (as was its session mate, "Steamboat Man Blues") by the otherwise unknown Bill Wallace, "Sobbin' Sister Blues" is performed almost as an imitation of Bessie Smith, complete with a similar melody featuring phrase endings on the third and a shouting vocal delivery similar to "Sobbin' Hearted Blues" recorded by Bessie Smith (Columbia 14056, January 14, 1925). That it was a conscious imitation is further proved by the trumpet accompaniment by Freddie Jenkins, which following the line, "I start weeping in the morning and crying till I go to bed," quotes Louis Armstrong's backing of the lyrics, "I'm gonna start walkin', 'cause I got a wooden pair of shoes" on the earlier record.

Armstrong himself recorded with Smith on two sessions in January and April 1925, but the synergy evident on his recordings with Bessie Smith is unfortunately not evident on those with Clara. While the Bessie Smith recordings afforded Armstrong a fair amount of freedom in terms of crafting background figures and even some solos choruses, only "Court House Blues" with Clara Smith allows him any opportunities for give and take. The tunes recorded in January, "Nobody Knows the Way I Feel Dis

Mornin'" and "Broken Busted Blues" (Columbia 14058-D and 14062-D, January 7, 1925) are simply too complex melodically for backgrounds to work well. The second session produced more compelling results, with "Court House Blues" being memorable enough for Armstrong to re-create it as part of his 1956 *Satchmo—A Musical Autobiography* album (Decca, 1957). For the most part, Clara Smith made her best recordings with simpler accompaniments; those with only Fletcher Henderson, Stanley Miller, Lemuel Fowler, Porter Grainger, and especially James P. Johnson by themselves, or with perhaps one discrete horn (clarinet, trumpet, or trombone), are in the end the most satisfying, suggesting a level of discomfort sharing the stage with major jazz players.

Of more interest is her performance of "Lowland Moan," recorded on September 9, 1930 (Columbia 14580-D). Credited to Clara Smith, the lyrics demonstrate a hard look at the lot of a displaced woman lamenting her hard life with numerous references to southern Black imagery, but the vocal performance represents a much more subtle approach to blues singing.

1. Got coal in my cellar, just got to shovel more [2x]
   But they stopped my credit, so did the mean old grocery store
2. Six months in the lowland, has made an awful change in me [2x]
   But give me the lowland, 'cause that's where I want to be

Smith's later recordings gravitate more toward novelty and comedy: salacious blues ("For Sale [Hannah Johnson's Jack Ass]"), songs of defiance ("So Long, Jim"), and vaudeville comedy duets (several with guitarist Lonnie Johnson). The two duets with singer Asbestos Jones (or Burns, depending on the source) are classic examples of what she must have done on stage in her shows to generate such praise for her comic abilities. "Unemployed Papa—Charity Workin' Mama" (Columbia 14619-D, August 4, 1931) includes a great deal of patter between the two characters built around a fairly complicated verse and leading into a chorus.

[female] Unemployed papa, unemployed papa, don't ask me to give you no more
[male] Charity workin' mama, charity workin' mama, you never talked like this before

[female] Keep away, for I don't wish to be annoyed, my stuff
is only for the poor and unemployed
[male] Then please tell me the reason why you give your meat
to the man who owns the house across the street
[female] he needs it!
[female] Unemployed papa, unemployed papa, where you get
your nerve I can not see
[male] that's 'cause you're blind!
[female] the other night you tried to crash my breadline twice
[male] Well I can't help baby if your bread is nice . . . I like
good bread!
[female] Unemployed papa,
[male] charity workin' mama,
[both] you can't take advantage of me

Very few "scripts" exist of what probably went on in a Black vaudeville act of the 1920s, but this recording seems to preserve the onstage dynamic between performers of significant experience and professionalism.

Smith continued to record throughout the 1920s, while simultaneously leading tours and headlining shows throughout the TOBA circuit. By June 1925, she had become successful enough to invest in real estate, buying a house in Macon, Georgia, for $2,500, and apparently she owned some property in New York City as well (William Smith, *Afro-American*, June 20, 1925, 5). Following a long two-month tour in Florida in early 1926, she married her show manager, Charles Wesley, who was known in the African American community for being a manager and player on several Negro Baseball League teams, including the Memphis Red Sox. He apparently traveled with her shows during the off season and filled numerous functions as manager and producer ("Clara Smith Is No Blues Singer," *Afro-American*, May 22, 1926, 4B). By the fall of 1927, she had assumed management of the show herself and presumably directed the *Black Bottom Revue*, *Clara Smith's Musical Revue*, and possibly other shows organized around her singing for the balance of the decade.

As the 1920s wore on and the vogue for the Vaudeville Blues singers waned, Smith began appearing in shows as a featured act, often performing with rising stars like Jackie (later "Moms") Mabley, George Dewey Washington, and Edgar Hayes. Smith and Mabley both starred in a curiosity, a Black western called *Trouble on the Ranch*, during the spring of 1931. While her star had fallen considerably, apparently she was in enough demand as a singer and comedian that she continued touring, living for a time in Chicago and Cleveland, where she died of heart disease in February 1935.

Martha Copeland

An excellent example of a vaudeville professional who was brought before the recording microphone based on audience appeal rather than exceptional musical ability, Martha Copeland had a full an active career in the 1920s, but then disappeared from view.

Born Martha Williams in the early 1890s in Portsmouth, Virginia, she was raised in Norfolk, making her theatrical debut at the Pekin Theater in Richmond in 1910 ("Sharing Earnings with Poor Blues-Singer's Idea of Fun," 1927). Shortly after that she left with a company led by Zack Copeland, whose name she adopted, even before marrying Isaac Copeland in 1912. She apparently barnstormed around the vaudeville circuit until the early 1920s found her in New York, where she was engaged to make her first records in the fall of 1923, for OKeh. Her first mention in the Black press came because of her first two records. Although her name was mentioned in passing, it was her accompanist, Eddie Heywood Sr. who was given the lion's share of the notice because of his exceptional playing and the fact that he composed both numbers ("OKeh Notes," *Chicago Defender*, October 6, 1923, 7). Apparently those records were not deemed successful and she was not invited back.

After several years of touring, she was engaged by Columbia for a two-year contract negotiated by her manager, Joe Davis. This series was obviously better received and Copeland was given a high percentage of pop and vaudeville material that emphasized her theatrical and comic abilities over her small voice. Songs like "Papa, If You Can't Do Better, I'm Gonna Get a Better Papa" (Columbia 14161, September 14, 1926) and "On Decoration Day They'll Know Where to Bring Your Flowers To" (Columbia 14189, December 21, 1926) were pure knockabout comedy of the sort she was noted for on stage.

She toured with comic and songwriter Sidney Easton in his trio in 1927, and was also in his show *Mayor of Jimtown*, which was a development of one act of the Sissle and Blake *Shuffle Along* of 1921. The two of them made two records that give a good impression of their stage presence at the time. Copeland's later recordings veered more toward the popular (such as the cover of "I Can't Give You Anything but Love"—an unusual assignment for inclusion in the Columbia race series—Columbia 14327, May 26, 1928), with more polite accompaniment by jazz players like Bubber Miley and James P. Johnson, as well as several violinists.

Ida Cox

Ida Cox occupies a unique place in the Classic Blues pantheon. While not a headliner, she was reviewed positively throughout the 1910s, and had a busy career until she began recording in June 1923, after which she toured the TOBA extensively. Based in Chicago, all her recordings during the 1920s were done for the Paramount label, and she was heavily advertised in the Black press along with Ma Rainey and, a bit later, Blind Lemon Jefferson and Papa Charlie Jackson. As with most of her contemporaries, Cox's recording career seemed to be over by 1930, although she was blessed with enough good health (and luck as well) to outlive Rainey and all the Smiths, enjoying a short rediscovery in the late 1930s, and emerging again for a final curtain call in 1961. Of her approximately ninety issued recordings between 1923 and 1929, about half were either her own compositions or co-compositions (many with either her first accompanist Love Austin or her husband and later accompanist, Jesse Crump; it is possible that songs not copyrighted by her were her own compositions). In this way she can be considered a bridge to the "Downhome" style of blues singers that will be considered in the next chapter, although her extensive theatrical credits definitely identify her with the Vaudeville Blues.

Furthering her association with the later singers, Cox's recorded repertoire was far more centered on the standard twelve-bar blues than that of any other Vaudeville Blues singer. While Rainey frequently recorded songs and song forms from an earlier part of Black entertainment history and both Bessie and Clara Smith (along with the earlier stylists) featured more contemporary popular and Tin Pan Alley fare, perhaps 70 percent of Cox's recordings were blues with various lyric patterns. Almost all the blues credited to Cox were twelve bars and in the familiar AAB lyric pattern, occasionally introduced by nonblues verses. Several songs by Lovie Austin took liberties with the form, for example, "Worried in Mind Blues" (Paramount 12237, August 1924, a ten-bar blues omitting the usual fourth and eighth measures) and "My Mean Man Blues" (Paramount 12237, same session, which omits the IV chords entirely) deviate from the established norm. The Cox compositions "Chattanooga Blues" (Paramount 12063, July or August 1923) and "Pleading Blues" (Paramount 12513, July 1927) are twelve bars, but in ABC form. Assuming that she in fact wrote the songs attributed to her, Cox was a remarkably prolific and poetic lyricist.

Cox was born Ida Prather in Toccoa, Georgia, although she was raised about 150 miles away in Cedartown, the county seat. The date usually given for her birth is 1896 (her gravestone and death record cite 1894), although several factors indicate an earlier date. Her parents, Lamax (or Lomax) and Susie Prather were listed as married and living in Toccoa in the 1880 census, and apparently had another daughter, Willie Bell, whose married name was Nelson and who died in Knoxville, Tennessee, in 1957, at the age of sixty-seven. Both parents were born in the 1850s, making it unlikely that they had another child when both were nearing (or past) forty. Also, Ida lived with her daughter, Helen Goode, in Knoxville throughout the 1950s and '60s and Helen's gravestone and death records indicate that she was born in 1908, making it almost impossible that her mother was only twelve when she was born. It is much more likely that Ida was born earlier in the decade and left to begin touring after the birth of her daughter, which was quite possibly out of wedlock.

In an unpublished interview late in life, Cox remembered leaving her rural, yet comfortable home as a teenager (probably around 1910) to join the Georgia Black and Tan Minstrels following several years of singing in church. After several barnstorming years with tent show companies in which she sang "Ragtime songs was what we called them in those days. Later years, of course, they started calling them blues" (Westergaard interview, in Neely, 2009). During her travels she became acquainted with Ma Rainey, who she said was much more popular and a longer tenured veteran from whom she learned.

The first mention of her in the Black press comes from January, 1913 (J. M. Means, "Rabbit's Foot Company," January 14, 1913, 6), with the announcement that she was touring with the Rabbit's Foot company in Florida, with her husband, cornet player Arthur (or Adler) Cox and soon went to the Douglas Theater in Macon, Georgia. At the time, she was considered a "soubrette" and sang popular material such as "Meet Me Tonight in Dreamland" (1910), as well as participating in a comic skit in the Russell and Owens show a few months later. The first mention of her singing a song that might be considered part of the blues tradition came in November 1914, when she was complimented for singing "Come Right In," which she later recorded and then in May 1915 where she was reported to be singing "Titanic Blues" (*The Freeman*, November 17, 1914). By 1922 she was being billed as a blues singer on the TOBA circuit (*Baltimore African-American*, April 17, 1922).

Cox's abilities as a singer and comedian were highly regarded by this time, and she was to show ability as a show producer as well, managing her own tours and later the companies she brought with her. With the success of Bessie Smith's Columbia recordings in the first half of 1923, Paramount began casting about for southern blues singers to bolster its catalog, usurping the cabaret artists of the previous three years. Mayo Williams must have heard her sing many times when she passed through Chicago, and in June 1923, signed Ida Cox to be the first blues singer to record in their Chicago studios (Alberta Hunter, Monette Moore, and Lucille Hegamin had been recording for Paramount in New York for several years by that point). Almost immediately advertised as "The Uncrowned Queen of the Blues," Cox was an instant success, especially in the South and Midwest.

Part of Cox's appeal on stage was her incisive yet unadorned delivery, qualities that come across on her recordings and are reflected by her repertoire. How much agency she had in her choice of songs to record is open to conjecture, but it is reasonable to conclude that singers recording for smaller companies had more control than did those involved with larger ones, accounting for the vastly different repertoires of Ida Cox and Ma Rainey, for example, when Columbia stars like Bessie and Clara Smith recorded far more cover material and pop songs from various eras.

This relatively conservative approach to repertoire is likewise reflected in the accompaniments provided by Paramount. While Columbia used a wide range of instrumental forces behind the Smiths from solo pianists to full jazz bands, country fiddlers, and single horns, Paramount was far more consistent with Cox and to a lesser degree Rainey in backing them up with either small combinations or solo pianists, initially organized around the person of pianist Lovie Austin (1887–1972).

Born Cora Taylor in Chattanooga, where she was a friend and neighbor of Bessie Smith, Austin was a great anomaly during her time, being a skilled pianist and arranger who directed the music at the Monogram Theater from 1913 until the late 1930s, acquainting her with virtually all the Black vaudevillians who passed through Chicago in the 1920s (Austin interview, Hogan Jazz Archive, 1969). As a technically trained musician (her father was a noted music teacher), Austin was invaluable to Paramount, which used her extensively as both accompanist and music director of jazz bands and particularly in connection with the wave of blues singers who began recording in 1923. Most of these singers were not musically literate, and it fell to Austin to transcribe the music and lyrics of their original songs for copyright. She also did transcription work for less literate musicians such as Jelly Roll Morton.

She supplied much material on her own and, unlike Mayo Williams, was generally credited with genuine composition. As a woman in what was an overwhelmingly a man's industry in control of musical decisions, Austin had an instant connection with singers such as Cox, Rainey, and even Alberta Hunter, who valued her honesty and talent. For her part, Austin recalled Cox as her favorite and the singer she worked with the most on recordings and occasional live performances, receiving co-composer credit on two of her first records and full credit on a half dozen more.

Austin was usually credited as an accompanist on record labels with her "Blues Serenaders," which was a stable personnel, including New Orleans cornetist Tommy Ladnier (1900–1939), clarinetist Jimmy O'Bryant (1896–1928), and occasionally other musicians (all of whom had regular jobs in other orchestras). Most of Cox's first series of recordings were done with these musicians in some combination with Austin serving as music director and supplying the functional arrangements. After Ladnier left to go to Europe with the Sam Wooding Orchestra, he was replaced by Dave Nelson, Theodore "Wingy" Carpenter, and a few others, and after O'Bryant's early death, Johnny Dodds filled on at least one session.

On Ida Cox's first session in June 1923, Austin was the only accompanist and she collaborated with the singer on "'Bama Bound Blues" (Paramount 12045, June 1923), which emphasizes the traditional blues theme of loss, both physical and emotional.

1. Mister engineer, please, turn your train around [2x]
   I believe to my soul my man is 'Bama bound

2. Take me back daddy, try me one more time [2x]
   And if I don't please you, break my neck for tryin'

3. But the train passed by with my daddy on the inside [2x]
   I could do nothin' but hang my head and I cried

4. My mama told me, my papa told me too [2x]
   Some brown-skin man is going to be the death of you

5. I'm 'Bama bound, ain't got no railroad fare [2x]
   If the blues don't leave me, I'll walk the railroad there

While fairly ordinary in terms of lyrics, "'Bama Bound Blues" presented a singer seemingly at home with the microphone and not demonstrating the discomfort that Bessie Smith, for example, had on her initial records.

More characteristic of Cox's later work was "Graveyard Dream Blues," recorded on the following session (Paramount 12044, June 1923):

1. Blues on my mind, blues all around my head [2x]
   I had a dream last night the man I love was dead

[clarinet solo]

2. I went to the graveyard, fell down on my knees [2x]
   I asked the gravedigger to give me back my good man, please

[cornet solo]

3. The grave digger looked me in my eye [2x]
   Said sorry for you lady, your man's said his last goodbye

Exploring the darker elements of love and death became a key component of Cox's discography, with titles like "Death Letter Blues," "Marble Slab Blues," and so on celebrating the morbid elements of the human experience. "Graveyard Dream Blues" was popular enough that Cox rerecorded it (a highly unusual occurrence for the same company), although with only Austin on piano (Paramount 12022, October 1923). The slightly brighter tempo and only one soloist allowed her to include the final verse, which changes the import of the song.

I was so worried I wanted to scream [2x]
But when I woke up, it was only a dream

A much more compositionally integrated piece from her early recordings (and one that had a compelling enough melodic structure to be covered by several Black Chicago bands in the 1920s, and revived by clarinetist Sidney Bechet in 1945) was "Weary Way Blues," composed by Cox and Austin (Paramount 12044, June 1923 on the flip side of "Graveyard Dream Blues").

[verse] Did you ever, did you ever, / feel just like you lost the best friend that you ever had?
And you wake up in the morning, head bowed down and sad
When you think about your daddy, it makes you feel so bad
[verse] Just like a mourner, just like a mourner, in the amen corner you will mourn
Hurry down sunshine, and let tomorrow come
When I think about my daddy, my heart beats like a drum
[chorus] Now I'm not rough, I don't fight, / the man that gets me got to treat me right
Lawd, I'm crazy 'bout my loving, / got to have my fun
And if you want me to love you, / do something that you've never done
[instrumental chorus—cornet solo]
[chorus] I can Eagle Rock, I can Ball the Jack, / I know just what it takes to get my daddy back
Now he's crazy but his lovin', / got to have his fun
And if you want me to love you, / do something that you've never done

Consisting of two distinct strains, "Weary Way Blues" is in the ABC lyric pattern not used often by Cox and includes several poetic blues lines that can be found in numerous later blues compositions and performances by other artists. Whether lines like "hurry down sunshine" or "I'm not rough" were originated by Cox is in some ways beside the point; her development of a coherent theme, coupled with the vivid lyrics and the tension created with the breaks in the initial two bars of what I am calling the chorus makes "Weary Way Blues" an excellent example of a blues composition, rather than just a collection of loosely related or completely unrelated stanzas.

From a melodic point of view, Cox's "Treetop Tall Papa" also stands out from the ordinary blues melody of the period (Paramount 12690, July 1928).

Clearly, Cox was ahead of her contemporaries in terms of the musical content of her compositions during the 1920s. While not musically trained as far as can be determined, she seems to have possessed an innate quality of both melodic organization and harmonic awareness that was doubtless aided by her two primary accompanists: Lovie Austin and Jesse Crump.

Tree Top Tall Papa

At some point in the 1920s, Cox began using Jesse Crump as her accompanist on tour (Austin was tied to her job at the Monogram and was not able to leave Chicago for extended periods), and they were married by 1927. Beginning with her July 1927 session for Paramount, Crump was the pianist, arranger and often composer for all of Cox's records for the next year. With the end of her recording career seemingly at hand and the generally diminished popularity of the Classic Blues as a genre, Cox and Crump developed a traditional southern tent show called *Raisin' Cain*, which toured under several names through the late 1930s and kept her name before the public. Trumpeter Clark Terry toured with this show in 1939, and left a vivid account of a late tent show, including dancers, singers, a swing band, and Ida herself, whose voice "could have knocked a fly off the back wall" (Terry, 2011, 35). This led to an encounter with jazz entrepreneur John Hammond, who engaged Cox to represent the Classic Blues in his 1939 *From Spirituals to Swing* concert celebrating the African American contribution to American popular music. This association in turn led to three recording sessions in 1939 and 1940, featuring Swing musicians such as Red Allen, Hot Lips Page, Edmond Hall, and J. C. Higginbotham, as well as prior associates James P. Johnson and Fletcher Henderson, giving us a much better recorded picture of how Cox sounded onstage in the previous decade.

Crump and Cox were apparently still married in 1947, when they were filmed doing two songs ("Fore Day Creep," and "Kentucky Man

Blues") for inclusion in the short film *Woman's a Fool* (1947, Astor Pictures Productions), which was a revue of several unconnected performances. Nevertheless, we can imagine a somewhat younger and more flashily attired Ida Cox performing on stage in the 1920s in just the same setting: standing beside a piano and delivering the lyrics in a clearly enunciated, vivid, yet nonhistrionic manner. With the Bessie Smith film, a few 1940s film appearances by Mamie Smith, and the very brief 1929 sequence that survives of Mamie Smith, this is the total of the filmed performances of Classic Blues singers in something like their natural stage presentation.

At some point shortly after she filmed those two performances, Cox had a stroke, which caused her to retire and to return to Knoxville to live with her daughter (her marriage to Crump must have ended about the same time). In 1961 she was interviewed and recorded singing some of her old songs at home and was brought to New York to record an album with jazz musicians such as Roy Eldridge, Coleman Hawkins, and Claude Hopkins, which showed her to have a remarkably well-preserved voice (at the age of at least seventy), in some ways sounding better than she had in 1939. After she returned home, she suffered several more years of poor health, passing away in 1967.

Sara Martin

In the 1920s, the recording industry made stars out of a number of entertainers who had labored on the margins of the Black entertainment universe, in some cases for decades, including Sara Martin. She was born in Louisville, Kentucky, in 1884, to Katie and William Dunn. By 1900 she was already married to Christopher Wooden, and they were living with her mother, Katie, who had been widowed and remarried to David Finchley. The Woodens apparently moved to French Lick, Indiana, shortly after, where Christopher either died or disappeared around 1901. This appears to be when Sara began to perform professionally, with her first press mentions dating from this period. Another marriage was to William O. Martin in Louisville in 1909, followed by a brief marriage to Abe B. Burton in 1919 (she was listed as a widow on that marriage certificate). Martin's professional activity seems to have been centered around the Louisville/French Lick area, until she moved to New York City in the early 1920s, establishing herself by 1922 with the *Oh, Joy!* show.

Her final marriage was to Hayes Buford Withers in 1925, apparently on tour while in Detroit. In the 1930 census, he was listed as an "advance

Figure 4.5. Sara Martin, ca. 1925. Courtesy David A. Jasen Collection. Public domain.

agent" in the theatrical profession, with both he and Sara residing back in Louisville. He also sang along with Martin and Sylvester Weaver on a recording session devoted to gospel music in 1927. A mention of Sara touring with her husband, "William Myers" and their son is located in the 1920s, but this might refer to her husband Martin in the 1910s (although no mention of a son was made again).

From the beginning of her recording career, Martin was closely associated with Clarence Williams. No one in the industry was more focused on the main chance than Williams, who parlayed one of the most prolific recording careers of any musician in the 1920s into an extraordinary business success. Martin, for her part, seems to have been part of the Williams publishing machine—in effect, a song demonstrator. At first she seems to have been given the more overtly blues numbers, while Williams's wife Eva Taylor did more of the pop songs (although these lines crossed back and forth). Most of the recordings for the first and last parts of her discographic career were of songs published and occasionally composed by Clarence Williams. Presumably, her reputation for professionalism and dependability were attractive to Williams, although her recordings with him are very uneven in quality. Perhaps because of her unfamiliarity with some of the material, she sounds uncomfortable and frequently out of tune.

Martin comes off far better when backed by larger groups. It might have been that the added parts and more flexible pitch control of wind instruments centered her sound more and inspired her to more impassioned singing. "Blind Man Blues" and "Atlanta Blues" (OKeh 8090, August 1, 1923) were done with Clarence Williams's Blue Five, a classic early jazz group featuring Sidney Bechet on soprano sax, with cornetist Thomas Morris and trombonist John Mayfield, along with Williams and Buddy Christian on banjo. Martin responds to the driving beat the band provides, giving a type of impassioned performance not evident over the course of her first year of recording. Later band recordings such as "Some of These Mornings" (OKeh 8292, November 24, 1925) with Harry's Happy Four (an unusual ensemble with two trumpets, a piano, and a banjo) give what might be a clearer picture of how she sounded on stage, with a rhythmic flexibility and assurance, as well as a shouting delivery that must have been quite exciting in person.

One remarkable example of a singer recording with her touring band came April 1923, with Martin backed by W. C. Handy's Orchestra, which had accompanied her on tour during that period. The well-rehearsed and

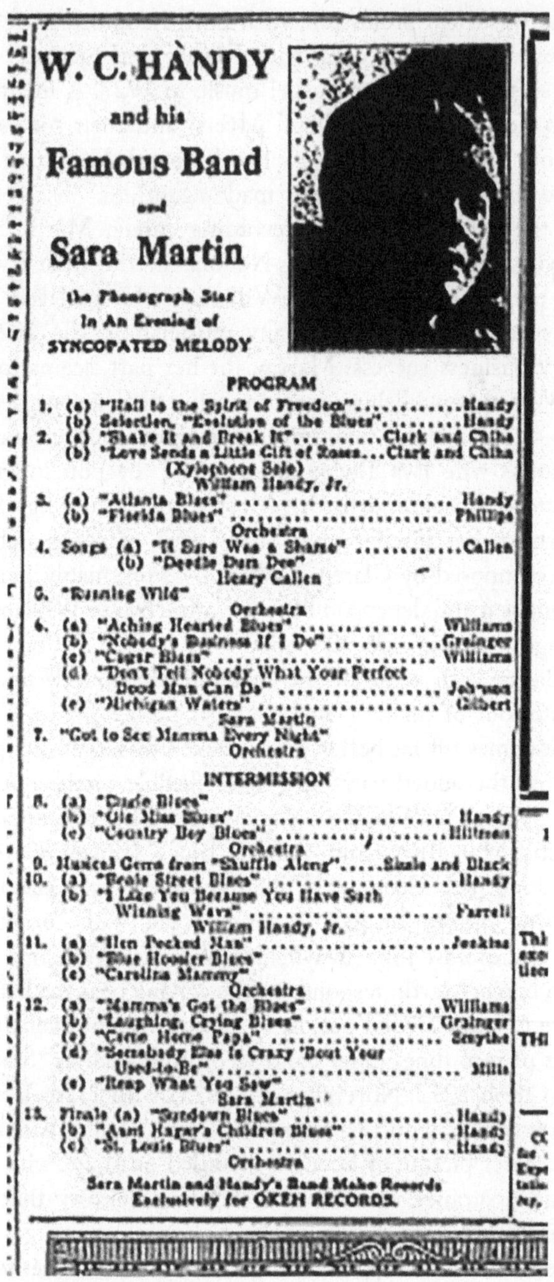

W. C. HANDY

and his

Famous Band

and

Sara Martin

the Phonograph Star

In An Evening of

SYNCOPATED MELODY

PROGRAM

1. (a) "Hail to the Spirit of Freedom" .... Handy
   (b) Selection, "Evolution of the Blues" .... Handy
2. (a) "Shake It and Break It" .... Clark and Chiha
   (b) "Love Sends a Little Gift of Roses ... Clark and Chiha
   (Xylophone Solo)
   William Handy, Jr.
3. (a) "Atlanta Blues" .... Handy
   (b) "Florida Blues" .... Phillips
   Orchestra
4. Songs (a) "It Sure Was a Shame" .... Callen
   (b) "Doodle Dum Dee"
   Henry Callen
5. "Running Wild"
   Orchestra
6. (a) "Aching Hearted Blues" .... Williams
   (b) "Nobody's Business If I Do" .... Grainger
   (c) "Sugar Blues" .... Williams
   (d) "Don't Tell Nobody What Your Perfect Good Man Can Do" .... Johnson
   (e) "Michigan Waters" .... Gilbert
   Sara Martin
7. "Got to See Mamma Every Night"
   Orchestra

INTERMISSION

8. (a) "Dixie Blues"
   (b) "Ole Miss Blues" .... Handy
   (c) "Country Boy Blues" .... Hillman
   Orchestra
9. Musical Gems from "Shuffle Along" ..... Sissle and Blake
10. (a) "Beale Street Blues" .... Handy
    (b) "I Like You Because You Have Such Winning Ways" .... Farrell
    William Handy, Jr.
11. (a) "Hen Pecked Man" .... Jenkins
    (b) "Blue Hoosier Blues"
    (c) "Carolina Mammy"
    Orchestra
12. (a) "Mamma's Got the Blues" .... Williams
    (b) "Laughing, Crying Blues" .... Grainger
    (c) "Come Home Papa" .... Smythe
    (d) "Somebody Else is Crazy 'Bout Your Used-to-Be" .... Mills
    (e) "Reap What You Sow"
    Sara Martin
13. Finale (a) "Sundown Blues" .... Handy
    (b) "Aunt Hagar's Children Blues" .... Handy
    (c) "St. Louis Blues" .... Handy
    Orchestra

Sara Martin and Handy's Band Make Records Exclusively for OKEH RECORDS.

Figure 4.6. Program from the Fall, 1923 tour of Sara Martin and W. C. Handy, presenting blues and Black music in a formal setting, perhaps for the first time in the 1920s. Public domain.

organized group recorded three tunes, the most successful of which was apparently "Laughin' Cryin' Blues" (OKeh 8064, April 21, 1923), which became a signature piece for her, mentioned in press releases for several years. Here, Martin's histrionic abilities are on display, giving another good picture of how she probably sounded on stage. Occasionally billed as "the Colored Sophie Tucker," Martin was known for putting over a song in a shouting, direct fashion not heard too often on her recordings. One late example that amply demonstrates this approach is "Don't Turn Your Back on Me," with Clarence Williams and His Orchestra (QRS R7035, November 1928).

> Look here papa, don't turn your back on me,
> 'cause it ain't never been your shoulder blades that mama wants to see
> Say, when a lady's speaking honey, don't you know your place
> How can I get results if I don't see your face?
> Get out there in that stable with them other mules
> 'cause it's too darn hot for anyone to be so cool
> Come on and treat your mama with some decency, and don't you turn your back on me

Initially, Martin's repertoire was focused on the current Williams publications but as OKeh began publicizing her aggressively in the Black press her releases became more varied in style and content. Beginning in October 1923, Martin began doing sessions with guitarist Sylvester Weaver, who also began recording solo sessions generally considered to be the first recordings of country blues guitar. These recordings (and a later date with Weaver in August 1927), plus the three sessions she did with "Her Jug Band" in the fall of 1924, represent an interesting change in direction for her; her singing comes off considerably better, perhaps owing to the more intimate sound of the guitar, which can more easily match her vocal quality. The first release with Weaver, "Longing for Daddy Blues" and I've Got to Go and Leave My Daddy Behind" (OKeh 8117 and 8104, October 24, 1923) are, in retrospect, more in line with the Downhome Blues style that would become popular within a year or two. This series was successful enough commercially to inspire Columbia to have its two singing stars Bessie Smith and Clara Smith record with similarly countrified accompaniment in the spring of 1924 (Bessie Smith) and early 1925 (Clara Smith). It is tempting to attribute the greater degree of artistic success on these Martin recordings to the more traditional aspect of the material, most of which are variations on standard twelve-bar blues.

Most of Martin's final recording sessions for OKeh in 1927, and a final two for QRS in 1928 featured her with a larger band led by Clarence Williams singing songs from his current catalog. A single film appearance came in the short *Hello, Bill*, starring Bill "Bojangles" Robinson (Famous Artists, 1929), which may have been filmed before she had a serious illness in the summer of 1928, requiring a temporary retirement of several months. After this, she retired permanently to Louisville with Withers, occasionally emerging to sing gospel music. After leaving the business entirely in the mid-1930s, apparently she took over management of a local nursing home and continued in that business until her death in 1955.

Josie Miles

Josie Miles's recordings run the gamut of African American popular music of the 1920s, from blues to gospel, comedy duets, and possibly religious sermons. Born around 1900, in Summerville, South Carolina, she was in New York by 1921, and performed with the Sissle and Blake show *Shuffle Along*, with which she was identified for the rest of her career. After her first recordings for Black Swan apparently were met with public approval, she went on a national tour heading a troop called the Black Swan Troubadours with a band called the Black Swan Jazz Masters, led by pianist Arthur Ray ("New Group," 1923). She appeared in several other shows in the New York area, and was obviously a seasoned stage professional, even if concrete information about her career is pretty severely lacking. That professionalism is the hallmark of her recordings, which show off a great variety of approaches and styles.

Miles's first recordings were made for Black Swan and were similar in style to the Ethel Waters sides had been making, but with one exception. Eight of the first ten sides were done with the usual arranged accompaniments, presumably done by Fletcher Henderson, who was the piano player on several or William Grant Still. The first two sides were done for Paramount with just a piano accompaniment (Henderson on one, Q. Roscoe Snowden on the other), which was quite unusual for the time, suggesting that it might have been an audition session that was deemed good enough to release. Miles indeed seems quite confident in front of the microphone, particularly on "Please Don't Tickle Me Babe"

(Black Swan 14121, August 1922)—a comedy tune by Snowden that she had perhaps already been performing.

The most remarkable of the early sides was "Love Me in Your Old Time Way" (Black Swan 14139, December 1922), a song by Willy M. Gant, who was responsible for a number of Black Swan recordings during this period. Presumably Still did the arrangement, which sounds two decades ahead of the other ones done for similar sessions. The integration of the voice into the orchestration is also remarkable, with at least four horns and rhythm creating a modern-sounding "groove" before Miles enters, soaring over the ensemble, seamlessly negotiating the ensemble, solo, and vocal breaks. The level of writing is matched by the playing, which combined to create an exceptional musical whole that was unfortunately lost once singers began routinely recording with just piano and a horn, or two doing largely improvised backgrounds. That Miles was able to deal so well with a complex arrangement is a tribute to her musicianship and, presumably, her experience doing similar work on stage.

Following her Black Swan recordings, Miles's tour with the Black Swan Troubadours took her away from New York at least until the summer, by which time the company was facing serious financial difficulty. In September 1923, she was signed to a contract for Gennett records, making her the "first race girl" to be signed to the company, putting them in competition with Paramount, OKeh, Ajax, and Columbia in the race records business ("South Carolina Girl Gets Big Recording Contract," 1923). Over the next five months, Gennett released twelve sides by Miles, most accompanied by Fletcher Henderson and a cornet player—later to be a regular in his band—Joe Smith. Most of these tunes were much more blues based, if not actual blues, than the earlier Black Swan records. On her cover of Ida Cox's "Graveyard Dream Blues" (Gennett 5292, October 26, 1923; one of the most frequently recorded tunes of the era), Miles is most convincing, even using the Bessie Smith third seeker device many other singers were beginning to copy.

For the rest of her recording career, Miles did most of her work for the Ajax company, except for a few sides for Edison and Banner (which seem to have had a connection with Ajax). Miles's accompanying groups during this period were by groups called the Choo Choo Jazzers or the Kansas City Five, which were made up of a small circle of musicians including trumpeters Bubber Miley, Louis Metcalf, clarinetist Bob Fuller, banjoist Elmer Snowden, and pianists Arthur Ray, Cliff Jackson, or Louis Hooper. This group had a way of creating spontaneous musical backgrounds that nevertheless sounded very organized, as demonstrated on "Mad Mama's Blues," recorded for Edison and taking advantage of the longer playing time of the Edison records (Edison 51477, November 21, 1924). The lyrics (by Duke Jones, aka Spencer Williams) are a triumph of violent expression

> Give me gunpowder, give me dynamite [2x]
> Yes, I'd wreck the city, blow it up tonight

Miles gives a forceful reading, omitting the sarcasm and wink-and-nod aspect some singers might have utilized. The instrumental parts are a combination of improvisation (including two double-time choruses introducing solo trumpet and clarinet breaks.

A significant number of the Ajax records are given over to Miles doing comedy duos with Billy Higgins, by 1924 one of the top stars in Black entertainment. Having been featured in shows since the early 1910s, Higgins headlined shows and made numerous recordings (sometimes credited as "Jazz Caspar") with Monette Moore and Kitty Brown, as well as under his own name, mostly for Ajax ("Dead—Billy Higgins, Noted Comedian," 1937). "Satisfied," for example, preserves some of the back-and-forth dialogue in addition to the song, by a composer named Briers.

> [Miles] If I could dress like quality, then I'd be satisfied
> Have all the women envy me, then I'd be satisfied
> If I could have a big sedan, lots of diamonds on my hand
> To hear them say now, "ain't she grand," then I'd be satisfied
> If I could lead the upper set, then I'd be satisfied
> If I could be the social pet, then I'd be satisfied
> If I could always wear silk hose if I could wear silk underclothes
> If I could smell just like a rose, then I'd be satisfied
> [Higgins] Well, baby, you does smell like a rose
> [Miles] Does I? What Kind of a rose does I smells like?
> [Higgins]—American Black Beauty! (*laughter*)
> If I could be what I'm not
> [Miles] Listen, man, I'll tell you what
> [Both] If we could have what we ain't got, then we'd be satisfied!

It is unknown if Miles and Higgins performed on stage together, but their rapport on the six sides they recorded for Ajax suggest they may have. Miles also recorded "There'll Be Some Changes Made," one of the relatively few songs to become a latter-day jazz standard done by 1920s blues singers (co-composed by Higgins with Benton Overstreet in 1921).

Two unusual records done for Ajax featured Miles singing gospel songs, accompanied by only Elmer Snowden on banjo, which may have been a foreshadowing of the 1928 records made for Gennett by Missionary Josephine Miles, fire and brimstone sermons that may or may not be by Josie Miles. By 1930, she had settled in Kansas City and concentrated on church work. Sources are unclear when she died, but it was apparently the result of an auto accident between twenty-five to thirty years later (Tracy, 1996).

Hazel Meyers

Hazel Meyers is another of the many singers about whom we know very little, who made a significant number of recordings during the period. Information as to her birth and death are completely lacking, with only the time beginning with her first recording and extending slightly more than a year after her last being accounted for.

As far as her professional activities outside the recording studio are known, she toured as the primary star with the Thomas and Russell show *Steppin' High* beginning in the fall of 1924 in Los Angeles and San Francisco, making her one of the few recorded singers to tour the West Coast ("Jazz as Is Jazz," *Los Angeles Times*, August 17, 1924, B28). One wonders what to make of the fact that, except for a single session producing two sides, her recording career was over at that point. She apparently continued with this show on an East Coast tour lasting into 1926, after which she was active in Chicago, at least until 1928 (Rye, 1996). After this, the trail goes cold.

About half of Meyers's thirty released recordings between September 1923 and August, 1924 were recorded for the Ajax label and probably published by the recording director, Joe Davis. Davis (a White producer and publisher) was connected to numerous songwriters and musicians in this "one hand washes the other" period of music publication. It is probable that he had an arrangement with Perry Bradford, whose tunes "Hateful Blues" and "Frankie Blues" had been recorded by Bessie Smith for Columbia in April 1924, and covered by Meyers for Ajax three months later (Ajax, 17048, July 1924). Meyer's blues singing here is somewhat contrived and more songlike than Smith's versions. She is more successful on her cover of Ida Cox's "Graveyard Dream Blues" (Vocalion 14688, October 1, 1923; Bessie Smith was first to record this and Cox's and Meyer's version were recorded almost simultaneously). While rhythmically stilted, her interpretation of Cox's dark tune is suitably heavy and serious from the point of view of delivery.

While not especially convincing as a blues singer, Meyers had a pleasant (if unremarkable) voice and was clearly at home with the more dramatic titles she was given, such as "You'll Never Have No Luck by Quittin' Me" which is aria-like in its composition and delivery. Here, Meyers sounds more like Sophie Tucker and presumably this is the sort of thing that went over especially well on stage. Meyers was also quite fortunate in her accompanists, having some of the Ajax house band (Bubber Miley, Louis Hooper, and Bob Fuller) on many of her sessions, and Fats Waller as an accompanist on others.

Margaret Johnson

Another well-recorded but ill-documented singer from the period is Margaret Johnson. Not mentioned by Abbott and Seroff in any of their research, Johnson apparently toured with several reasonably well-known companies in the 1920s, including a tour in Puerto Rico with Gonzelle White (Rowe, 1996). Johnson's birth and death dates are unknown, but she is well represented on disc, with about thirty issued sides ranging from country blues to fairly sophisticated jazz performances accompanied by several different Clarence Williams groups, including Louis Armstrong, Sidney Bechet, and Bubber Miley.

Johnson had a remarkably deep and resonant voice and seemed to have no trouble at all dealing with sometimes noisy band accompaniments (suggesting extensive experience on large stages or tents) such as on the unusually highly arranged "Nobody Knows the Way I Feel This Mornin'" (OKeh 8162, September 5, 1924). She also could restrain herself when singing with just a piano, as on "Nobody's Blues but My Own" with Clarence Williams, who has to adjust his introductory tempo to match her entry (OKeh 8220, June 9, 1925). Johnson also was one of the first singers to record a double entendre song of the sort that became overwhelmingly evident in the later part of the decade; her catalog of inquisition on "Who'll Chop Your Suey When I'm Gone?" (credited to

Bechet and Rousseau Simmons; OKeh 8193, January 7, 1925) includes the lines "Who'll clam your chowder Friday night / who'll toot your fruity nice and tight?" and provides a good prototype for many later songs.

Virginia Liston

Virginia Liston was born Virginia Crawford, apparently in the Gulf Coast region, in the early 1890s, although census information is inconclusive. Her family may have lived in New Orleans by 1900, from which city she began a career in entertainment on the Black vaudeville circuit. She was reported as touring with the George Lewis stock company in the fall of 1909 and the Kenner and Lewis stock company (which may have included Jelly Roll Morton) two years later (Abbott & Seroff, 2017, 45, 55). After divorcing her first husband, David Liston, she apparently stayed in New Orleans before moving to the East Coast, making a base in Washington, DC. Liston was appearing at the Minihaha Theater in Washington, and for the next three years was reported in places along the Eastern seaboard, traveling as far afield as Kansas City and Indiana (Abbott & Seroff, 2007, 134). Members of Tolliver's *Smart Set* company who were wintering in New Orleans during the first months of 1916 recalled meeting Liston.

In 1913 she was touring as half of "Jones and Liston," with her partner Hambone Jones singing and doing comedy. This association apparently lasted until the end of 1914, after which she toured as a single until 1919, when she rejoined Jones as part of his touring company. Following his death in late 1919, Liston took over management duty (Abbott & Seroff, 2017, 192). It was as part of this company that she teamed with and married pianist and comedian Sam Gray, partnering with him (for some reason sometimes billed as "Liston and Liston") until their divorce in the mid-1920s. It was during this period that she relocated to New York and began recording at the behest of producer and pianist Clarence Williams, whom she may have known from their early days in New Orleans.

During her long career in Black vaudeville prior to her recording career, Liston was regarded as a popular singer of the "coon shouter" and blues variety. In an unsigned review of her performance with Jones in 1914, she was cited as a "blues girl," although she

> sings popular songs and in good style. She is tall and of good stage appearance, having that winning combination of sad and sweet when she gets down into her work, giving that fervor that seems to go with the kind of singing called the blues. There come times when one feels to reply to her as if soul were answering soul, and especially the soul of black folks as Prof. Du Bois speaks so glorious of. She reminds us of the old days, the days we read about, when singers told the history of their nations on public stages to the tune of the harp. It is just so when Miss Liston sings "The Titanic Blues"—she recites in song what she conceives to be the last scenes and words of the ill-fated set. ("At the New Crown Garden in Indianapolis," *The Freeman*, 1914)

This remarkably detailed review locates her firmly in the blues and folk sphere, although it takes pains to credit her with a wide repertoire. Her rendition of "Titanic Blues" was still topical, the sinking of the ship having occurred only two and half years earlier. She recorded the song on the last record date under her own name in May 1926 (Vocalion 1031, May 29, 1926). Liston's first recording date was done for OKeh (as were all her subsequent ones, save for the last) on September 18, 1923, on which she was accompanied by Clarence Williams. The first six tunes released were all compositions by her and Sam Gray and were presumably ones they used in their act.

On "You Thought I Was Blind, but Now I See" (OKeh 8092, September 18, 1923) the verse introduces some perceived autobiography to set up the tune.

> [verse] Virginia Liston, a Creole queen, met a Baltimore Boy who was long and lean
> Sam liked to strut both night and day, it seems like his wife couldn't see it that way
> Sam came home one night at twelve, right at him Virginia yelled . . .
> [chorus] You thought I was blind, but now I see
> You needn't think you can stay all night trying' to two time me
> Now daddy, late or early, you're bound to fall
> But I'm so glad that one man ain't got it all
> You thought I was blind, but now I see

Gray makes an appearance on a session duetting with his wife on two songs. "Just Take One Last Lingering Look" (OKeh 8126, January 2, 1924) presents a take on the standard battle of the sexes theme in a well-rehearsed and compelling performance.

> [Virginia] Just take one long last lingering look, 'cause you don't linger longer here no more
> [Sam] Baby, can't you read my mind? [Virginia] yes, just like a book
> [Sam] Now, Virginia . . . [Virginia] Sam, there's the door!
> [Sam] You know my heart burns with a fire so true
> [Virginia] Yes, but here's one old long tall gal who will extinguish you
> [Sam] Baby don't say you're gonna shake me [Virginia] No, you're already shook
> [Both] So take a long last lingering look

After the initial sessions with Sam Gray and Clarence Williams, OKeh obviously wanted to try her as more of a pop/jazz singer, backing her with jazz groups, which at various times include Sidney Bechet, Louis Armstrong, and several unknown horn players. At times she didn't seem comfortable or overly familiar with the material; on "You've Got the Right Key, but the Wrong Keyhole" her delivery is very stilted and not at all rhythmically secure. Covers of tunes recorded by other singers, such as "Jail House Blues," and "Weeping Willow Blues" (both done by Bessie Smith) are not especially convincing and obviously pale in comparison with the originals.

In general, Liston's voice was not great by the time her recording career began. A scratchy sound combined with poor pitch and a very limited range suggests that she was past her peak by the mid-1920s, and she didn't seem to be able to handle new material well. Nevertheless, some of her finest moments came in her last session where she recreated her success from the previous decade, "Titanic Blues" as well as her own tune "Rolls Royce Papa" (Vocalion 1032 and 1031, May 29, 1926), which mined the double entendre lyrics in vogue at the time.

> Your carburetor's rusty, this I really mean
> Your gas tank's empty, won't hold gasoline
> Your windshield it is broken, it ain't worth a cent

Your steering wheel is wobbly, your piston rod is bent
Your fender's all broken, your wheels ain't tight
And I know doggone well your spark plugs ain't hittin' right

On this Chicago session (her others were all done in New York), Liston sounds much more at ease with the material, suggesting that she had been performing it regularly. She apparently retired from show business in 1929, and moved to St. Louis after remarrying and becoming involved in a church, dying in 1932.

Edmonia Henderson

One singer who was in the wrong place at the wrong time was Edmonia Henderson. A seasoned stage performer who had been recognized in the Black vaudeville circuit since the mid-1910s, Henderson had toured extensively with Ma and Pa Rainey for a few years and then was featured headlining bills herself. She was in Chicago in the mid-1920s and was engaged to record for Paramount records, producing about a dozen sides with backing by Lovie Austin's Blues Serenaders and Bernie Young's band, which were primarily blues but very much in the vaudeville tradition. Her bad luck was that when Mayo Williams became the main talent scout for the company, shortly after she was signed on, he began focusing on more Downhome singers with less professional background with the theory that they would be easier to deal with, cheaper, and probably bring more of their own material to record. Henderson recorded a few more sides in 1926 for Vocalion, with her final two of songs by Jelly Roll Morton with an accompaniment by the composer himself. Her later life is also obscure, with some sources saying she returned to her hometown of Louisville, Kentucky in the late 1920s, and became involved with gospel music.

Helen Gross

Helen Gross made a series of twenty-one issued records for the Ajax company in 1924 and 1925. Accompanied by the house band, called variously the Choo Choo Jazzers or the Kansas City Five, she sang almost exclusively twelve-bar blues songs published by Joe Davis, who was the recording director for Ajax. One startling exception to that rule was a version of Irving Berlin's brand new "What'll I Do?," from August 1924, featuring cornetist Bubber Miley, then about to begin a profitable association with Duke Ellington. Virtually unique in the discography of African American women singers in the 1920s, "What'll I Do?" (Ajax 17049, August 1924) is performed as a straight waltz, as it was in Berlin's *Music Box Revue.* Also of interest is "Ghost Walkin' Blues" (Ajax 17051, July 1924), referring to the theatrical expression "The Ghost Walks," meaning the time when actors are paid (taken from Shakespeare's *Hamlet*). Gross was apparently not an especially active (or at any rate successful) stage performer, as almost no mention can be found of her in the trade press of the period. Her recordings are remembered primarily for their accompanying groups, which at various times included Miley, clarinetist Bob Fuller, pianist Louis Hooper, banjoist Elmer Snowden, and cornetist Rex Stewart (in his first recordings).

Laura Smith

One of the most mysterious (and, ultimately, tragic) figures of the 1920s blues scene is Laura Smith. Documentation exists of her varied and extensive theatrical appearances beginning in 1909, but very little information exists of her early years. Her birth name may have been Laura or Loretta Bryant (based on a marriage certificate from 1916), and she possibly came from either Indiana or Illinois. It is possible that she was born in 1882, making her and Essie Whitman the oldest African American singers to record, although the marriage certificate to Olanda Sharpe puts her birth date at 1888.

The first mention of Laura Smith (whether this was a birth, stage, or married name is unclear) is as part of a show at the Peekin Theater in Memphis, doing a blackface comedy act (Abbott & Seroff, 2017, 53). She was accomplished enough to have been hired by Ma and Pa Rainey to replace the departed Bessie Smith in 1910 (Abbott & Seroff, 2017, 164), and thereafter toured various vaudeville theaters throughout the South and Gulf Coast, where she was renowned as both a "coon shouter" and a comedienne. For a period in 1912, she was with Alexander Tolliver's Smart Set company in Chicago.

Smith apparently made comic hay out of her appearance, in which she was similar to Ma Rainey. In an extensive review, she was described as "a favorite of the Crown Garden patrons. She's a little dump of a thing, almost as broad as she is long, but she's there with the fun" ("Smith and Redmond," 1913), and identified as a dancing comedienne who sang blues such as "Baby Seals Blues" and "Memphis Blues" during this period. By 1914 she was being called the "queen of grotesque and eccentric comediennes" in an appearance at the Monogram Theater in Chicago (Bragg, 1914). According to Abbott and Seroff, Smith and her contemporary Virginia Liston were as popular on stage as Ma Rainey and Bessie Smith were during the late 1910s (Abbott & Seroff, 2017, 178).

Following her marriage in 1916 (if indeed it is she), Smith apparently based herself in her husband's hometown of Detroit, where she performed locally with very little national press coverage. One rare mention came in March 1918, when she was reported to be drawing much praise for singing the popular "A Good Man Is Hard to Find" at the Vaudette Theatre in Detroit ("Laura Smith Back," *Chicago Defender*, March 23, 1918, 7). It is possible she went into a temporary retirement, but she begins to resurface in the press in the early 1920s, appearing in a stage show in Baltimore in January 1920 (Rye, 1996). By the fall of 1922, she was headlining her own company, called the Ginger Pep Workers, in a series of Southern tours, featuring the dancer Slim Jones, whom she married during this period. Presumably this show brought her to or near New York in the summer of 1924, when she was signed by OKeh to make a series of recordings.

A flurry of recording that fall and some personal appearances (as well as twenty years on the road) may have contributed to a physical breakdown that laid her up for the first half of 1925, during which time she lived with her sister in Chicago. Following her recovery, she stated her intention to retire from the stage and make religious recordings for OKeh ("Laura Smith Better" and "Laura Smith Up Again," 1925). She did in fact make two somewhat odd recordings of standard hymns that were totally out of step with the rest of her discography. Following this, she returned to the land of the secular and began touring again after the end of her recording career with various shows in Chicago, New York, Denver, and Philadelphia between 1929 and 1930, although no longer as a headliner. By 1931 she was in Los Angeles, where she hoped to begin getting film roles, but a long-standing issue with high blood pressure limited her activities and ultimately killed her in 1932.

Smith's recording career is divided in two parts. The first part was done from her first session in August 1924 through October of that year, producing eight released sides, all accompanied by Clarence Williams and his stable of musicians. Most of the tunes were either composed or published by Williams and are excellent examples of full-throated blues singing with well-organized accompaniments. Smith demonstrates the superb blues feeling and rhythmic instincts that are complimented by the full front line (Thomas Morris on cornet, Charlie Irvis on trombone, and clarinetist Ernest Elliott), particularly on her first side, "Texas Moaner Blues," co-composed by Williams and Texas blues singer Fae Barnes (aka Maggie Jones) (OKeh 8157, August 1, 1924). From two months later came several sides with just Williams, but the final session of 1924 had Williams, Buddy Christian on banjo, and Elliott again on clarinet. "Lake Ponchatrain Blues" and "Gravier Street Blues" (OKeh 8179, October 10, 1924) were Williams's compositions recalling his early days in New Orleans, and Smith does not hold back in her shouting delivery that allows Elliott room to provide responses to her phrase endings.

Following this date was a year of silence, during most of which Smith was recovering from what was called a nervous breakdown, but which might have been a preview of the heart disease that ended her life eight years later. When she returned to the studio, she recorded the two hymns with a strange accompaniment bordering both on classical and folk style. This may have been the delivery of a promise to God for her recuperation, but her next several releases that fall featured a similarly odd accompaniment by "Perry Bradford's Mean Four," which consisted of a country-style ensemble of harmonica, fiddle, guitar, and piano. "Lucy Long," Bradford's adaption of a traditional minstrel song was also recorded by the Original Jazz Hounds and twice by the composer, but this is the only version that was completely vocal, and was probably similar to the comic material Smith was singing on the stage a decade before (OKeh 8366, October 3, 1925).

The difference in Smith's voice is evident; she no longer sings with the power she demonstrated in the previous year's recordings and this vocal deterioration is progressively evident through the balance of her recordings. Her final session, done for Victor in Chicago in 1927, has her virtually whispering the lyrics (made possible by the electric process). On a tune like "Mississippi Blues" she seems to have trouble sustaining her lines, a problem made all the more evident by the accompaniment being only pianist Clarence M. Jones (Victor 20775, June 7, 1927). Her health problems were getting more serious (and perhaps not touring had made her a bit rusty), and her return to the stage may have been done out of economic necessity.

Maggie Jones

Another of the mysterious singers of the 1920s, Maggie Jones also recorded under the name Fae Barnes, which might have been her birth name. Census records mention a Fae Barnes born in Hillsboro, Texas, in 1900, and a Maggie Jones in the same place in 1894, but the evidence in either case is inconclusive.

What is known is that Jones was likely from Texas—she was occasionally billed as the "Texas Nightingale"—and she began to appear in the press in New York by the early 1920s. Whatever her background, she was a very accomplished singer who could do convincing blues as well as up-tempo dance numbers, and had a measure of success on the New York stage until she returned to Texas around 1930. After that, nothing is known.

In August 1923, Jones (as Fae Barnes) recorded two sides for Black Swan, one of the first singers from Texas to record and among the last recorded for the label. Also, her accompaniment was a solo piano—an unusual economy for Black Swan that might reflect the financial difficulties it was experiencing. Two more recordings the following month for Pathe accompanied by Fletcher Henderson seemed to situate her as a singer of Tin Pan Alley songs, but sales apparently did not encourage any more sessions.

It was not until April of 1924 that Jones returned to the studios, recording two tunes for Paramount with only guitar accompaniment, strongly suggesting her Texas roots and looking forward to the country blues of a few years later. By October she signed a contract with Columbia that occupied her for the next year and half (the rest of her career) and brought her into the studio with Charlie Green and Louis Armstrong at first, singing primarily Spencer Williams blues. "Box Car Blues" (Columbia 14047, November 13, 1924) with Charlie Green is particularly impressive—a driving performance that sounds fifteen years ahead of its time with a proto–boogie-woogie feel that enlivens even the usually sedate Henderson. Her recordings with Armstrong are generally considered to be some of his most effective accompaniments and some of his favorites as well. "Poor House Blues" (Columbia 14050, December 9, 1924) bears comparison with Bessie Smith's records with Armstrong, and almost sounds like a cover, although Smith did not record that particular tune.

One of the only tunes Jones recorded on which she had composer credit (with Henderson) was "Screamin' the Blues," with Armstrong and Henderson (Columbia 14055, December 17, 1924).

1. Talk about blues, you ought to hear mine [2x]
   The man I love keeps me worried all the time
2. One thing I hate, I can't have my way [2x]
   The man that mistreats me is being buried today

Taken at a suitably funeral tempo about one beat per second, the song features a passionate vocal that is well supported by Armstrong, who solos only in the introduction and coda while using his plunger mute to make dark comments to fill out the singer's phrases. This recording stands comparison to the best of the era despite its relative obscurity, perhaps due to the better-known singers Bessie and Clara Smith being competitors at Columbia at the time.

Clearly Columbia felt that Jones had abilities beyond that of a standard blues singer; she was tapped to share, with Bessie Smith, the first electrically recorded session the company attempted. Smith's portion came to a stunning close when the tent that housed the singer, band, microphone, and sound engineers came crashing down. Prior to that, Jones was able to record two pop songs: "Cheatin' on Me" and "Mamma, Won't You Come and Ma-Ma Me," accompanied by a large group for the day—cornet, trombone, clarinet, piano and banjo—all from Fletcher Henderson's band (Columbia 14074, May 5, 1925). Following that session, Jones was paired with musicians from the Louis Hooper/Elmer Snowden stable, recording tunes that were mostly Joe Davis publications.

Maggie Jones was one of the more interesting singers of the period. With an undeniable affinity for the more rural elements of the blues, yet a voice and musicality that was clearly adept at more sophisticated material, she represents a transitional figure between the vaudeville and Downhome blues. In that, she was similar to Ida Cox, although unlike Cox she composed very little of her own material. Nevertheless, her total discography is among the strongest of any of the singers of the period.

Other Vaudeville Singers

Many African American women were introduced to the microphone in the wake of Bessie Smith's success at Columbia and they were largely drawn from the rosters of Black vaudeville shows, mostly with a southern heritage and pedigree. The great majority of them were not successful and made only a handful of recordings or, in some cases only a single record.

Many of them are remembered solely for having as their accompanists noted jazz players who were usually at the very beginning of their careers and added to provide some more interesting background to the vocals. Julia Moody is a good example of a better than average singer who is remembered chiefly due to her accompanists, Bubber Miley in particular. While no biographical information is available, she is well represented on sixteen recordings for Black Swan, Banner, and Columbia.

One interesting sidelight to the era that presaged the some of the performers in the next chapter was an Atlanta field trip in 1923 by OKeh. This trip produced records by Lucille Bogan and Fannie Mae Goosby, among other local bands. Bogan recorded a few more times in the 1920s and then frequently (as "Bessie Jackson") in the 1930s, becoming known for her pornographic rendering of "Shave 'em Dry" (which was not supposed to have been released) and many of her own compositions, locating her as a "Downhome" singer. Goosby did several more sessions in New York, largely of her own material, which might suggest she was a "Downhome" singer, but her extensive theatrical work in the Atlanta area and her precise diction and good intonation make it clear she was primarily a Vaudeville Singer.

Husband-and-Wife Duos

One of the most venerable traditions on the African American stage was the husband and wife cross-talk act. Usually a blend of music, dancing, and casual insults, these duo acts had extremely long careers; the marriages of Billy and Mary Mack, Butterbeans and Susie, Grant and Wilson, and George Williams and Bessie Brown outlasted the vaudeville era by a considerable margin. Other singers such as Ma Rainey and Virginia Liston were also known for duo acts in marriages that did not last. These acts were brought into the recording studios, often during the 1920s and occasionally thereafter.

Billy and Mary Mack

Billy McBride was born in Mobile, Alabama, on February 26, 1884, and was touring the South in minstrel shows by 1900. Renowned as a comic and singer, by 1910 he had become a highly accomplished promoter and tour director. When an early show was stranded in New Orleans in 1908,

McBride met Mary Thacker, who was born in Algiers, Louisiana, on July 28, 1891, but grew up in New Orleans, listening to Buddy Bolden and numerous early jazz performers and eventually singing professionally. She was performing with a Creole society band led by violinist John Robichaux when McBride heard her, after which they began performing together, marrying in around 1910 (Mack interview, Hogan Jazz Archive, 1959).

Even with three children born in the first several years of their marriage, the McBrides toured extensively in tent shows, eventually gravitating to vaudeville. They were doing the standard Black theater circuit in 1911, traveling from New Orleans to Memphis and Atlanta, with numerous stops in between. Their first press mention was of a date in New Orleans in 1913, performing as McBride and McBride at Stroder's Airdome with a small troupe ("New Orleans Theaters," *The Freeman*, May 31, 1913, 5). Shortly after this they took a theater manager's advice and simplified their billing to Mack and Mack, which was how they toured before changing the name to the Merrymakers, and crediting the leadership sometimes to Billy and sometimes to Mary Mack.

By the late 1910s, they were headlining shows throughout the South and sometimes venturing north as well. In 1914, they appeared in New York for the first time, with Mary recalling being nervous about the "northern acts" and how they would compare. Billy's insistence on maintaining their act succeeded and they began to make forays further afield. By 1918 they were traveling with their own band, which was unusual for the day in Black vaudeville shows. Using some of Mary's acquaintances from New Orleans such as Johnny Dodds, Mutt Carey, and even Tony Jackson and Jelly Roll Morton, the Macks were credited with being the first variety show to carry a jazz band. An article in 1922, reviewing an appearance at the Lincoln Theater in Baltimore, mentioned Billy as the principal comic with Mary, who did most of the singing, lead a troupe of girl singers/dancers. It also detailed their "New Orleans Jazz Band," which included William Paris (possibly Wilbur DeParis, whom Mary later remembered fondly) and pianist Wesley Wilson (later known as "Kid Socks"), neither of whom was from New Orleans ("Lincoln—Billy Mack's Company," *Afro-American*, July 7, 1922, 5).

It was around this time that the Macks relocated to Chicago for a while, singing as a duo at the Royal Gardens, while King Oliver's Creole Jazz Band was playing on the stage for dancing, they strolled among the diners. For the balance of the 1920s, they toured the TOBA circuit, finally settling in Chicago in retirement. (Their second child, Billy Mack

Jr., was a noted artist and collector whose papers at the Chicago Library contain quite a number of photos and reminiscences of his parents' career.)

The handful of recordings Billy and Mary Mack made are very much in the old-style tradition of the vaudeville husband and wife, battle of the sexes. The good-natured ribbing and easy interaction between them on their first recording—"Black but Sweet, Oh God" (OKeh 8195, recorded in New Orleans, January 22, 1925)—features Mary praising her boyfriend, a "brown" who is "little and cute, chocolate to the bone," while Billy retorts that she needs a man like him, "black and ugly," who "ain't good looking" because "good looks ain't gonna carry me through this world"—although he's "black but sweet, oh God!" The chorus of the flip side of that record begins with a reference to their embrace of jazz—"I'd rather hear you say one word than hear that Jazz Band play" ("My Heart-Breakin' Gal," same date and matrix)—and features a solo by New Orleans cornet player Punch Miller, who the Macks recalled using on several tours before his alcohol problems made it impossible. Later duets backed by Clarence Williams in 1926, and then a last record in Chicago in 1936, continue the tradition.

In their 1959 interview, Mary Mack recalled that their act was one of the first husband-and-wife or family duos on the Black stage; she points out that they preceded Butterbeans and Susie and only the Whitman Sisters came before. In addition to their early stake in the game, the Macks were also responsible for bringing a great deal of early jazz to the stage, a contribution for which they have never been sufficiently credited.

Butterbeans and Susie

The comedy team known professionally as Butterbeans and Susie might hold the record for the longest continuous career in African American entertainment, performing together from 1916 until Susie's death in 1963. Likewise, their marriage (beginning in 1917) proved to exemplify a level of durability virtually unknown in any entertainment circle.

Jodie (sometimes credited in the press as "Joddie") Edwards was born in Marietta, Georgia, in 1893, and began dancing on street corners and singing with a string band by the age of ten (Butterbeans and Susie interview, 1960). Susie Hawthorne was born in 1894, in Pensacola, Florida, and also began singing as a child. By 1913, she was touring with Alexander's Tolliver's Smart Set, continuing that association with Tolliver's Big Show in 1915, performing in a sister act called Poteet and Hawthorne, in which she sang "Memphis Blues" and "That Animal Rag," combining the two primary strains of music popular at the time on the Black stage ("Alexander Tolliver's Big Show," *The Freeman*, November 20, 1915, 6). Apparently it was here that she and Jody met, although they did not perform together until the 1916 version of the *Big Show*, beginning in New Orleans and also featuring Ma and Pa Rainey.

After leaving the Tolliver show, Edwards and Hawthorne entered the world of TOBA vaudeville, touring with the already legendary Butler "String Beans" May, and his wife Sweetie Matthews. Edwards and Hawthorne were married during that tour and mentored by the older couple, who were among the most popular acts in vaudeville at the time. When May died in November 1917, Edwards was encouraged to assume the name "Butterbeans" in tribute, along with appropriating much of the older man's humor and stage presence.

From that point through the 1930s Butterbeans and Susie toured the upper regions of Black vaudeville and stage shows, creating and maintaining a reputation of dependable professionalism as well as generosity to other performers. Their act generally consisted of Susie singing a blues number or two, Butterbeans doing an eccentric dance specialty, and the two of them performing broad comedy numbers and skits exploring marital and relationship conflicts that were staples on the Black stage. By 1924 they were touring in a show featuring the veteran singer Sara Martin, who was enjoying a flurry of success in her recording career for OKeh following a decade on stage.

Martin (who was also known for professional generosity) recommended the team to OKeh record executives and apparently also conspired to have one in the audience for an audition during a performance. Jody for his part was reluctant, feeling that he wasn't enough of a singer and that their act was in any event more dependent on comedy than music. Nevertheless, they made their first record in New York in May 1924, accompanied by Clarence Williams.

For the most part, Butterbeans and Susie's records were representative of their stage show, with songs often emphasizing the male or female perspective, with a good deal of exaggerated violence or misdirection providing the humor. Their first recording date produced two sides: "When My Man Shimmies" and "A Married Man's a Fool" (OKeh 8147 and 8140, May 22, 1924). The first was largely given over to Susie Edwards's good if unexceptional blues singing of her own composition, joined by her husband at the end. The second was a showpiece for Butterbeans, who takes on the role of a preacher quoting the Bible to support his cheating habits over a four measure vamp that was actually the bridge of the AABA Vaudeville Blues form (with his wife adding some commentary, as she likely would have done on stage).

It was not until their third session that the team was allowed to record one of their stage routines emphasizing marital themes.

> [Susie] If I had you [Butterbeans] If you had me
> [Susie] I'd make you get you a job, working all day long carrying a hod
> Your company I would ignore, I'd make you sleep down on the kitchen floor
> I wouldn't allow [Butterbeans] You wouldn't allow?
> [Susie] You a decent suit, I'd make you wear a shoe and a boot
> I would not care if you did get mad, I'd keep you looking like something the buzzard had
> So nowadays girls, it pays to treat them rough, so get yourself a monkey man and make them strut their stuff
> [Butterbeans] Come here, come here, if I had you [Susie] What would you do?
> [Butterbeans] I'd make you get you a job, massaging clothes in some one washtub [Susie] That's a lie!
> I'd whup your head every time you breathe, rough treatment, woman, is exactly what you need
> I'd go out every night with my gals and I'd get full of gin, and you'd be hospital bound if you asked me where I'd been
> I can make you climb up a slippery elm tree and if you slip, [Susie] 'spose I slip? [Butterbeans] your hips would belong to me
> Now you know a man was put on this earth to rule, so take a tip from me and don't be no woman big fool

This gives a good idea of the back-and-forth aspects of the team's shows and the delivery demonstrates superb comic timing, even without a live audience. As the 1920s continued, they like so many other singers and blues performers, began exploring the mine of double entendre and sexual metaphor, although it is possible that Butterbeans and Susie were pioneers of this sort of song from their vaudeville days, possibly inspired by the example of String Beans May. The notorious "I Want a Hot Dog for my Roll" was left unreleased by OKeh, although it was issued years later.

For the duration of their professional career, Butterbeans and Susie worked consistently in their own shows (including *Heebie Jeebies* in 1927) primarily in Black theaters. During their last two decades, when they were based in Chicago, they mentored and financially assisted numerous Black stars, including Moms Mabley and Stepin Fetchit. They also continued making recordings for OKeh until 1930, making a final visit to the studios for an LP made shortly before Susie died in 1963. Jody lived until 1967, but did not perform again.

Coot Grant and Kid Wilson

The comedy duo known as Grant and Wilson were modeled after the example of Butterbeans and Susie and countless other husband and wife teams on the Black vaudeville circuit. Leola Henton was born in Alabama in 1893, and by the time she was able to walk and talk she was on stage. Tours to South America and Europe gave her an exceptionally broad perspective in the entertainment industry and by the mid-1910s she was working extensively in tent shows and theaters, sometimes with her husband Isaiah Grant, whom she married in 1913. By 1920, Grant had died and Leola partnered, both professionally and domestically with pianist Wesley Wilson. Wilson had been born in 1893, in Jacksonville, Florida, and, like his wife, had knocked around the African American entertainment industry doing a variety of acts under a variety of names during the 1910s, before marrying Leola and becoming identified with the team as its chief accompanist (on piano) and songwriter.

It was as a songwriter that Wilson was perhaps best known. All the songs they recorded together and many that Grant sang by herself were composed by him or by both of them. Their abilities in that direction were respected in the entertainment community as well. In 1933 for Bessie Smith's last recording session, Wilson was hired to provide all four tunes (apparently to the consternation of John Hammond, the producer, who wanted her to revisit some of her early blues repertoire). "Take Me for a Buggy Ride" and "Do Your Duty" were both recorded by the duo for Vocalion and then again by Smith with a jazz band backing. Both Grant and Wilson also recorded quite a bit apart from each other—Grant made two records for Paramount in 1926 that were the first appearance of

Downhome blues artist Blind Blake, while Wilson recorded in a hokum, country blues series with Harry McDaniel (called, among other things, Pigmeat Pete and Catjuice Charlie), during the early 1930s.

Numerous theatrical appearances and a small but apparently successful series of recordings, beginning in 1925, kept the couple busy into the mid-1930s, although a flirtation with the movies did not develop beyond some extra work on the Paul Robeson film *Emperor Jones* in 1933. A recording session with Trixie Smith and Sidney Bechet for Decca in 1938, failed to ignite much interest; however, a short bloom came in the mid-1940s, when the team was engaged by the White clarinetist Mezz Mezzrow to compose and record for his King Jazz label, which led to some New York engagements, including two appearances on Rudi Blesh's *This Is Jazz* radio show in 1947. Following this came another decade of scuffling, until Wilson died in 1958, after returning to the East Coast from a period in California. Grant returned to California where she lived until her death in 1970, apparently in poverty and never able to reignite her career.

George Williams and Bessie Brown

After Butterbeans and Susie, the most recorded husband-and-wife duo of the period was George Williams and Bessie Brown. Both were from Texas and were born around the turn of the century, but little is known of their lives outside of a handful of press mentions during the 1920s. The commonness of each of their names leads to further confusion; several different singers recorded under names similar to "Bessie Brown" but it appears that they are all different people (especially "Original Bessie Brown" who had a long career in her own right). Williams and Brown led vaudeville revues throughout the 1920s, capitalizing on their Columbia recordings, which were apparently very popular. By 1929 they began the *Happy Go Lucky* show, lasting into the early 1930s (Blind Blake may have toured with them).

In "Bald-Headed Mama Blues" (Columbia 14065, February 28, 1925) Brown comments to Williams that she's been "looking at you for the last twelve years," so their association would have begun in 1913 or so. They were known for an "argumentary act" and apparently their son, George Jr., appeared with them as well (Russell, 1927). A profile of Williams in 1936 mentions that he and Brown had been married for eighteen years and that they were still performing, although they made their last records

Figure 4.7. Bessie Brown, ca. 1925. Courtesy David A. Jasen Collection. Public domain.

together in 1926 (Williams did a solo session in 1930) (Matthews, 1936). Press mentions of them continue at least until 1941, and they may have been performing as late as 1949 (Rowe, 1949), although what happened to them after that is unknown.

Their recordings, made for Columbia between 1923 and 1926 range from standard vaudeville crosstalk performances to solos by each performer. Very few (if any) of their recordings are of their own material. Most are credited to one of their accompanists—Lem Fowler or Fletcher Henderson (as George Brooks), with the others being a smattering of Vaudeville

Blues composers and this reliance on outside sources presumably impacted their popularity and future. While they were very positively reviewed in the press, the recordings tend to sound rather dull, with Williams's nasal voice furthering the case that he was better known as a comic (and often sounding more like a White country singer, yodels and all), while Brown comes off a good deal better as a blues singer with a heavy delivery and obvious affinity for the material.

On "Mississippi Delta Blues" (Columbia 14036, August 19, 1924—a Spencer Williams tune)—she sings very much in a style comparable to her label-mate Bessie Smith, with accompaniment by Henderson and his star tenor saxophonist Coleman Hawkins. This is presumably one of the sessions that Hawkins later denigrated as "cotton field" music he had to play early in his career, although Brown's performance is very convincing.

Chapter 5

"It's Tight Like That"

Downhome Blues

Following the first rush of Cabaret Blues singers, and then the Vaudeville Blues, the way was clear for the Downhome Blues. (*Downhome Blues* is a term used by Jeffrey Todd Titon [1994] to describe the blues that is dominated by male singers in the second half of the 1920s, but I will include some of the female singers of the period as well.) Just as the market was perceived as changing in the early part of 1923, some business-minded recording executives, particularly J. Mayo Williams of Paramount, identified the end of the vaudeville trend by about the middle of 1924, and began casting about for something new. Williams was of the opinion that African American audiences wanted more elemental, rural blues material, without the show business trappings of the female blues singers who had dominated the market up to that point. While sales figures for Bessie Smith, Ma Rainey, and the other top singers of the time were still very encouraging, Williams felt that the available talent was largely tapped out by 1924, with the top Vaudeville and Cabaret Singers already signed and in most cases exhausted.

Another reason for the shift was economic; just as the Vaudeville Singers had represented a more cost-effective way of recording blues with fewer accompanists and no need to create the fully realized arrangements that the earlier singers required, the Downhome singers were often (at least in the case of the men) self-accompanied or only used a single accompanist. Also, the singers (both male and female) were more adept at providing their own material, which would be free from copyright restrictions. These songs could then be bought for a set fee by the producers and published by their own companies, creating an additional revenue stream.

Even before this, some interesting experiments had been made within the previous style. Sara Martin recorded "Longing for Daddy Blues" and "I've Got to Go and Leave My Daddy Behind" (OKeh 8117 and 8104, October 24, 1923) in the fall of 1923, accompanied only by Sylvester Weaver on guitar, creating what is generally recognized as the first country (or Downhome) blues record. Martin apparently composed the two songs and publisher/producer Clarence Williams was given (or rather, took) co-composer credit. Weaver also recorded a series of solo guitar and vocal blues as well, although he was alone among the influential male performers to record primarily in New York (although some of his records with Martin were done while they were on tour in Atlanta and St. Louis).

Columbia, seeing the popularity of Martin and Sylvester on OKeh, began trying to use more rural accompaniment behind their stars Bessie Smith and Clara Smith, although those experiments were largely unsuccessful. The field recording units by OKeh and other companies began to record actual rural singers by the early months of 1924. Ed Andrews is usually acknowledged to be the first of the male blues singer/guitarists to record, making two recordings in Atlanta in the spring of 1924. He was closely followed by Stovepipe No. 1 (Samuel Jones) and Daddy Stovepipe (Johnny Watson), who traveled to the Gennett studios in Richmond, Indiana, in May, although their recordings did not make much of an impact.

Mayo Williams's first notable signing was of Papa Charlie Jackson in the summer of 1924, after he heard him singing on the street in Chicago. Paramount fairly dominated the market with Jackson and its two subsequent acquisitions, Blind Lemon Jefferson and Blind Blake, although OKeh had a strong contender in Lonnie Johnson, who made more records in the 1920s than the other three combined.

Recording companies also cast about for women for their race record series who were not as closely identified with professional entertainment, preferring singers who were active in local rural markets. Paramount found Elzadie Robinson and Sodarisa Miller; OKeh had Sippie Wallace, Bertha "Chippie" Hill, and Victoria Spivey; Vocalion signed Luella Miller; and numerous other singers made a handful of records for those and various other companies. These women were overwhelmingly devoted to the standard twelve-bar blues with a country flavor, often composing their own material, especially in the case of Wallace and Spivey.

Sippie Wallace

By 1925, there was a changing market in the Race Records industry. After five years of African American female vaudeville and tent show entertainers dominating the sales of most companies, the pendulum was swinging more in the direction of jazz and dance bands. In addition to this, male singers began to break into the top-sellers' charts. Papa Charlie Jackson began his long series of records for Paramount in August 1924, and by the middle of 1926 both Blind Lemon Jefferson Blind Blake had also established success for the same company.

A look at the discographies of singers popular in the early 1920s (Mamie Smith, Lucille Hegamin, Mary Stafford, Trixie Smith, and even Alberta Hunter) show a sudden decrease if not a complete cessation of recording activity after 1925. Of the early singers, only Ethel Waters continued recording frequently, although she was primarily featured on tunes from her popular shows and other Tin Pan Alley fare and her records released on the general (as opposed to the "race") series. The next iteration of "blues" singers (Bessie Smith, Ma Rainey, Clara Smith, Ida Cox, and Rosa Henderson) continued to record, but with a broader range of material, including the popular double entendre, "racy" songs.

The next generation of women singers to be promoted as blues singers was for the most part too young to have been active professionals during the 1910s. Wallace, Victoria Spivey, and Memphis Minnie were all born around the turn of the century but did not tour for any length of time with the better-known traveling companies or appear in vaudeville much if at all.[1] These singers were much more rooted in the "folk" element of blues expression and, in Spivey's case, composed a significant part of her own material.

Beulah Thomas was born in Jefferson County, Arkansas, in 1898 but by the 1900 census her family had moved to Houston, where she spent her childhood and teen years. By 1910 the family included at least nine children, most of whom were apparently musical. Thomas's father, George Thomas Sr., was a laborer who apparently also functioned as a deacon

1. Memphis Minnie was active in the late 1910s in the South (particularly in Memphis), and was in Chicago by the late 1920s, but did not begin her recording career until 1929, and in any event did not exert much influence until her series of blues records in the 1930s and 1940s, so she will not be dealt with here. Other African American women who began recording in the 1920s but who found lasting fame and influence in later decades were Adelaide Hall, Helen Humes, and Josephine Baker.

in the local church, and Beulah began singing and playing for church services, which she did for much of her life. Her eldest brother, George Jr., was an accomplished pianist and composer who was responsible for Beulah's introduction to blues and ultimately her first recording. George's daughter Hociel was also a recorded blues singer in the 1920s, and again in the 1940s, although she did not have a consistent career. The youngest sibling Hersal was considered the best musician in the family and had a flurry of successes accompanying Beulah (who as a child was known as "Sippie" due to eating habits), as well as composing blues numbers and recording some early boogie-woogie piano solos before dying in 1926 at the age of twenty.

George Jr. moved to New Orleans in about 1915, and made the acquaintance of Clarence Williams, as well as noted jazz players like King Oliver, who became important to his career in the next decade. Within a year, Sippie had joined him (bringing Hociel, whom she largely raised) and began singing in clubs around town under her brother's tutelage. By the late 1910s George had moved to Chicago, where he began publishing some of his best-known tunes, including "New Orleans Hop Scop Blues" and "Muscle Shoals Blues," both of which were probably composed during his New Orleans sojourn. Sippie and Hersal both joined him in Chicago by the early 1920s, becoming active in the publishing and song-demonstrating industry.

Sippie Thomas became Sippie Wallace in 1923, with her marriage to Matt Wallace who was occasionally credited as a gambler, promoter, and her theatrical manager, although the paucity of mentions of her in the Black press suggests she did not tour or even appear in vaudeville very often. She apparently toured as a dresser for the headliner in a low-budget medicine show in 1919, and may have had some opportunities to sing and play, leading to local jobs after she returned to Houston (Harrison, 1988, 119–20). Her collaborations with her brother George resulted in her first record date in October 1923, for OKeh. The two tunes recorded that day were both composed by George Thomas in the style of "country blues" using rural imagery, although accompanied by the very sophisticated and highly esteemed vaudeville pianist, Eddie Heywood ("Up the Country Blues/Shorty George Blues," OKeh 8106, October 26, 1923). "Up the Country" was cocredited to Wallace and "Shorty George" to Hersal.

Following her initial recording session Wallace may have done some touring, but the press is mum about her whereabouts, although in a 1982 interview she said she toured the TOBA circuit between 1924 and 1926, probably on the strength of her recordings (Townley, 1983). She may also have stayed in Chicago with her brothers and niece, collaborating on songs and playing in clubs there until the end of the decade.

When she returned to the studios on a half-dozen occasions during May and December 1924, she was apparently either living or appearing in New York, where she was accompanied by various members of the Clarence Williams music circle. Recording mostly compositions by George or herself, Sippie Wallace is supported by either Williams alone or his Harmonizers or Blue Five, which at various times included Sidney Bechet, Louis Armstrong, and Buddy Christian, all New Orleans natives, and probably acquaintances of the Thomas family from their sojourn there in the middle 1910s. Wallace comes across best on tunes with more spare accompaniments, such as "Underworld Blues" (OKeh 8144, May 26, 1924).

Credited to George Thomas and Wallace, "Underworld Blues" is a dark blues of the sort to which Wallace seemed attracted during her career.

1. I keep on dreaming, just can't help myself [2x]
   It's about my man, I mean all by nobody else

2. Sometimes I think my man's too good to die [2x]
   Then again I think he ought to be buried alive

3. My man don't treat me like he used to do [2x]
   He keeps me always worried with those underworld blues

In addition to her very convincing blues expression (triumphing over Clarence Williams's wrong chords in places), Wallace uses the third seeker associated with Bessie Smith and the long, sustained lines made necessary by the lack of any horns in the band.

By early 1925, she was back in Chicago for a short period at least and made three of her best recordings, backed by Hersal on piano and Joe "King" Oliver on cornet. On "Devil Dance Blues" (her own composition, OKeh 8206, February 24, 1925), Wallace weds the shouting, moaning sound of country blues with an air of religiosity that came out of her own dual career of blues singing and church music.

1. I had a dream last night and it filled me full of fright [2x]
   I dreamed I was in a dancehall where the devil danced at night

2. I saw the sweet missus devil standing in her hall [2x]
   He was out with the devil band and he was giving a ball

3. He had on a robe that was made of gold [2x]
   I never seen no devil look so sweet before
4. It was a dream, a dream I've never had before [2x]
   I dreamed we all were dancing and put on a great big show

Oliver's plaintive cornet and Thomas's rolling piano highlight Wallace's confident delivery of lyrics that seem closer to Irving Berlin's 1913 "At the Devil's Ball" than any contemporary blues song.

Wallace's recordings from the beginning of 1926 until the end of the decade were also made in Chicago, presumably because of its relative proximity to her home in Detroit. In these she was backed at first by Louis Armstrong (himself recently returned from New York) and Hersal, who seemed to draw a darker quality from Wallace's voice on material primarily written by her, Hersal, or George Thomas. Records such as "Mail Train Blues" (OKeh 8345, March 3, 1926) and "The Flood Blues" (OKeh 8470, May 6, 1927) are far more informed by a rural sensibility than most of the material by earlier Black women singers other than Ma Rainey, and provide a bridge to the rural blues singers just then beginning to record.

By the first half of 1925, she and her husband apparently relocated to Detroit, where she would be based for the rest of her life, although she also had a simultaneous residence in Chicago, keeping house for her brothers. Matt Wallace may have used the location as a base for his gambling enterprises, and by the end of the 1920s his wife gradually began focusing her musical efforts on church work, especially following the sudden death (apparently due to food poisoning) of Hersal in 1926, and then the deaths of both her husband and George in 1937. She continued to make occasional trips to Chicago to record in 1926, 1927, and 1929 (occasionally accompanying herself on piano), but, except for one record session for Mercury in 1945, largely dropped out of the industry until she retired from her church work in the mid-1960s and was discovered by a younger blues and folk audience. She made numerous recordings and toured extensively until her death in 1986.

Victoria Spivey

Victoria Regina Spivey was born in Houston, Texas in 1907 (her birth certificate has that date crossed out and "1910" written in, but the earlier date is almost certainly correct). Her mother Addie worked for a time as a practical nurse and her father Grant was a railroad worker who was killed in an accident when Victoria was seven. Both parents were musical and shared their musical abilities with their eight children, several of whom became professional musicians. In addition to Victoria, Willie was a pianist who instructed her in the rudiments and took her on gigs, while Elton and Addie both became singers (Elton was known as the "Za Zu Girl" and Addie as "Sweet Pease").

By her early teens, Victoria was playing piano and singing in various clubs in Houston, many of which were not of the wholesome variety. It was during this period that she was exposed to the rich Texas blues tradition, making the acquaintance of many blues performers, especially Blind Lemon Jefferson who became a particular friend and influence. Due in some part to her mother's objections, she attempted to get a stable job playing in one of the local theaters, but her lack of reading ability ended that job as quickly as it began. Her attendance at the local Black theaters introduced her to Ida Cox (who encouraged the young singer) and another older singer active in Houston, Sippie Thomas (who became known as Sippie Wallace).

In part due to Cox's encouragement, Spivey left Houston just before she turned twenty and moved to St. Louis where she performed in clubs and made her first recordings. Unlike virtually any of the blues singers of the 1920s, Spivey composed almost all the songs she recorded and they can thus be seen as an accurate reflection of her influences and experiences.

Within three months of her initial recording sessions, she had moved to New York and began performing locally as well as recording frequently, often with the pianist John Erby, who himself was a significant blues composer, using the pen name J. Guy Suddoth. Possessing a voice with, as Daphne Duval Harrison called it, "a distinctive nasal quality" (Harrison, 1988, 148), Spivey recorded primarily blues and was employed in live dates in that way, although she had a well-reviewed run in the show *Africana* (starring Ethel Waters) in 1927 ("Hit Bits from Africana," 1927). Spivey was called "an entirely different type of blues singer" suggesting the differences between her and the more stage-oriented singers such as Waters or Alberta Hunter.

An interruption in her recording career between November, 1927 and September, 1928 coincided with her marriage to trumpeter Reuben Floyd and the apparent indecision of OKeh about how to present her. Up to that point she had sung almost exclusively blues (most self-composed) but several sessions were produced featuring her with first-class jazz accompaniment, including King Oliver, Louis Armstrong, Red Allen,

Eddie Lang, and members of the Louis Armstrong Hot Five and the Luis Russell Orchestra. Simultaneous sessions with guitarist and singer Lonnie Johnson (a friend from her St. Louis days) were perhaps deemed more successful and less adorned blues (often fairly dirty ones) filled out much of her remaining 1920s discography, much of which was done for the larger and more stable company, Victor.

On the heels of her recording and theatrical success, Spivey was engaged to play the role of "Missy Rose" in King Vidor's film *Hallelujah* of 1929, the first large-scale Hollywood picture with an all-Black cast. Following this success, Spivey began touring with Lloyd Hunter's Serenaders (which included her husband), recording with them in 1931, returning to New York and working in a series of Black shows. By 1936 she was in Chicago, where she remained at least until then end of the decade making numerous blues recordings for Decca and Vocalion and performing with her next husband, dancer Billy Williams, whom she married in 1937.

After a few more film appearances and local Chicago engagements, Spivey essentially retired from blues performance by 1950, focusing her efforts as a singer and piano player on her church work, which occupied her for the next decade. By 1960, the nostalgia boom was in full swing for performers who had been active in the 1920s, and she along with Sippie Wallace, Lucille Hegamin, and Alberta Hunter were coaxed out of retirement or alternate careers to sing again on records as well as for personal appearances, primarily on the folk music circuit. For her part, Spivey also utilized her significant business acumen and formed her own record company (with her last domestic partner, blues enthusiast and journalist Len Kunstadt) both to record and reissue sides by blues stars of the past. She was in constant demand as a performer and interview subject until her death in 1976.

Listening to Victoria Spivey's recordings in order actually becomes somewhat tedious; virtually the first two-thirds of her issued recordings are self-composed twelve-bar blues with a relatively static accompaniment and emotional intensity. Her voice also can be quite abrasive in the style of the country blues singers she was influenced by in her youth. Where the interest comes is in the lyrics; no other blues singer of the 1920s (even Ma Rainey) produced such a catalog of songs reflecting country themes and an intimate acquaintance with her audience. A song like "Hoodoo Man Blues" (OKeh 8370, August 12, 1926) from one of her early sessions combines the lost man theme with the traditional acceptance of supernatural forces and the power of an individual who could control such forces.

> He's sent the hoodoo man, / everybody's talking 'bout the
> hoodoo man.
> The women's all raving 'bout him,
> I'll pick a man for you, / now, if that'll do
> Your man is nearly through, / I know he's through with you
> And I mean that I am just the hoodoo man

On the darker side is "Blood Thirsty Blues" (OKeh 8531, October 31, 1927), which celebrates the murder of a faithless lover.

1. Blood, blood, blood look at all that blood [2x]
   Yes I killed my man, a low-down good for nothing clown
2. I told him blood was in my eye, and still he wouldn't listen to me [2x]
   Yes instead of giving him sugar, I put glass in his tea
3. Another thing folds, you can put me down and let me walk [2x]
   You know I'm a mighty mean woman and won't stand for no back talk
4. The only man I ever loved, out of thin air to his ruin [2x]
   Yes I know I'm blood thirsty, worryin' what my man's doin'

The architecture of the song is also unique among blues compositions of this period; the first and last verses are in minor while the two interior ones are in major, heightening the emotional intensity.

Spivey's songs had an emotional directness to them that had far more in common with the rural country blues singers of the time than did the slicker and "show-biz" songs that made up the repertoire of most of the 1920s "Blues Queens" who had done long apprenticeships on vaudeville and tent show stages before entering the recording studio. Her work also pointed to the urban blues scene of the next decade, which in turn led to the Chicago blues style of the 1940s and '50s.

Hociel Thomas

The Thomas clan was one of the premier blues families of the 1920s, although they did not receive a great deal of recognition at the time. The most prominent of the family (largely due to more extensive recording opportunities and a long professional life) was Beulah Thomas, known professionally as Sippie Wallace (discussed above).

The eldest of the clan was George Washington Thomas Jr., who played piano and many other instruments, but was best known as a composer of blues songs from the 1910s when he lived in New Orleans through the 1920s, when he was in Chicago. He had married at some point between 1900 and 1904, when Hociel was born in Houston. By the 1910 census, his wife had died and his daughter was being largely raised by Beulah. The two of them (and another brother, Hersal) followed George to New Orleans in the late 1910s, where they constituted a family unit, surviving on George's performance and publication income, with Beulah occasionally singing and the barely teenaged Hersal playing piano as well.

By 1920 the family had relocated to Chicago, where all four became active performers in clubs and on record, with George continuing his publishing business and composing more songs. Hociel began recording in 1925, accompanied by Hersal and featuring George's songs. These are very elemental blues performances, with the eighteen-year-old Hersal creating some inventive and energetic backgrounds that veer close to boogie-woogie, while Hociel infuses the traditional lyrics with a drive and varied approach using moans and growls. "I Must Have It" (Gennett 3006, April 6, 1925) is a particularly compelling performance, marking one of the earliest recordings of a woman singing what can only be called country blues.

By the end of 1925, the Thomas family was obviously becoming a force on the Chicago blues and race records scene (Beulah had been recording as Sippie Wallace for two years at that point). The newly returned Louis Armstrong was rushed into the OKeh studios as the behest of producer and pianist Richard M. Jones to join several singers, including Hociel on November 11, and six sides were released as "accompanied by Louis Armstrong's Jazz Four," including Hersal, Johnny Dodds on clarinet, and Johnny St. Cyr on banjo (the latter two joining Armstrong on the first recording with his Hot Five the following day). These sides are all credited to "Thomas," which I assume means George. As Steve Tracy points out, the vocal ranges seem uncomfortable for Hociel, suggesting that maybe they were written for another singer, possibly Sippie (Tracy,

1996). Thomas's recordings the following February feature just Hersal and Louis Armstrong and are more successful, with "Lonesome Hours" being most compelling, featuring superb work from both accompanists (OKeh 8297, February 24, 1926). The lyrics of capture and loss are uniquely expressed and may well represent a blues from the earliest part of the century.

1. The reason I love him, I stole him from my best friend [2x]
   But she good lucky, stole him back again
2. Ever since he left me, I've been wondering what must I do [2x]
   'Cause these lonesome hours always keeps me blue

Thomas herself uses some of the devices associated with Bessie Smith, including her third seeker. Along with Armstrong's backing, this makes comparison with Smith inevitable, although in general those comparisons should be favorable.

After Hersal's sudden death in July 1926, Hociel lost her interest in performing and settled down to a common-law marriage with Arthur Tebo in 1929 (according to his later marriage certificate to his second wife), moving to the Oakland area and having at least two children. Rudi Blesh brought her out of retirement to make some excellent records for his Circle label in 1947 (on which she also played piano), and she seemed primed for a comeback until a physical fight with one of her relatives left her blind and the other woman dead. Hociel Thomas lived in ill health until her death in 1952.

Elzadie Robinson

In the middle 1920s, the Chicago branch of Paramount records began recording singers who were not active on the vaudeville stage. J. Mayo "Ink" Williams was largely responsible for this direction, feeling that the market for "race" records was by that point driven more by lyrics than individual personality, and in that conclusion he was proven correct by the success of otherwise unknown singers like Elzadie Robinson.

Robinson, who made about thirty-four sides for Paramount between 1926 and 1929, as well as two (as "Blanche Johnson") for Herwin in 1927, is largely unknown as a personality outside of the recording studio. She was apparently born in Louisiana in 1901, near the Texas border, and made the acquaintance of Texas pianist Will Ezell. The two may have been a performing duo when they were "discovered" by Paramount recording director Art Laibly, who brought them into the studio in September 1926 (Montgomery, 2019). Ezell was a blues piano player who was about a decade older than Robinson and had been playing in the Southwest for twenty years before his recording debut.

Most of the songs Robinson recorded were credited either to her or Ezell and reflect a very rural, downhome sensibility that is much more reflective of country blues rather than any type of stage presentation. Titles such as "Barrel House Man" and "Sawmill Blues" (Paramount 12417, October 1926), as well as songs commemorating Galveston and Houston support the assumption that the duo was active in Texas before their recording career began. In general, the songs are straight-ahead twelve-bar blues with very limited melodic variation (many seem to put new lyrics to an all-purpose melody), sung with conviction, although no particular individuality, and, on her first few sessions, seriously marred by the recording balance, which makes her sound as if she is in a different room.

Robinson is remembered mostly for the half-dozen records she made accompanied by legendary jazz players Johnny Dodds, Jimmy Blythe, Jimmy Bertrand, and Richard M. Jones's Jazz Wizards, but these were presumably set up in an attempt to assess her appeal to an audience that might prefer more jazz-oriented sounds. The lack of follow up to any of these would seem to provide the answer.

At some point after her last recording in 1929, Robinson apparently married and moved to Flint, Michigan, where according to the 1940 census, she (as "Edlazie") was listed as a seamstress, living with her husband, Perry Henderson.

Irene Scruggs

Born in Mississippi, Irene Scruggs was apparently raised in St. Louis, but did not begin her stage career until about the time she made her first records in 1924. Her first appearance in the studio came about because of a triumph in a blues singing contest in St. Louis, which won her a trip to New York, and two days in the OKeh studio with Clarence Williams, which produced four sides, three composed by Scruggs herself (unsigned article, *Chicago Defender*, September 20, 1924, 6).

Those first records are clearly impacted by nervousness on the part of the singer as well as unfamiliarity with the process. Far more successful are the records that were made for a variety of other companies between 1926 and 1930, many of which were her own compositions. "Sorrow Valley Blues" was a tune of hers she recorded both with King Oliver (Vocalion 1017, April 23, 1926) and when back home in St. Louis with Lonnie Johnson (OKeh 8476, May 2, 1927). With Oliver she sounds comfortable with a full band (a small group from Oliver's dance band).

1. You got your hammer, you're knocking me from morn to night [2x]
   Well no matter what you say, you really got to treat me right
2. If I could lose this lonesome feeling baby I have now [2x]
   Anywhere I go, people talk any old how
3. Now this sorrow valley is a big old lonesome place [2x]
   Where people lose their sorrow and a gravedigger pleads your case

With Johnson (and pianist De Loise Searcy) the tempo is slower and the omission of the clarinet solo on the Oliver version allows for another verse further describing the insincere residents of Sorrow Valley, although the consistency of the text over the course of at least a year demonstrates that Scruggs actually composed the song (rather than compiling it in the studio).

> When you talk about me here and you knock me everywhere you go [2x]
> I'm just a good old girl, but bad luck's going 'round my door

Scruggs's later recordings were done with more rural-sounding backing, including duet sessions with Blind Blake (where she was billed as "Chocolate Brown") and pianist Eurreal "Little Brother" Montgomery (with whom she was touring in 1930), as well as an unusual series done with pianist and singer Johnny Hodges (or Hardge), where she was called

"Dixie Nolan." These recordings (and the ones with Johnson) situate her very firmly in the Downhome tradition, although she is convincing in a more up-to-date setting, as the sides with Oliver demonstrate.

By 1930 Scruggs was appearing on stage with her daughter Lazar, who was billed as "Baby Scruggs" and sang and danced. By the 1940s, both were in Europe, where Lazar appeared in stage shows while Irene sang in clubs (Johnson, 1952). Celebrated in Europe for her singing and her history on records, Scruggs passed away in Germany in 1981.

Luella Miller

Very little is known about Luella Miller, although she is presumed to have been born in St. Louis, where she was active in the mid-1920s, when she made her first recordings. All of her two dozen issued sides were for Vocalion and are of standard twelve-bar blues in the country tradition. Most utilize a single, all-purpose melody, colored by moans and long lines. Generally, the song topics are from a rural perspective: "Rattle Snake Groan" (Vocalion 1081, January 28, 1927), "Muddy Stream Blues," "Tornado Groan," (Vocalion 1147, January 24, 1928), and so on.

Her first session was done in St. Louis and she benefited from the accompaniment of the Johnson brothers—Lonnie on guitar and violin and James on piano—lending a particularly country air to the sound (particularly on the tracks with Lonnie's elementary fiddle playing). Her subsequent sessions were done in New York and Chicago, although the Johnsons and some other St. Louis musicians were with her on them, suggesting that they were all imported by Vocalion, which had ceased or greatly limited their location recordings by the late 1920s.

Most (if not all) of the songs recorded by Miller were originals, which doubtless made her attractive to the recording executives of the period and put her in a category with the male singers of the day. In "Tornado Blues" she recounts a familiar Midwest experience linking both meteorological and romantic events with a poetic and visual flair.

1. Tornado swept out this little town today [2x]
   And taken away everything I had

2. Lightning flashed, wind rattled around my door [2x]
   Every since that time, I haven't seen my house no more

3. It ruined my clothes and blowed my bed away [2x]
   I ain't got no place to lay my weary head
4. The storm came back and blowed my man away [2x]
   That's the reason why I ain't got a good man today
5. I'm lonesome now, I have to walk the street [2x]
   I'm like a stranger to everyone I meet
6. Mmmmm . . . tornado ruined my home [2x]
   And left me turnin' with the tornado groan

Where Luella Miller went from there is a mystery, suggesting that she was probably either an amateur performer or that her standard performance venues were far away from the reporting of the standard Black press.

Sylvester Weaver

If he had not been one of the first to record blues solos and accompaniments, Sylvester Weaver would likely be merely a footnote to the era. As it is, he made fewer than two dozen sides under his own name as well as a handful of accompaniments to female singers, most notably Sara Martin.

Born in the blues-drenched area around Louisville in 1896, Weaver somehow learned how to play guitar in a ragtime style which he later adapted to the blues repertoire. Based on his later recordings he must also have learned elements of Hawaiian slide guitar, which was finding a vogue in the United States during the 1910s and 1920s. After serving in World War I, he began playing around Louisville with fellow city dweller Martin and other singers and gradually began appearing in vaudeville.

By the fall of 1923 Weaver and Martin were performing as a duo and made their first recording together in October (see chapter 4). The popular success of this disc led OKeh recording executive Ralph Peer to write to Martin during a tour and strongly suggest that she retool her stage show to feature the country sound that she and Weaver had produced (Obrecht, 2015, 11). It was during one of their tours that Lonnie Johnson heard Weaver and came away profoundly impressed, although Johnson was Weaver's technical superior even at that time.

The success of the first Martin/Weaver disc and several follow up sessions (including one devoted to religious songs) encouraged OKeh to begin using Weaver by himself. The first session generally acknowledged to be by a solo country-styled guitarist produced "Guitar Rag" and "Guitar Blues" (OKeh 8109, November 2, 1923). These two tunes represent the two main facets of Weaver's style, a melding of Hawaiian and country slide guitar techniques on the blues and a very straight, unbluesy ragtime piece done in simplified style. Both of these styles were presumably common in Louisville in the early 1910s, when he was developing his technique and playing casual engagements.

In an answer to the market success of Papa Charlie Jackson, Blind Lemon Jefferson, Lonnie Johnson, and Blind Blake, OKeh brought Weaver back under his own name in the spring of 1927 after a nearly three year hiatus. "Poor Boy Blues" (OKeh 8522, August 31, 1927) is his own composition and features his unadorned guitar playing supporting a simple singing style that impresses with its directness, if not its diction, which is nearly impenetrable in places. "Can't Be Trusted Blues" (OKeh 8504, August 31, 1927) is a similar blues (credited to "Jones") that also seems to appropriate the melody of Ida Cox's "Death Letter Blues."

More successful is "Devil Blues" (OKeh 8534, November 27, 1927), credited to Williams (presumably Clarence Williams, although the subject matter seems to suggest Weaver was the composer). The vocal delivery is not especially involved with blues phrasing, although in places Weaver seems to be using some gospel-like inflections, which are in line with the hellfire and brimstone lyrics (Weaver was known to be religiously observant throughout his life), although tongue is planted firmly in cheek by the end.

1. Hellhound starts to chasing me, and I was a running fool [2x]
   My ankles caught on fire, couldn't keep my puppies cool.
2. A thousand devils with tails and sharp horns [2x] my lawdy!
   Everyone wonders, try to step on my corns
3. For miles around me, heard men scream and yell [2x] my lawdy!
   Couldn't see a woman, I said Lord, ain't this hell!

Weaver's most significant contribution is in his playing; his later recordings feature him with Walter Beasley, and the two guitars create an integrated blend of ragtime and blues in equal measure, with Weaver's very early slide guitar technique on display on tunes such as "Bottleneck Blues" (OKeh 8530, November 27, 1927). The B side of this record is a wonderfully relaxed version of Handy's "St. Louis Blues," which comes to a very inconclusive ending (omitting the last four bars for some reason, suggesting a rehearsal take), but which probably gives a good idea of how this music might have sounded on the street in a casual setting. After these last sessions for OKeh, Weaver largely retired from show business and worked as a personal chauffeur until his death in 1960, with even his second wife not entirely aware of his relative fame as a performer in the 1920s.

Papa Charlie Jackson

As with most of the male singers of this period, Papa Charlie Jackson is a nearly complete mystery in terms of early influence and experience. He was probably born in New Orleans around 1887, and one could surmise he left home early to tour with minstrel and medicine shows shortly after the turn of the century. His recorded repertoire is a wide one, encompassing a range of material that he presumably would only have gotten by extensive performance experience. His instrument of choice was a "banjo-guitar," which utilized the six strings of a banjo tuned like a guitar with a guitar neck and a very large head that softened the sound somewhat. With that, Jackson evolved a highly refined and remarkably sophisticated technique that provided him with a full sounding background to his vocals.

According to Abbott and Seroff, Jackson played a vaudeville engagement in Chicago with clarinetist Jimmy O'Bryant in 1925, and was reported doing a similar date at the Lyric Theater in New Orleans. His other theatrical performances are unknown, or at least undocumented. The engagement in New Orleans was organized by Mayo Williams, the talent scout and producer for Paramount who had "discovered" him busking on Maxwell Street in Chicago. Williams was always on the lookout for new talent to record for his race records, and by the middle of 1924 he was beginning to feel that the pool of women singers was getting shallow.

Williams was, in a word, a snob. Born in Arkansas in 1894, he was one of the first African American graduates of Brown University, and had high expectations of Black artists. "You didn't have a chance with me if you split a verb, even if you were a hell of a singer," he said, remembering some of the singers he recorded during his time at Paramount (Galt, part 4, 1989, 20). On the other hand, he was enough of a hardheaded businessman that he had no reservations hiring singers like Ma Rainey, who was quite unsophisticated even by standards of blues women. He felt that the darker the complexion, the more in touch a singer was with the potential audience for their records.

It was partly due to that opinion that he was first attracted to Jackson when he heard him entertaining on the street in the summer of 1924. Going with his instinct, Williams brought him into the studio the following month and quickly realized he had a popular artist on his hands. While Jackson was not the first solo male blues singer or performer on record (Sylvester Weaver and Ed Andrews beat him to it), he became the most prolific before his label mates Blind Lemon Jefferson and Blind Blake. To his credit, Williams realized the significance of the talent Jackson (and later, Blind Blake) had and apparently helped them find work outside the studio.

Jackson's first Paramount release was "Papa's Lawdy, Lawdy Blues" and "Airy Man Blues" (Paramount 12219, August 1924). These two sides give a good capsule look at his recorded repertoire and it is reasonable to surmise that these were songs Williams heard him perform on the street. "Papa's Lawdy" is a slightly adapted refrain blues, showing off Jackson's baritone/bass vocal range, while "Airy Man" (which might be a mistranslation of "Hairy Man Blues") has him negotiating the wordy, up-tempo melody in the tenor range. More of a folk song, "Airy Man" cites State Street in Chicago and uses a sixteen bar form with a verse and chorus, suggesting it was a preexisting song.

From his second session comes what was one of his biggest hits, "Salty Dog Blues" (Paramount 12236, September 1924). Built on the older, probably preblues, eight-bar structure with a standard cyclic chord progression to which endless verses could be fit, the form accounts for several of Jackson's first twenty records. This was a significant enough success for Jackson that he was brought in to the studio two years later to guest with a jazz group led by New Orleans cornetist Freddie Keppard and clarinetist Johnny Dodds and to contribute a truncated version of his vocal, ending the record with a stentorian "Papa Charlie done sung that song!" to be sure no one would miss his efforts (Paramount 12399, July 1926).

Salty Dog
Refrain
Jackson/Rainey
F♯7 F♯7
Now the scared est I ev er been in my life Un cle
B7 B7 E7 E7
Bud liked to caught me kis sin his wife you sal ty dog oh you
A A C♯7
sal ty dog

Another older form used frequently by Jackson during his early recording period was the eight bar form exemplified by "Shave 'em Dry," a tune with a history of fairly pornographic references greatly diluted here (Paramount 12264, February 1925). The other recording from this period is by Ma Rainey and features similarly sanitized lyrics (the Jackson version credits Rainey as co-composer), but an alternate take of a 1935 recording by Bessie Jackson (earlier known as Lucille Bogan) gives an idea of the unexpurgated lyrics one might have heard in a bordello or buffet flat in the 1920s.

The progression here is similar to "Trouble in Mind" and many other songs (including Jackson's "Alabama Bound"/"Don't You Leave Me Here" variation) considered to be early versions of the blues, allying Jackson to the earlier style probably common when he began his professional career (e.g., see chapter 2).

By the spring of 1926, Jackson's repertoire on disc had shifted dramatically to twelve-bar blues, suggesting both that the audience favored that and that Paramount and Mayo Williams were pressuring him to bring in more new material that could be copyrighted. "Bad Luck Woman Blues" was a straight-ahead blues making use of some of the imagery of superstition frequently used in traditional songs (Paramount 12383, May or June 1926).

1. She keeps a rabbit's foot in her hand at night when she goes to sleep [2x]
   She keeps it with her so I won't make no midnight creep
2. My bad luck woman keeps me feeling blue [2x]
   I can't get rid of her, she sticks to me like glue

Earlier Tin Pan Alley tunes were also recorded; "Bright Eyes" (Paramount 12574, November 1927) was a 1905 tune by Harry H. Williams and Egbert van Alstyne (credited to Jackson on the label) that he presumably knew from his early days on the entertainment circuits.

Jackson continued recording for Paramount career until May 1930, including doing duets and accompaniments for Ma Rainey, Ida Cox, Hattie McDaniel, and even Blind Blake (who Jackson apparently viewed as an influence, although Blake was almost a decade younger). The label limped on for another two years after releasing Jackson before ceasing production. He did two more sessions for OKeh in 1934, and then an unreleased one in 1935 for ARC with Big Bill Broonzy (one of his former students), most of which were devoted to dirty blues, but audiences were apparently not buying what he was trying to sell. Papa Charlie died in 1938, largely forgotten. While not a virtuoso, Jackson was a repository of African American folk and popular songs from the beginning the twentieth (and probably the end of the nineteenth) century and was in many ways the male counterpart to Ma Rainey in that regard.

Blind Blake

We know considerably more about Arthur Blake than we do about other performers of his generation, largely because of intrepid sleuthing by blues scholars in the early 2000s. Due in large part to Alex van der Tuuk and several others, Blake's birthplace has been established as Newport News, Virginia, in 1896, and his death as being caused by the effects of tuberculosis in 1934.

How Blake came to be in Chicago in 1926 when he began his recording career is not known; his name does not appear in any contemporary source before advertisements for his Paramount recordings began to appear in the Black press. It is possible that he was recommended by record dealers in Virginia or Florida (where he apparently lived for much of his life), a not uncommon means of professional accession at the time. By that point he had evolved a complex and highly technical guitar technique that is an example of what has been called "Piedmont" style, which makes sense given his birthplace. Based to some degree in the style of ragtime piano, this guitar style emphasized a highly syncopated treble over a loping bass line and required an advanced technique, especially when the performer also sang, as Blake usually did.

Blake must have been an experienced entertainer by the time Paramount brought him into the studio; the company used him extensively to back other singers and instrumentalists. Discovered by producer J. Mayo Williams (possibly in retaliation over Williams's rival Art Laibly's success with Blind Lemon Jefferson), Blake brought a level of sophistication and showmanship that was well beyond any of the other male singers of the time (Galt, part 4, 1989, 11). In addition to his singing and guitar playing, he was an adept piano player as well, backing singers Bertha Henderson and Elzadie Robinson on several sides in an effective ragtime/blues style. Williams, who we have seen had a certain measure of prejudice about blues singers, felt that Blake was an artist and sought to help him find outside work as well.

Over the course of six years, Blake was on about eighty records that range from country blues and old-fashioned minstrel songs to ragtime to jazz. He appeared with other blues instrumentalists like Papa Charlie Jackson, Gus Cannon, and Charlie Spand; singers Ma Rainey, Leola Wilson, Laura Rucker, Bertha Henderson, and Irene Scruggs; jazz players Johnny Dodds, Tiny Parham, and Jimmy Bertrand; and even an unidentified bones player on one session. In addition to his own tunes he recorded somewhat camouflaged versions of songs by Clarence Williams and other composers and even did a gospel number.

With that type of variety in his repertoire he might be considered a songster, although he apparently did not travel a great deal. According to van der Tuuk, Blake lived in Jacksonville, Florida for most of the 1920s, traveling to Chicago (and then later to Richmond, Indiana and Grafton, Wisconsin) for his recording dates. He apparently toured with George Williams's *Happy Go Lucky* show in Black vaudeville in 1932 (Pecknold, 2013, 153) but no other theatrical association has come to light. The initial sales of Blake's records (especially "West Coast Blues"; Paramount 12387, August 1926) were extremely vigorous and encouraged Paramount to sign him to a contract of some sort that kept him recording sessions every spring and fall until June 1932 (although the last two years had significantly fewer issued records). He apparently earned fifty dollars per side and supplemented his income while in Chicago playing rent parties with other blues musicians (Obrecht, 79).

"West Coast Blues" (credited to Blake) was a significant hit for Paramount and was remarkable in that it was an instrumental with verbal interjections from Blake. Not a blues at all, it was essentially a dance number along the lines of "Ballin' the Jack," and in the square dance tradition with the performer calling out instructions to the dancers. After beginning with "Now we're going to the old country route" suggesting square dance, Blake then goes on to comment on women, supposedly in the audience, teasing the listeners with what he was going to be playing later in the tune, and even referencing "Maxwell House Coffee—good to the last drop." Based on a cyclic progression (C-E7-A7-D7-G7) common to many ragtime tunes and used by Blake on numerous recordings, "West Coast Blues" combined his finger picking virtuosity, humorous showmanship and the relentless beat that must have made him enormously popular at rent parties and functions.

A further testament to Blake's abilities comes on "Tootie Blues" (Paramount 12643, May 1928), in which he talks and sings his own lyrics on the refrain-styled blues, which repeats the middle four measures in an interesting variation. The real interest comes in his guitar accompaniment to his own vocals, which vary from a straight four to double-time figures. At the same time he sometimes harmonizes his own vocal line while not interrupting the rhythm and then answering his own phrases with extended single-note runs.

> Let me tell you what your sweet patootie will do, / take all
> your money and stay all night from you
> I'm wild about my tootie, only thing I crave [2x]
> Sweet patootie gonna carry me to my grave

Blake made relatively few purely instrumental sides, but "Guitar Chimes" and "Blind Arthur's Breakdown" (Paramount 12892, October 1929) are quite remarkable. Credited to "Blind Arthur," these two recordings demonstrate a significant virtuosity and a willingness to stretch some of the conventions of the blues as well. "Blind Arthur's Breakdown" uses shifting harmonies and a multistrain structure as well as a solid, dance-influenced rhythm. Chicago pianist Little Brother Montgomery recalled Blake playing in bands during the 1920s and knowing many popular tunes but preferring the blues (Barlow, 1989, 86).

By the end of his recording career, Blake's voice had taken on a rougher quality and his playing began to reflect some of the more "up-to-date" dance rhythms that presumably he was being required to play. A copy of "Miss Emma Liza," for years thought to be a lost record, turned up in a flea market in 2012 (Paramount 13115, January 1932). One of Blake's last recordings, it must be a fairly accurate representation of his abilities as a showman. Although he is credited as composer, the song is actually "Sweet Emmalina" by Andy Razaf and Jack Palmer. Blake's recording is clearly based on the Clarence Williams's Jazz Kings recording of April 10, 1928, even down to the falsetto vocals (imitating Emmalina/Emma Liza) (Columbia 145992), and his enthusiasm and humor are wonderfully evident on this track more than probably on any of his other recordings. If Papa Charlie Jackson is analogous to Ma Rainey, Blind Blake would have to be like Bessie Smith in his mastery of the newer styles of Black music and his unsurpassed musical abilities.

Blind Lemon Jefferson

Other than Bessie Smith, the most popular and influential African American artist to record in the 1920s was a somewhat rootless guitar player and singer from Wortham, Texas. Robert Springer presents a compelling case that Jefferson's (and to a lesser extent Ma Rainey's) records were so well known in rural Black areas that his lyrics influenced many subsequent singers, with certain formulas becoming virtually ubiquitous, largely due to his popularity (Springer, 2006, 164). Various accounts of his life suggest numerous birth dates, but census records indicate that he was born in 1893. His actual name was Lemmon, and he was born to Alex and Clarissa Jefferson as one of at least five children and several stepchildren from his mother's earlier marriage.

Born blind, Jefferson began playing guitar as a youth and by his teens was an active street performer in the surrounding areas, amassing a wide repertoire of pop songs, ballads, spirituals, and folk material, in addition to the emerging blues songs for which he later became known. He occasionally played with other musicians—mostly guitar and mandolin players—and he began singing to expand his audience. In addition to his performing, he also took advantage of his physical heft to supplement his income as an amateur wrestler, which would later expand to a bootlegging business.

Around 1912, Jefferson moved to Dallas where he played regularly in Deep Ellum, the Black section of town that was a center of music and carousing. Making his living as a street musician, he accumulated experience that was invaluable to his later recording career. During this period he traveled and performed with Huddie Ledbetter, a somewhat older musician who nevertheless looked up to Jefferson for his performing abilities, especially on guitar. He often had younger musicians leading him around in order to absorb some of his technique and style; the later blues star T. Bone Walker recalled helping Jefferson during the early 1920s, and passing the cup for audience tips.

By 1920 he had moved back to Wortham, at least for a while, although he would frequently return to Dallas and tour throughout the Delta and Texas panhandle regions. The White pianist John "Knocky" Parker recalled meeting Jefferson as well as other Black musicians in a Dallas bar when he was five or six years old (he was born in 1918), and being allowed to play piano with them (Parker interview, Hogan Jazz Archive, 1963). Parker's father was an employment agent for an agricultural company and would hire out-of-work musicians. The boy had been playing piano for several years and was adopted as a mascot by the older Black musicians.

It was during this phase of his career that Jefferson came to the attention of Paramount. Several stories exist of how the introduction came to pass, but the most likely is that a young record store clerk named Sammy Price (later to become a well-known blues and jazz pianist) or a record dealer named R. T. Ashford wrote a letter to Art Laibly, who came down and heard a street performance and was impressed enough to engage him to come to Chicago at the end of 1925 to begin recording.

Laibly may have heard Jefferson do some spirituals on the street, because the product of his first Paramount session was a pair religious songs that were released later in the year as by "Deacon L. J. Bates." The following session produced four sides, one coupling ("Got the Blues" and "Long Lonesome Blues," Paramount 12354, March 1926) becoming an unexpected success with the Black public. Although self-accompanied male performers had been making records for several years (most notably Papa Charlie Jackson), Jefferson was a very different prospect. With little or no professional stage experience, Jefferson represented a very new demographic. Laibly was extraordinarily lucky to find a performer as versatile; Jefferson was a singer with an exceptional range. His spiritual recordings have him singing in a resonant baritone while his later, more traditional blues extends his voice to a high tenor. In addition to that he was a guitarist of such remarkable technique that he was able to accompany himself in a free-floating and independent way (Parker recalled the guitarists he met as playing a "free" style of accompaniment that was not necessarily wedded to any metrical considerations).

As Calt and Wardlow pointed out, Jefferson's recordings were so unique as to be virtually uncoverable by other artists (unlike the efforts of most female singers of the day). This encouraged Paramount and other companies to begin hiring male performers with similar backgrounds to make original blues records. Laibly returned to Dallas to get Dad Nelson, Ramblin' Thomas and pianist Will Ezell (also remembered by Knocky Parker) and to Birmingham to find Bo Weevil Jackson (James Jackson). None of these artists made much of an impact, although as will be seen, Blind Blake (discovered by Mayo Williams) overshadowed all but Jefferson with his records. For most of his recording career Jefferson was a Paramount artist, although he did one session for OKeh in Atlanta in 1927, of which only two titles were issued. The Paramount publicity arm described Jefferson as "a sterling old-time guitar strumming blues singer from Dallas," clearly intending to locate him as an untutored performer in the oldest tradition (Obrecht, 2015, 59).

Perhaps of significance is the fact that those two OKeh titles were, if not actual covers, then at least inspired by earlier pieces. "Matchbox Blues" (OKeh 8455, March 14, 1927; he also recorded it twice in April 1927 for Paramount, both takes released as 12474) has as its centerpiece the verse that Ma Rainey used in "Long Lost Wandering Blues" (Paramount 12098, March 24, 1924).

> Sitting here wondering, would a matchbox hold my clothes [2x]
> I ain't so many matches, but I got so far to go

"Black Snake Moan" may have been inspired by Victoria Spivey's "Black Snake Blues," although it is difficult to hear much in common between the songs in terms of theme or even style. Spivey flatly accused Jefferson of co-opting her song, which she said originally had no overt sexual reference, but Jefferson is clearly mining the dirtier aspects of the imagery than was present on her first recording (OKeh 8338, May 11,

1926). Spivey's later "New Black Snake Blues" (a two-sided performance with Lonnie Johnson; OKeh 8626, October 13, 1928) seems to bow to the inevitable and meets Jefferson on his own ground. Jefferson recorded "Black Snake Moan" twice—Paramount 12407 (November 1926) and OKeh 8455 (March 14, 1927)—and also the related but much more driving "Black Snake Dream Blues" (Paramount 12510, June 1927).

"Beggin' Back" is an interesting and somewhat atypical performance by Jefferson. With a remarkably steady rhythm, even underneath his "talking vocal" sections, one can imagine this as a dance tune, although most of the performances we know of him doing are in the "songster" or busking tradition, with no mention of playing for formal dances. Most of the lyrics and form are redolent of a Victorian parlor song, although the second verse hints at some social protest (not a common thing during this period).

> Every evening, half past eight, / I'm laying around rich man's gate
> Workin' and studying, thinkin' out the plan, / How to get that biscuit out that rich man's hand
> Rich man's hand, rich man's hand, / how to get that biscuit out the rich man's hand

An example of Jefferson's guitar prowess (if not virtuosity) is on "Black Horse Blues" (Paramount 12367, April 1926). Interrupting his sung verses twice with long solos as well as an instrumental introduction, he focuses the record on the guitar, a very unusual procedure for him. This performance also highlights his well-recounted habit of adding or subtracting bars from a song's form to fit his accompaniment figures. Unfortunately, one of the unreleased OKeh records was a guitar solo on "English Stop Time," which would doubtless provide some fascinating perspective on his guitar influences (Monge & Evans, 2003). The lead sheet filed with the Library of Congress suggests that it was a simplified, single-strain ragtime tune.

Many of Jefferson's original tunes are clearly inspired by (if not based on) floating blues verses that can be found in many other blues of that period, as well as later eras (later recordings were more often than not directly inspired by his 1920s records). "Change My Luck Blues" (Paramount 12639, February 1928) uses the traditional "Elgin movements" image that Abbott and Seroff (2017, 70) have attributed to String Beans May as early as 1911.

> She's got Elgin movements, from her head down to her toes [2x]
> And she can break in on a dollar most anywhere she goes

Several of his tunes utilize the same basic melody, allying the practice with that of the early American hymn tradition, which fit many lyrics to preexisting tunes based on certain metric patterns.

Jefferson's recording career continued with numerous sessions for Paramount in Chicago in the winter/spring and then the fall from 1926 to 1929, ending with a marathon session in Richmond, Indiana, on September 24, 1929, producing twelve released sides. That date included the extraordinary "That Crawlin' Baby Blues" (Paramount 12880, September 24, 1929), which developed a layered text recounting infidelity, illegitimacy, and a female-centered narrative. Within three months, Jefferson had died on a street in Chicago under somewhat suspicious circumstances, although it was likely due to a heart attack.

Blind Lemon Jefferson might rightly be called the first "crossover" artist of the 1920s. His records were tremendously popular with African American communities who identified with his themes and delivery (Paramount also targeted those communities—even in rural areas—with their advertisements and marketing). White audiences also responded to his blend of humor and for the most part comprehensible singing, making him one of the best-selling artists of the decade (Obrecht, 58).

Lonnie Johnson

One of the most versatile musicians of the 1920s and well beyond was Lonnie Johnson. Born in New Orleans in 1894, Johnson began playing guitar and violin in his family band by the time he was a teenager. Bass player Pops Foster recalled the Johnsons playing on street corners in New Orleans, probably in the early 1910s (Foster and Stoddard, 1971, 107). By 1917 he had joined a theatrical company and made his way to England and Scotland, where he toured until about 1919, fortunately removing him from New Orleans at the height of the flu epidemic, which killed all his brothers and sisters except for the other musical son, James. Known as "Steady Roll," James played piano, guitar and violin (as did Lonnie) and spent most of his career in St. Louis.

In 1920 Lonnie Johnson left New Orleans following the close of Storyville and the deaths of his siblings and followed James to St. Louis, where he played frequently as well as working as a day laborer. The Johnsons were both able to read music and Lonnie began playing with cornet player Charlie Creath's orchestra, both locally and on the riverboats, recording with them in 1925. It was also in 1925 that he won a series of talent contests at a local theater, with the result being a record contract for OKeh, which was making regular recordings in St. Louis.

A series of featured records with either pianist De Loise Searcy or John Arnold and his brother James (on which both Johnsons played violin, piano, and guitar and sang) were made in St. Louis (and two sessions in New York, presumably during a theater tour) from November 1925 until the spring of 1927, when he moved to New York. These forty or so records supplanted those by Sylvester Weaver in the OKeh catalog and gave that company a bona fide star singing Downhome Blues.

Until the end of his life Johnson bristled at any suggestion that he was a "country blues" player or singer. He insisted that he had been raised in the city and his playing technique and experiences came from that background, which involved a wide variety of musical expression, only one of which was traditional blues. Part of his reason for moving to New York was apparently at the behest of OKeh, which saw him as a valuable commodity in the recording studio as well as commercially. During his first period there he recorded another dozen sides under his own name, although interestingly he only rarely appeared by himself; OKeh always paired him with at least a piano player, perhaps to deemphasize the rural taste of the Paramount records.

Johnson's next stop was Chicago at the end of 1927, where he remained for several months, making records under his own name as well as guesting with other OKeh stars—Bertha "Chippie" Hill, and especially, Louis Armstrong's Hot Seven and Hot Five—seamlessly fitting in with cutting edge jazz as well as blues players. The next three months found him going with the OKeh field unit (probably in tandem with a TOBA tour) to Memphis, San Antonio, and Dallas, recording with local musicians in each place.

The fall of 1928 found Johnson returning to New York and beginning the most fertile time of his recording career. In addition to continuing with his own series, he guested with Duke Ellington's Famous Orchestra,

McKinney's Cotton Pickers (as the Chocolate Dandies), Bessie Smith, King Oliver, and Victoria Spivey (who had recorded with him in St. Louis). His most remarkable collaboration was with the white jazz guitarist Eddie Lang, with whom he recorded ten duets, credited to "Lonnie Johnson and Blind Willie Dunn." These were remarkable tours de force that Johnson raved about later in life and balanced rural-sounding blues with amazingly sophisticated interplay and harmonic subtlety.

From the beginning of 1930 until his contract was not renewed in the middle of 1932, Johnson was compelled to record in the now popular "hokum" blues format with either Spivey, Clarence Williams, or the unrelated Spencer Williams, supplying songs that ranged from suggestive to downright pornographic. These records had reasonable sales but the Depression had put a virtual pause on the recording industry and also finished the TOBA circuit (which Johnson had toured throughout the 1920s, including a 1929 experience with a Bessie Smith show in which he and the star apparently carried on a lively affair). Johnson's marriage to Mary Johnson, who began an active blues singing career herself in 1929 for Brunswick, Paramount, and Decca, ended in 1932, which added to the difficulties that the early 1930s presented for most Black musicians. Johnson found work as a menial laborer in Chicago until his career was resuscitated with a series of solo and accompanying records for Decca and then Bluebird in the late 1930s.

After a switch to electric guitar in the 1940s, Johnson made a stab at playing rhythm and blues that did not succeed, and spent most of the 1950s working as a janitor and giving guitar lessons in Philadelphia. Another rediscovery in 1960 brought him to the attention of the blues revival community and he began touring the festival circuit and making records with jazz groups and even reuniting with Victoria Spivey. He lived his final years in Toronto as a respected historical figure, passing away in 1970.

It is difficult to draw many conclusions about Johnson's popularity based on his recorded repertoire, which covered more bases than practically any other performer of the day. His singing was doubtless a commercial asset on these records, although his voice was unremarkable and his blues singing seemed to favor one melodic form for the most part. The first series of recordings he did with his brother are interesting for the constantly shifting textures with all the different instruments. James also sings on two numbers issued under his own name, but his stentorian delivery did not succeed well enough to justify another session. The two did a guitar duet on "Nile of Genago" (OKeh 40695, January 20, 1926; it was the only one of Johnson's OKeh records to be issued in the general catalog, rather than the 8000 Race series), which sounds like the sort of Mexican waltz the Johnson family might have played on the streets of New Orleans fifteen years earlier; it can also be heard as a prototype for the Johnson/Lang duets of a few years later.

Johnson's own tunes are sometimes more interesting than his singing might suggest. "A Good Happy Home" (OKeh 8340, May 14, 1926) is one on which he sings and plays violin simultaneously, a trick he said guaranteed him a certain amount of work in St. Louis in his early days. A two-strain tune with the first being a minor AABA song of the "My Daddy Rocks Me" type, it changes to a major blues.

> (minor) I used to be happy, but I would not let that do [2x]
> I used to be happy but that wouldn't do I got no sweet woman to tell my troubles to
> I'm all alone baby, so are you
> (minor) I used to go out from my baby, I wouldn't stay the whole night long
> I used to go out from my baby, I wouldn't stay all night long, now someone's got my baby and gone
> Now I'm all alone, I mean I'm all alone
> (major) There is nothing like a good woman and a happy home [2x]
> There is nothing to worry 'bout—you don't have to be all alone

Johnson's singing here is more convincing than elsewhere, and his very elemental country fiddle style highlights both the dark mood of the verse and the positive answer of the chorus.

As mentioned earlier, OKeh seemed reluctant to present Johnson on record as a self-accompanied singer, although by the time he began traveling in the summer of 1927 to be featured with other OKeh stars, the company seemed more willing (perhaps because his usual accompanists were not with him). "Low Land Moan" (OKeh 8677, December 12, 1927) is one of his own tunes and comes as close as he ever did to a fundamental Downhome Blues.

> I went down to the levee, and over to the freight house yard [2x]
> They paid a dollar an hour, but the work was too long and hard.

There follow several fairly standard floating verses, but the song ends with

> Six months in the lowlands, has made some change [2x]
> To go back to my home baby, it'll be murder in the first degree.

The only giveaway that Johnson is not in fact a country blues singer is his precise attention to the meter of the song and his precise (almost studied) diction.

In some ways Lonnie Johnson's career trajectory is comparable to that of Ethel Waters. Both rose to national prominence as blues stars, although neither could be defined by any narrow category. While Waters went on to Broadway, film, and television, Johnson found artistic expression and probably fulfillment in playing with some of the most advanced and influential jazz players of the 1920s and 1930s, leading to his reinvention as a leader in several more idioms, including the party blues of the 1930s, rhythm and blues in the 1940s, and the revival movement of the 1960s.

Other Singers

By 1924 and 1925, Paramount began a program of recording practically any singer they could find in an effort to see what might resonate with the record-buying public. Mayo Williams and Art Laibly were apparently in competition to find Black performers to make race records and, as was inevitable, there were more misses than hits. Alice Pearson, Marie Bradley, Mattie Dorsey, and Star Page were all female singers who recorded a handful (or, in Page's case, just two) sides and then disappeared when the records failed to make a hit.

Sodarisa Miller was somewhat more successful, recording twelve sides over the course of her one year with the company from August 1924. On tunes such as "Sunshine Special" (Paramount 12276, April 1, 1925) she demonstrates a convincing blues feel, backed up by Jimmy Blythe's rolling piano accompaniment that clearly set the stage for the blues and boogie-woogie pianists of the next decade. Virtually nothing is known of her background, but according to census records she was born in Kentucky in or about 1900, and died in Chicago in 1973. On her death certificate she was listed as a "domestic," while the 1930 census does not list her occupation as "none," suggesting that she was not a professional entertainer, despite her recording career (she made two further records in 1927 for Victor following her year with Paramount but is not mentioned in any press releases other than record advertisements). It is tempting to assume her southern background gave her an exposure to country blues that resulted in her style, as well as the compositions credited to her—"Hot Springs Blues" (Paramount 12231 and test pressing, August 1924) and "Reckless Don't Care Mama Blues" (Paramount 12306, August 1925)—each of which allies itself more to the Downhome style with sequences of traditional blues verses.

One singer who does not fit easily into any category was Lillie Delk Christian. Born in 1896 in Mobile, Alabama, she lived her entire adult life in Chicago until she died in 1966. During the 1920s, she and her husband ran a rooming house where one of her tenants was the New Orleans banjo player Johnny St. Cyr, who was an active performer with a number of bands, including ones led by King Oliver, Louis Armstrong, Doc Cook, and Jelly Roll Morton. He had heard her singing around the house and brought her to the attention of OKeh, which engaged her to do a series of records that are chiefly remembered for the accompanying musicians, including St. Cyr, Jimmie Noone, Armstrong, and Earl Hines. Christian did not compose any of her material and her singing was definitely of the amateur variety, although by the 1930s she was touring with Carroll Dickerson's Orchestra (Christian interview, Hogan Jazz Archive, 1961).

Various road trips by record companies during the 1920s began turning up a large number of singers who would be classified as "Downhome." In New Orleans, trips by OKeh in 1924 and 1929, Columbia in 1926 and 1927, and Victor in 1927, recorded Lela Bolden, Ruth Green, Willie Jackson, Ann Cook, Alberta Brown, Genevieve Davis, Florence White, Dorothy Everetts, and Christina Gray, all accompanied by very traditional jazz bands or solo pianists. From Atlanta came Fannie Mae Goosby, Lucille Bogan, and Billy Bird; Dallas produced Ben Norsingle, Hattie Burleson, Lillian Glinn, Ollie Ross, and Hattie Hudson; while St. Louis was home to Mae Smith, Helen Humes, Ada Brown, Mary Bradford, Bertha Henderson, Cora Perkins, Missouri Anderson, Luella Miller, Irene Scruggs, Alma Henderson, and Mary Johnson.

Hokum

The final blues style to emerge in the 1920s came to be called "Hokum" and led directly into the "City Style" blues of the 1930s. Papa Charlie

Jackson is usually credited with beginning the style with his recording of "Shake That Thing" in 1925, but elements of the style can be heard in other blues as well as string band recordings and even some of the husband-and-wife cross-talk acts.

Roberta Schwartz proposes using the term *city style* to cover the party blues of the 1930s that ran the gamut from the Decca recordings of the Harlem Hamfats and Big Bill Broonzy to the "Bluebird Blues" that Lester Melrose recorded on the Bluebird label. The early 1930s recordings of the Hokum Boys, the State Street Ramblers, and Memphis Ramblers are also part of this continuum (Schwartz, 2018).

Hokum as a style was defined by humor, double entendre, and a generally upbeat tempo that went over well at rent parties, speakeasies, and other situations known as "temporary entertainment venues" (Schwartz, 2018, 368). One element embraced by the hokum musicians was boogie-woogie, which became a key component of the 1930s scene as well. Following Jackson's lead, the guitarist and singer Tampa Red joined forces with pianist Georgia Tom Dorsey to compose a follow-up, which became one of the most popular tunes of the 1920s, "It's Tight Like That."

Georgia Tom was in fact Thomas A. Dorsey, who had been active as a blues composer and performer since the late 1910s, when he was learning his craft in Atlanta while listening to Bessie Smith and Ma Rainey. Following his move to Chicago in the early 1920s, he became known as a composer and bandleader, leading Rainey's band following her initial success on records. By the late 1920s, he had been working as an arranger and transcriber for Paramount Records but had entered a fallow professional period as a performer. Tampa Red was born Hudson Woodbridge in Georgia in 1903, but was raised in Florida, where he took on the surname Whittaker and learned to play guitar. By the 1920s he was in Chicago and playing rent parties and even on the streets when he met Dorsey and began recording with Ma Rainey.

By 1928, the race recording industry had moved toward less professional performers, ideally ones who would bring their own material that was free of copyright restrictions. After making the acquaintance of Mayo Williams at Paramount (which Williams was about to leave), Woodbridge enlisted Dorsey to write some songs that Williams would be interested in recording. They apparently composed "It's Tight Like That" in the fall of 1928, and made several unsuccessful attempts at recording it, but finally they succeeded in September, waxing a version that became a runaway hit (Vocalion 1216, October 24, 1928).

It's Tight Like That

First Chorus
Dorsey/Whittaker
F F7 B♭ B♭m F C7 F F7 B♭ B♭m
Lis ten her folks I'm gon na sing a little song but you mus n't get mad 'cause I
F F7 B♭7 B♭7 Fm7 F
mean you no wrong, oh it's tight like that be edle um bum oh it's tight like that
F C7 F♯dim G7 C7 F B♭ F
be edle um bum hear me talk in to you you know it's tight like that

Basically a refrain blues using some of the melodic material of "Shake That Thing," "It's Tight Like That" capitalized on a common phrase in African American culture at the time and produced a string of re-recordings (several by Tampa Red and Georgia Tom) and covers (by Jimmie Noone, McKinney's Cotton Pickers, and Clara Smith, among others). Along with the trend toward the "smutty" blues sung by most of the established blues singers, Hokum extended the life of the race records industry at least to the Depression. Woodbridge is given credit for taking the rural blues style he presumably learned as a boy and gentrifying it through a spotless guitar technique and clean vocal style, which allowed him to have a busy career up through the 1940s, both as a performer and as a producer/composer of the city blues style.

Conclusion

The End of the Era

Following the example of Blind Lemon Jefferson's success at Paramount, other companies began recording solo blues guitarists and singers from the country tradition. Many of these were discovered as a result of the company's field trips to various southern locations, which were done in the interest of casting a wide net in the hopes of catching a few lucrative fish. As Paul Oliver details in *Barrelhouse Blues*, by the late 1920s many companies were making regular trips to centers like Atlanta, Memphis, Dallas, San Antonio, and New Orleans in the hopes that a regional singer or act might hit it big. While relatively few Black performers were so fortunate, White entertainers like Jimmie Rodgers and the Carter Family became nationally known through their records made at these sessions.

Nevertheless, a large number of Black musicians were captured on records in this manner—some on only a few, some for much longer. Barbecue Bob (Robert Hicks) was a successful recording artist for Columbia from 1927 to 1930, after his initial session in Atlanta. Blind Willie McTell occupied the same territory for Victor, although he also recorded at the same time for Columbia as Blind Sammie, and his career continued into the 1950s. Peg Leg Howell also emerged from Atlanta to make a long series of recordings for Columbia from 1926 to 1929. Jim Jackson began recording for Vocalion in 1927, and then switched to Victor the following year before returning to Vocalion in 1929, creating a series of about forty very elemental rural blues performances that had a measure of popularity. Furry Lewis's recording career was an almost exact duplicate of Jackson's, although with only half the released sides.

Mississippi and Delta-style guitarist/singers became popular at the very end of the 1920s with Mississippi John Hurt, Son House, Tommy

Johnson, Joe McCoy, Memphis Minnie, and even Big Bill Broonzy beginning their recording careers in the last year or so of the decade. Although he recorded a handful of sides in Chicago that fall generally into the Hokum category in the late 1920s, Broonzy did not hit his stride until the next decade in the "City Blues." Far more important and productive in the transitional phase were the recordings by guitarist Scrapper Blackwell and pianist Leroy Carr, who combined rural blues with hokum in a long series of recordings for Vocalion from 1928 to 1934, and then a short series for Victor (Blackwell had a concurrent series of solo recordings for Vocalion and Gennett).

String bands also became targets of recording director's plans as well. The Mississippi Sheiks and the Beale Street Sheiks were two groups whose records (for Paramount and OKeh, respectively) became surprisingly popular at the very end of the decade, and even more at the beginning of the Depression. The example of these groups caused some Black string bands exploring earlier repertoire to record during the 1930s, but their real influence came on White groups who were initially marketed as "hillbilly" bands.

These above-mentioned singers and instrumentalists were much more allied with the music that was to come in the 1930s, rather than what was going on in the 1920s. By 1929, the recording companies and directors such as Mayo Williams and Ralph Peer were beginning to realize the sales potential for rural, Downhome Blues records. The fact that there was little or no overhead associated with these sessions (which generally included only one or two musicians performing original songs not encumbered by copyright) made them even more attractive. The death of vaudeville and the touring entertainment circuits (including the TOBA, which essentially struck its tent in 1930, when Sherman Dudley sold off his theaters) caused by a combination of the Depression, radio, and sound film, signaled an end to the recording careers of most of the vaudeville and cabaret singers of the previous decade (Oliver, 2009, 116), although some transitioned into other branches of performance and several saw career revivals in subsequent decades.

While the two greatest stars of the era, Bessie Smith and Ma Rainey, did not live long enough to benefit by rediscovery, several of their contemporaries did; Ida Cox and Trixie Smith both began recording again in the late 1930s and continued touring into the 1940s, while Mamie Smith found work in the movies during the 1930s and '40s. Ethel Waters never retired; she continued her movie and Broadway career in the 1930s, and even performed on television in the 1950s and '60s; while Edith Wilson had a lucrative (if controversial) endorsement career as the face of Aunt Jemima. After a long second career as a nurse, Alberta Hunter emerged from retirement in the late 1960s, still singing well and embarking on a third career as a touring and recording singer, as did Victoria Spivey, Sippie Wallace, and even Ida Cox and Lucille Hegamin.

The vast majority of the entertainers I have discussed here did not have the opportunity for a second act, as it were. Many died—often from the long-term results of the touring lifestyle some had endured for decades—and some simply disappeared, their identities possibly merging with a new husband's and a devotion to domesticity. Even in that case, they doubtless had many exciting memories to look back on from their more peaceful and anonymous final years.

Bibliography

General

Abbott, Lynn, and Doug Seroff. *Out of Sight: The Rise of African American Popular Music, 1889–1895*. Jackson: University Press of Mississippi, 2002.

———. *Ragged but Right: Black Travelling Shows, "Coon Songs," and the Dark Pathway to Blues and Jazz*. Jackson: University Press of Mississippi, 2007.

———. *The Original Blues: The Emergence of the Blues in African American Vaudeville 1899–1926*. Jackson: University Press of Mississippi, 2017.

Albertson, Chris. *Bessie: Expanded and Revised Edition*. New Haven, CT: Yale University Press, 2003.

Allen, Walter C. *Hendersonia: The Music of Fletcher Henderson and His Musicians*. Highland Park, NJ: Jazz Monographs No. 4, 1973.

Antelyes, Peter. "Red Hot Mamas: Bessie Smith, Sophie Tucker and the Ethnic Maternal Voice in American Popular Music," in *Embodied Voices: Representing Female Vocality in Western Culture*, edited by Leslie C. Dunn and Nancy A. Jones. Cambridge, UK: Cambridge University Press, 1994.

Arvey, Verna, with B. A. Nugent. *In One Lifetime*. Fayetteville: University of Arkansas Press, 1984.

Baker, Jean-Claude, and Chris Chase. *Josephine: The Hungry Heart*. New York: Cooper Square Press, 2001 (originally published 1993).

Baker, R. S. "Justin Ring's Fifty Years on Record." *Syncopated Times*, https://syncopatedtimes.com/justin-rings-fifty-years-on-record/, July 25, 2019. Accessed March 9, 2022.

Balfour, Alan. Notes to *Eva Taylor in Chronological Order Volume 1* (DOCD 5408), *Volume 2* (DOCD 5409), and 3 (DOCD 5410). Document Records, 1995.

Barlow, William. *Looking Up at Down: The Emergence of Blues Culture*. Philadelphia, PA: Temple University Press, 1989.

Bastin, Bruce, with Kip Lornell. *Melody Man: Joe Davis and the New York Music Scene, 1916–1978*. Jackson: University of Mississippi Press, 2012.

Bernhardt, Clyde, with Sheldon Harris. *I Remember: Eighty Years of Black Entertainment, Big Bands, and the Blues*. Philadelphia: University of Pennsylvania Press, 1986.

Blesh, Rudi. *Shining Trumpets: A History of Jazz*. New York: A. A. Knopf, 1946.

Bogle, Donald. *Heat Wave: the Life and Career of Ethel Waters*. New York: Harper Collins, 2011.

Bradford, Perry. *Born with the Blues: Perry Bradford's Own Story*. New York: Oak Publications, 1965.

Brayboy, Bryan McKinley Jones, "Toward a Tribal Critical Race Theory in Education." *Urban Review* XXXVII, no. 5 (December 2005).

Breaux, Michael Shane. "Just a Buncha Clowns: Comedic Anarchy and Racialized Performance in Black Vaudeville, the Chop Suey Circuit, and las Carpas," PhD diss., Graduate Center, City University of New York, 2019.

Brooks, Edward. *The Bessie Smith Companion: A Critical and Detailed Appreciation of the Recordings*. New York: Da Capo Press, 1982.

Brooks, Tim. *Lost Sounds: Blacks and the Birth of the Recording Industry, 1890–1919*. Urbana: University of Illinois Press, 2004.

Brundage, W. Fitzhugh, ed. *Beyond Blackface: African-Americans and the Creation of American Popular Culture, 1890–1930*. Chapel Hill: University of North Carolina Press, 2011.

Bushell, Garvin, as told to Mark Tucker. *Jazz from the Beginning*. Ann Arbor, MI: University of Michigan Press, 1988.

Calt, Stephen, with Gayle Dean Wardlow. "The Anatomy of a 'Race' Label" in seven parts. *78 Quarterly*, no's. 3–7 (1988–1992).

Charters, Samuel B., with Leonard Kunstadt. *Jazz: A History of the New York Scene*. New York: Da Capo, 1981.

———. *Country Blues*. New York: Da Capo, 1975.

Cheatham, Adolphus "Doc," with Alyn Shipton. *I Guess I'll Get the Papers and Go Home: The Life of Doc Cheatham*. London: Cassell, 1995.

Cherry, Randall. "Ethel Waters: Long, Lean, Lanky Mama," in *Nobody Knows Where the Blues Come From: Lyrics and History*, edited by Robert Springer. Jackson: University of Mississippi Press, 2006.

Chilton, John. *Ride, Red, Ride: the life of Henry Red Allen*. New York: Cassell, 1989.

Clark, John. *Experiencing Bessie Smith: A Listener's Companion*. Lanham, MD: Rowman and Littlefield, 2017.

Cone, James H. *The Spirituals and the Blues: An Interpretation*. Maryknoll, NY: Orbis Books, 1991.

Coolen, Michael Theodore. "The Fodet: A Senegambian Origin for the Blues?" *The Black Perspective in Music* 10, no. 1 (Spring 1982): 69–84.

Crenshaw, Kimberle. "Demarginalizing the Intersection of Race and Sex: A Black Feminist Critique of Antidiscrimination Doctrine, Feminist Theory and Antiracist Politics," *University of Chicago Legal Forum* I, no. 8 (1989).

Cushing, Steve. *Blues before Sunrise: The Radio Interviews*. Urbana: University of Illinois Press, 2010.

Dahl, Linda. Stormy *Weather: The Music and Lives of a Century of Jazzwomen*. London: Quartet Books, 1984.

Davis, Angela Y. *Blues Legacies and Black Feminism*. New York: Vintage Books, 1998.

Davis, David, and Ivo De Loo. "Black Swan Records, 1921–1924: From a Swanky Swan to a Dead Duck." https://journals.sagepub.com/doi/abs/10.1177/103237320300800203. Accessed January 2, 2022.

Decker, Todd, "The 'Most Distinctive and Biggest Benefit That Broadway Has Ever Known': Producing, Performing and Applauding across the Color Line in the Twilight of the Jazz Age," in *Rethinking American Music*, edited by Tara Browner and Thomas L. Riis. Urbana: University of Illinois Press, 2019.

Dinerstein, Joel. *Swinging the Machine: Modernity, Technology, and African American Culture between the World Wars*. Amherst: University of Massachusetts Press, 2003.

Dixon, Robert M. W., John Goodrich, and Howard W. Rye. *Blues and Gospel Records: 1890–1943*. Oxford, UK: Clarendon Press, 1997.

Dolan, Mark K. "Extra! Chicago Defender Race Records Ads Show South from Afar." *Southern Cultures* XIII, no. 3 (fall 2007): 106–24.

Dunn, Leslie C., and Nancy A. Jones, ed. *Embodied Voices: Representing Female Vocality in Western Culture*. Cambridge. UK: Cambridge University Press, 1994.

Durham, Topsy M. *Swingin' the Blues: The Virtuosity of Eddie Durham*. Self-published: 2021.

Evans, David. *Big Road Blues: Tradition and Creativity in the Folk Blues*. Berkeley, CA: Da Capo Press, 1982.

———, ed. *Ramblin' on My Mind: New Perspectives on the Blues*. Urbana: University of Illinois Press, 2008.

Field, Andrew David. "The Fate of the Low-Key Bill Hegamin, Jazz Pianist, in Shanghai,"

http://shanghaisojourns.net/shanghais-dancing-world/2018/6/27/the-fate-of-the-low-key-bill-hegamin-jazz-pianist-in-shanghai. Accessed December 14, 2021.

Filzen, Sarah. "The Rise and Fall of Paramount Records." *Wisconsin Magazine of History* 82, no. 2 (Winter 1998–1999).

Floyd, Samuel A., Jr. *The Power of Black Music: Interpreting Its History from Africa to the United States*. New York: Oxford University Press, 1995.

Foster, Pops, with Tom Stoddard. *The Autobiography of Pops Foster: New Orleans Jazz Man*. Berkeley, CA: University of California Press, 1971.

Gates, Henry Louis, Jr. *The Signifying Monkey: A Theory of African American Literary Criticism*. Oxford, UK: Oxford University Press, 1989.

Gates, Henry Louis, Jr., and Evelyn Brooks Higginbotham, ed. *Harlem Renaissance Lives: From the African American National Biography*. Oxford, UK: Oxford University Press, 2009.

Gelatt, Roland. *The Fabulous Phonograph: 1877–1977*. New York: Macmillan, 1977.

Gilbert, Douglas. *American Vaudeville: Its Life and Times*. New York: Dover Publications, (1940) 1963.

Gittelman, Lisa. *Scripts, Grooves and Writing Machines: Representing Technology in the Edison Era*. Stanford, CA: Stanford University Press, 1999.

Griffin, Farah Jasmine. "When Malindy Sings: A Meditation on Black Women's Vocality," in *Uptown Conversation: The New Jazz Studies*, edited by Robert G. O'Meally, Brent Hayes Edwards, and Farah Jasmine Griffin. New York: Columbia University Press, 2004.

Gottschild, Brenda Dixon. *Waltzing in the Dark: African American Vaudeville and Race Politics in the Swing Era*. New York: Palgrave, 2000.

Gushee, Lawrence. *Pioneers of Jazz: The Story of the Creole Band*. London: Oxford University Press, 2010.

Gussow, Adam. "W. C. Handy and the 'Birth' of the Blues." *Southern Culture* XXIV, no. 4 (Winter 2008).

Handy, W. C. *The Father of the Blues: An Autobiography*. New York: Macmillan, 1941.

Harris, Michael W. *The Rise of Gospel Blues: The Music of Thomas Andrew Dorsey in the Urban Church*. Oxford, UK: Oxford University Press, 1992.

Harrison, Daphne Duval. *Black Pearls: Blues Queens of the 1920s*. New Brunswick, NJ: Rutgers University Press, 1988.

Harrison-Kahan, Lori. *The White Negress: Literature, Minstrelsy, and the Black-Jewish Imaginary*. New Brunswick, NJ: Rutgers University Press.

Harwood, Ronald P. "Mighty Tight Woman: The Thomas Family and Classic Blues" *Storyville* 17 (June–July 1968).

Haymes, Max. Liner notes to "Ma Rainey: Mother of the Blues," 5-CD set. JSP Records, 2007.

Hennessey, Thomas J. *From Jazz to Swing: African-American Jazz Musicians and Their Music, 1890–1935*. Detroit, MI: Wayne State University Press, 1994.

Hillman, Chris. "Ida Cox: Last Mile Blues," *Jazz Journal* XXI, no. 6 (June 1968).

House, Roger. *Blue Smoke: The Recorded Journey of Big Bill Broonzy*. Baton Rouge: Louisiana State University Press, 2010.

Horton, Luke. "Perry Bradford: The Man Who Sold the Blues." *Australasian Journal of American* Studies XXXI, no. 2 (December 2013).

Hunter, Alberta, with Frank C. Taylor and Gerald Cook. *Alberta Hunter: A Celebration in Blues*. New York: McGraw Hill, 1987.

Iyer, Vijay. "Beneath Improvisation," in *The Oxford Handbook of Critical Concepts in Music Theory*, edited by Alexander Rehding and Steven Rings. www.oxfordhandbooks.com.

Kent, Drew. "Blind Blake: The Vanished Bluesman," liner notes to *Blind Blake Remastered: All the Published Sides* (four CDs). JSP Records, 2003.

Komara, Edward. "Suitcases full of Blues: The Revenant/Third Man Paramount 'Cabinet of Wonder.'" *ARSC Journal* 46, no. 2 (Fall 2015).

Kunstadt, Len. "Rosa Henderson, Yesterday and Today," 1963 interview. *Record Research 75* (April 1966).

Laird, Ross, and Brian Rust. *Discography of OKeh Records, 1918–1934*. New York: Greenwood, 2004.

Levine, Lawrence W. *Black Culture and Black Consciousness: Afro-American Folk Thought from Slavery to Freedom*. Oxford, UK: Oxford University Press, 1977.

Lieb, Sandra. *Mother of the Blues: A Study of Ma Rainey*. Amherst: University of Massachusetts Press, 1981.

Lief, Shane, http://www.bluescenter.com/tag/anthony-maggio/. Accessed July 22, 2021.

Lindstrom, Bo. Oh Joe, Play That Trombone: The Life and Music of George L. Brashear. Sweden: self-published, 2018.

Lomax, Alan. *Mister Jelly Roll: The Fortunes of Jelly Roll Morton, New Orleans Creole and "Inventor of Jazz."* Berkeley: University of California Press, 1970."Looking Back with Eva, Part I." *Storyville* 14 (December 1967–January 1968).

"Looking Back with Eva, Part II." *Storyville* 14 (February–March 1968).

Luhrssen, David. "Blues in Wisconsin: The Paramount Records Story." *Wisconsin Academy Review* (1988).

Mahar, William J. *Behind the Burnt Cork Mask: Early Blackface Minstrelsy and Antebellum American Popular* Culture. Urbana: University of Illinois Press, 1999.

Malone, Jaqui. *Steppin' on the Blues: Visible Rhythms of African American Dance*. Urbana: University of Illinois Press, 1996.

Mazor, Barry. *Ralph Peer and the Making of Popular Roots Music*. Chicago: Chicago Review Press, 2015.

Millard, Andrew. *America on Record*. Cambridge, UK: Cambridge University Press, 1995.

Miller, Karl Hagstrom. *Segregating Sound: Inventing Folk and Pop Music in the Era of Jim Crow*. Durham, NC: Duke University Press, 2010.

Monge, Luigi, and David Evans. "New Songs of Blind Lemon Jefferson." Berkeley Electronic Press. http://citeseerx.ist.psu.edu/viewdoc/download?doi=10.1.1.544.8941&rep=rep1&type=pdf, 2003. Accessed January 23, 2022.

Montgomery, R. C. http://oldtimeblues.net/tag/elzadie-robinson/, 2019. Accessed January 11, 2022.

Morgenstern, Dan, edited by Sheldon Meyer. *Living with Jazz: A Reader*. New York: Pantheon Books, 2004.

Muir, Peter. *Popular Blues in America: 1850–1920*. Urbana: University of Illinois Press, 2010.

Neely, Jack. *Knoxville: The Obscure Prismatic City*. Charleston, SC: History Press, 2009.

Niles, John Jacob. "Shout, Coon, Shout," *Musical Quarterly* XVI, no. 4, October 1930.

O'Meally, Robert G., ed. *The Jazz Cadence of American Culture*. New York: Columbia University Press, 1998.

Oakley, Giles. *The Devil's Music: A History of the Blues*. New York: Da Capo Press, (1976) 1997.

Obrecht, Jas. *Early Blues: The First Stars of Blues Guitar*. Minneapolis: University of Minnesota Press, 2015.

Oliver, Paul. *Blues Fell This Morning: Meaning in the* Blues. Cambridge, UK: Cambridge University Press, 1960.

———. Screening *the Blues: Aspects of the Blues Tradition*. New York: Da Capo, 1968.

———. *Songsters and Saints: Vocal Traditions on Race Records*. Cambridge, UK: Cambridge University Press, 1984.

———. *Barrelhouse Blues: Location Recording and the Early Traditions of the Blues*. Philadelphia, PA: Perseus Books, 2009.

Pecknold, Dianne, ed. *Hidden in the Mix: The African-American Presence in Country Music*. Durham, NC: Duke University Press, 2013.

Ramsey, Guthrie P., Jr. "Bodies of Music/Songs of Magic," in *Rethinking American Music*, edited by Tara Browner and Thomas L. Riis. Urbana: University of Illinois Press, 2019.

Riis, Thomas, L. *Just before Jazz: Black Musical Theater in New York, 1890–1915*. Washington, DC: Smithsonian Institution Press, 1989.

Rimmer, Caitlin Margaret. "Queer and Moaning: Queen of the Moaners Clara Smith," Master of Arts Thesis. Chapel Hill: University of North Carolina, 2018.

Robinson, Cedric J. *Forgeries of Memory & Meaning: Blacks & the Regimes of Race in American Theater & Film before World War II*. Chapel Hill: University of North Carolina Press, 2007.

Rodger, Gillian M. *Champagne Charlie and Pretty Jemima: Variety Theater in the Nineteenth Century*. Urbana: University of Illinois Press, 2010.

Rowe, Mike. Notes to "Margaret Johnson, 1923–1927." Document Records, 1996.

Russell, Tony (series edited by Paul Oliver). *Blacks and Whites and Blues*. New York: Stein and Day, 1970.

Rust, Brian. *Jazz on Record, 1897–1943* (two volumes). New York: Arlington House, 1978.

Rye, Howard. Notes to "Viola McCoy/Julia Moody: Complete Recorded Works, Volume 2." Document Records, 1995.

———. Notes to "Laura Smith: Complete Recorded Works in Chronological Order, Volume 1, 1924–1927." Document Records, 1996.

Schwartz, Roberta Freund. "How Blue Can You Get? It's Tight Like That and the Hokum Blues." *American Music* XXXVI, no. 3 (Fall 2018).

Shapiro, Nat, and Nat Hentoff. *Hear Me Talkin' to Ya: The Story of Jazz as Told by the Men Who Made It*. New York: Dover Publications, 1966.

Slout, William L. *Theatre in a Tent: The Development of Tent Repertoire*. San Bernadino, CA: Emeritus Enterprise Book, 2000.

Smith, Willie. "The Lion" with George Hoefer. *Music on My Mind: The Memoirs of an American Pianist*. New York: Da Capo, 1978.

Southern, Eileen. *The Music of Black Americans: A History*. New York: W. W. Norton, 1971.

———, ed. *Readings in Black American Music*. New York: W. W. Norton, 1983.

Stallings, L. H. *Intersections of Folklore, Vernacular, Myth and Queerness in Black Female Culture*. Columbus: Ohio State University Press.

Stein, Charles W., ed. *American Vaudeville as Seen by Its Contemporaries*. New York: Alfred A. Knopf, 1984.

Stewart-Baxter, Derek, "Farewell Rosa Henderson," *Jazz Journal* (July 1968).

———. *Ma Rainey and the Classic Blues Singers*. New York: Stein and Day, 1970.

Stoever, Jennifer Lynn. *The Sonic Color Line: Race and the Cultural Politics of Listening*. New York: New York University Press, 2016.

Strausbaugh, John. *Black Like You: Blackface, Whiteface, Insult & Imitation in American Popular Culture*. New York: Jeremy P. Tarcher/Penguin, 2006.

Suisman, David. "Co-Workers in the Kingdom of Culture: Black Swan Records and the Political Economy of African American Music." *Journal of American History* XC, no. 4 (March 2004).

Sylvan, Robin. *Traces of the Spirit: The Religious Dimensions of Popular Music*. New York: New York University Press, 2002.

Taylor, Frank C. *Alberta Hunter: A Celebration in Blues*. New York: McGraw-Hill, 1987.

Terry, Clark, with Gwen Terry. *The Autobiography of Clark* Terry. Berkeley: University of California Press, 2011.

Tick, Judith, and Paul Beaudoin, ed. *Music in the USA: A Documentary Companion*. Oxford, UK: Oxford University Press, 2008.

Titon, Jeff Todd. *Early Downhome Blues: A Musical and Cultural Analysis* (2nd ed.). Chapel Hill: University of North Carolina Press, 1994.

Toll, Robert C. *Blacking Up: The Minstrel Show in Nineteenth-Century America*. London: Oxford University Press, 1974.

Townley, Eric, with Ronald P. Harwood. "The Texas Nightingale: Sippie Wallace." *Storyville* 108 (August–September 1983).

Tracy, Steven C., ed. *Write Me a Few of Your Lines: A Blues Reader*. Amherst: University of Massachusetts Press, 1999.

———. Liner notes to *Josie Miles Complete Recorded Works in Chronological Order, Volume 1* (DOCD 5066) and *Volume 2* (DOCD 5467), Document Records, 1996.

———. Liner notes to *Hociel Thomas and Lillie Delk Christian in Chronological Order, 1925–1928* (DOCD 5448), Document Records, 1996.

Van Der Merwe, Peter. *Origins of the Popular Style: The Antecedents of Twentieth Century Popular Music*. Oxford, UK: Clarendon Press, 1989.

Van Der Tuuk, Alex. "Aletha Dickerson: Paramount's Reluctant Recording Manager." http://www.vjm.biz/new_page_18.htm. Accessed January 2, 2022.

———. "In Search of Blind Blake." Paramount 12231 and test pressing, recorded August 1924. https://sundayblues.org/wp-content/uploads/2012/06/BR263-Blind-Blake.pdf. Accessed January 16, 2022.

"Victoria Spivey." https://blues.org/blues_hof_inductee/victoria-spivey/. Accessed December 26, 2021.

Vincent, Ted. "The Social Context of Black Swan Records," *Living Blues* 86 (May–June 1989).

———. *Keep Cool: The Black Activists Who Built the Jazz Age*. London: Pluto Press, 1995.

Waters, Ethel, and Charles Samuels. *His Eye Is on the Sparrow: An Autobiography by Ethel Waters*. Garden City, NY: Doubleday, 1951.

Watkins, Mel. *On the Real Side: Laughing, Lying, and Signifying: The Underground Tradition of African-American Humor That Transformed American Culture from Slavery to Richard Pryor*. New York: Simon and Schuster, 1994.

Weusi, Jitu K. "The Rise and Fall of Black Swan Records." https://syncopatedtimes.com/the-rise-and-fall-of-black-swan-records/. Accessed January 2, 2022.

White, Alan. "Blues Locations: Georgia, Columbus." http://earlyblues.org/blues-locations-georgia-columbus/. Accessed January 2, 2021.

Wilson, James F. *Bulldaggers, Pansies, and Chocolate Babies: Performance, Race, and Sexuality in the Harlem Renaissance*. Ann Arbor: University of Michigan Press, 2010.

Wilson, Karen. "Harlem Wisdom in a Wild Woman's Blues: The Cool Intellect of Ida Cox." *Afro-Americans in New York Life and History* 30, no. 2 (July 2006).

Woll, Allen. *Black Musical Theatre: From Coontown to Dreamgirls*. Baton Rouge: Louisiana State University Press, 1989.

Young, Alan. *Woke Me Up This Morning: Black Gospel Singers and the Gospel Life*. Jackson: University Press of Mississippi, 1997.

Newspaper Articles

Afro-American. December 2, 1921, 10.

———. April 27, 1922.

"Alexander Tolliver's Big Show." *The Freeman*, November 20, 1915, 6.

"At the New Crown Garden in Indianapolis." *The Freeman* December 21, 1914.

"Beans and Susie Observe 30th Year in Show Whirl." *Afro-American*, November 1, 1947.

"Billboardings." *Chicago Defender*, January 3, 1925, 7.

Bragg, Columbus. "On and Off the Stroll." *Chicago Defender*, October 10, 1914.
———. "On and Off the Stroll." *Chicago Defender*, November 7, 1914, 6.
"Butterbeans Breaks Down and Gives Secret of Tight Pants." *Afro-American*, January 14, 1928.
Calvin, Floyd. "Monette Moore Rises from Scrubbing Hotel Floors to Broadway Stardom." *Pittsburgh Courier*, March 4, 1933.
"Champion Blues Singer Here." *African-American*, April 11, 19
Chicago Defender, September 20, 1924, 6.24.
"Clara Smith Is No Blues Singer." *Afro-American*, May 22, 1926, 4B.
"Crown Garden Opens . . ." *The Freeman*, December 9, 1911, 5.
"Dead: Billy Higgins, Noted Comedian." *New York Age*, April 24, 1937.
"Ethel Waters Hurt." *Afro-American* October 23, 1922.
"F. A. Barrasso." *The Freeman*, February 11, 1911.
"Fame and Fortune: 'Blues' on Discs Making Race Composers Rich." *Chicago Defender*, October 6, 1923.
Hayes, Bob. "In Bamville in for a Run at Illinois: Grand, Monogram and Avenue and All Have Vaudeville." *Chicago Defender*, April 12, 1924.
———. "Let's Go . . ." *Chicago Defender*, February 23, 1924, 6.
———. "Ma Rainey Packs 'em in at the Monogram." *Chicago Defender*, February 21, 1925.
———. "Ma Rainey Review." *Chicago Defender*, February 13, 1926.
———. "Here and There." *Chicago Defender*, November 23, 1929.
———. "Here and There." *Chicago Defender*, February 13, 1936.
"Hit Bits from Africana." *New York Amsterdam News*, November 9, 1927.
Jackson, J. A. *Afro-American*, May 11, 1923.
"Jazz as Is Jazz." *Los Angeles Times*, August 17, 1924, B28.
Johnson, Ziggy. "Zagging with Ziggy." *Michigan Chronicle*, November 15, 1952.
Jones, William H. "Ma Rainey's Gang Invades Chicago." *Pittsburgh Courier*, July 2, 1927.
"Laura Smith Back." *Chicago Defender*, March 23, 1918, 7.
"Laura Smith Better." *Chicago Defender*, May 30, 1925.
"Laura Smith Up Again." *Chicago Defender*, December 19, 1925.
"Lincoln: Billy Mack's Company." *Afro-American*, July 7, 1922, 5.
"Lincoln Theater, New Orleans." *The Freeman*, October 7, 1916, 4.
Loomis, Joe, *Chicago Defender*, May 29, 1920, 4.
Matthews, Ralph. "A Comic with a Number of Odd Records," *Afro American*, February 22, 1936.
Means, J. M., "Rabbit's Foot Company," January 14, 1913, 6.
"Musicians Will Not Follow Star into Crackerland." *Afro-American*, February 9, 1922.
"New Group." *Chicago Defender*, January 23, 1923.
"New Orleans Theaters." *The Freeman*, May 31, 1913, 5.

"Notes from Florida." *The Freeman*, January 1, 1916.
"OKeh Notes." *Chicago Defender*, October 6, 1923, 7).
"Palace Theater at Houston, Texas." April 2, 1910.
"Perry Bradford Sent to the Penitentiary." *New York Amsterdam News*, January 17, 1923.
"Perry Bradford Will Face Jury." *New York Amsterdam News*, August 1932.
Ready, William. *Afro-American*, November 20, 1923.
Reeves, Walter L., Jr., *Afro American*, July 2, 1927.
Rowe, Billy, "Billy Rowe's Notebook," *Pittsburgh Courier*, November 19, 1949.
Russell, Sylvester. "Chicago Weekly Review." *The Freeman*, May 9, 1914, 5.
———. "Sylvester Russell's Review." *Pittsburgh Courier*, August 6, 1927.
"Savoy Theater." *The Freeman*, October 22, 1910.
"Sharing Earnings with Poor Blues-singer's Idea of Fun." *Afro American*, December 10, 1927.
"Sippie Wallace's Nephew Dies." *Chicago Defender*, July 18, 1925.
"Slim Henderson Dead." *Chicago Defender*, May 19, 1928.
"Smith and Redmond." *The Freeman*, May 17, 1913.
Smith, William. *Afro-American*, June 20, 1925, 5.
"South Carolina Girl Gets Big Recording Contract." *Pittsburgh Courier*, November 3, 1923.
"Spark's Minstrel." *The Freeman*, May 27, 1916.
"Trixie Smith Wins Big Blues Contest." *Savannah Tribune*, February 9, 1922.
"Trixie Smith." *Afro-American*, August 1, 1924, 10.
"Viola at It." *Chicago Defender*, August 2, 1924.
Wells, Al. "Alex Tolliver's Big Show," *The Freeman*, March 4, 1916.
Wilson, John. "Surviving Stylist: Ida Cox Sings Blues in 'Classic' Way." *New York Times*, September 10, 1961.

Oral History

Austin, Lovie. Interview by William Russell. https://musicrising.tulane.edu/listen/interviews/lovie-austin-1969-04-25/, April 25, 1969. Accessed September 24, 2021.
Butterbeans and Susie. Interview as part of recording. King (FRC 7000), 1960.
Christian, Lillie Delk. Unknown interviewer. https://musicrising.tulane.edu/listen/interviews/lillie-delk-christian-1961-04-25/, April 25, 1961. Accessed January 29, 2022.
Dean, Demas. Interview by Bill Reed. http://people-vs-drchilledair.blogspot.com/2010/02/meeting-with-remarkable-man.html, 1988.
Dorsey, Thomas A. Interview. https://musicrising.tulane.edu/listen/interviews/thomas-andrew-dorsey-1980-08-06/, August 6, 1980. Accessed October 1, 2021.

Mack, Billy and Mary. Interview by William Russell. https://musicrising.tulane.edu/listen/interviews/billy-and-mary-mcbride-mack-and-mack-1959-07-01/, July 1, 1959. Accessed October 1, 2021.

Miles, Lizzie. Interview by Richard B. Allen and Robert Greenwood. https://musicrising.tulane.edu/listen/interviews/lizzie-miles-1951-01-18/, January 18, 1951. Accessed January 12, 2022.

Morand, Herb. Interview by Robert Greenwood, Bernard Steiner, Edward Lehman, and Robert Matthews. https://musicrising.tulane.edu/listen/interviews/herb-morand-1950-03-12/, March 12, 1950. Accessed January 23, 2022.

Parker, Knocky. Interview by Paul Crawford and Ed Cann. https://musicrising.tulane.edu/listen/interviews/john-knocky-parker-1963-08-28/, August 8, 1963. Accessed January 23, 2022.

Wynn, Albert. Interview by William Russell. https://musicrising.tulane.edu/listen/interviews/albert-wynn-1958-05-29/, May 29, 1958. Accessed October 1, 2021.

Subject Index

Song Index